WORKINGCLASS GIANT

The Life of William Z. Foster

By Arthur Zipser

INTERNATIONAL PUBLISHERS, NEW YORK

To Pearl

Copyright © 1981 by
International Publishers

First edition, 1981

Manufactured in the
United States of America

Library of Congress Cataloging in Publication Data

Zipser, Arthur, 1909-
    Workingclass giant

        Includes bibliographical references and index.
        1. Foster, William Z., 1881-1961.   2. Labor and
laboring classes—United States—Biography.   3. Trade-
unions—United States—Biography. 4. Communists—United
States—Biography.   I. Title.
HD8073.F6Z5   331.88′092′4 [B]   81-2503
ISBN 0-7178-0590-5   AACR2
ISBN 0-7178-0582-4 (pbk.)

Contents

Preface

I was secretary and research assistant to William Z. Foster from 1951 to 1957. Being with Foster six days a week and observing him in all aspects of his work and in the bosom of his family qualified me, I suppose, to undertake the present book. But the principal sources for a William Z. Foster biography are his own autobiographical writings— *From Bryan to Stalin* (1937), *Pages from a Worker's Life* (1939) and *More Pages from a Worker's Life* (a posthumous collection I edited in 1979).

There are other sources, mostly in his own writings and in the writings of others, and I have generally credited these in the reference notes. Facts and anecdotes not otherwise credited are, in most instances, the fallout of many hundreds of hours of informal conversation with my subject.

A few passages in this book have previously appeared in other publications in somewhat altered form.

Although I had thought for several years of writing this short biography of a man who deserves a longer one, I might not have actually written it if I had not been goaded and driven to do so by my friend Gil Green who was a long-time associate of Foster's. Gil Green also was kind enough to read the manuscript and make valuable recommendations.

I am also deeply indebted to William Weinstone, a charter member of the Communist Party, whose advanced age has not dimmed his extraordinary mental and physical vigor. Will Weinstone gave the manuscript a careful and constructive reading and made numerous perceptive suggestions. In his characteristic way he monitored my project beyond the call of duty and friendship. His help and concern are deeply appreciated.

Gus Hall, Henry Winston, and James E. Jackson, leaders of the Communist Party and colleagues of William Z. Foster, read all or parts of the manuscript and made invaluable suggestions.

Special mention must be made of my wife, Pearl Zipser, without whose dedicated and patient assistance this would still be a work-in-progress.

With due thanks to all who helped me it is necessary to add that I alone am responsible for whatever errors of fact or judgment this book may contain.

WORKINGCLASS
GIANT

1

A Bit of Background

"Let Foster do it," said P.J. Conlon in 1925. Conlon was head of the International Association of Machinists' national organization department. Foster was William Z. Foster, the secretary-treasurer of the Trade Union Educational League (TUEL).

"Let Foster do it," was a sneer, of course. What Conlon was inviting Foster to do was to organize the huge and growing automobile industry. "The Machinists and the AFL," said Conlon, "will be quite willing to hand over the job in Detroit to any of the radicals who think they can organize the proletariat that is out of the craft unions."[1]

The American Federation of Labor had assigned Conlon's Machinists the leading role in bringing the vast and complex auto industry into the organized sector of American labor. With eighteen other craft unions also claiming a share of the pie—a pie which hadn't been baked yet—it is no wonder the IAM had only a handful of union garages and repair shops to its credit, while the manufacturing sector stood like a steel and concrete fortress against Conlon's bows and arrows.

There was nervous bravado in Conlon's "Let Foster do it" because Foster had done it before. In the meatpacking industry and in mighty steel, Foster had shown that it could be done.

What had to be done was not just a matter of organizing auto. It was the building of industrial unions all over North America, especially in the basic mass production industries. Beyond that was the need to socialize the ownership of all these industries under a workingclass government. But Conlon was not urging that—not even in jest.

That Foster would some day have to "do it" seems almost to have been ordained: both he and the American Federation of Labor were born in 1881.

The labor movement of the United States was almost one hundred years old by then. In 1792, soon after the Bill of Rights had been adopted, labor took its first halting steps towards organizing. The cordwainers, as shoemakers were then called, seem to have been the first.

The cordwainers of Philadelphia organized to defend their wages and by 1799 they were on strike to enforce their demands. Other trades—printers, cabinet makers, shipwrights, tailors—followed suit. In its fetal form the U.S. labor movement suggested vaguely the shape it was to take a hundred years later, when its long gestation was over. In the years since then changes have been many.

The early capitalists, themselves a primitive version of what that class was to become, displayed an easily recognizable response: In 1809 the cordwainers of New York City were under injunction and on trial for conspiring against free trade.[2]

Nevertheless more and more crafts became organized into unions. By the time of the War of 1812, a war which challenged the continued independence of the young United States, there were a number of craft unions whose members put their strength—physically and organizationally—on the line for defense of the country against the British aggressors. In this they were joined by a number of free Blacks.

Capitalism helplessly followed its inevitable cycles of boom and bust even in its fledgling period. Some unions were doomed by the strain of strikes and legal persecutions; the rest were finished off by the vicissitudes of the 1819-1822 economic depression.

With economic recovery came a regrowth of unionism culminating in 1837, when economic crisis again wiped out most unions. This demise included the National Trades Union which, in 1834, was the first effort at creating a federation of labor unions.

But the unions had registered gains which persisted—the 10-hour day in some areas, abolition of imprisonment for debts, a mechanics lien law, a common school system, and the practical elimination of property qualifications for voting (though Blacks were still barred from using the ballot). Starting in 1828 labor parties were formed, marking the beginning of more than 150 years of struggle for the elusive goal of independent labor political action.

The depression set off by the 1837 crisis was a long one, lasting 12 years. The cruelties of capitalism generated a search for a better way. This led to the growth of utopian socialist communities. The United States, with its seemingly endless space, and without tradition to inhibit it, became the testing ground for experiments in communalism, testing in practice the ideas of such outstanding European thinkers as Robert Owen, Claude Saint Simon and Charles Fourier. The communities recognized, in one form or another, the truth that an equitable society based on the common ownership of the means of production must end the dog-eat-dog of capitalism. These experiments all crumbled eventually on their unscientific and utopian foundations. But their efforts helped prepare the ground for the ideas of scientific socialism.

Such scientific, non-utopian ideas crossed the ocean westward in the form of the writings of Karl Marx and Frederick Engels and in the physical form of German Marxist immigrants. Their ideas and activities led, by 1876, to the founding of the Workingmen's Party of America, the antecedent of all U.S. socialist parties (including the Communist Party).[3]

Of course, the development of a labor movement was at first a phenomenon affecting only the white sector of the U.S. labor force. The millions of Black chattel slaves, like the system that employed them, were outside the scope of unionism just as their owners were outside of, though sometimes in collusion with, the capitalist sector of the economy.

A class struggle went on, nevertheless, in the slave South. Slave rebellions, runaways, sabotage were manifestations of the struggle, as was the organized Abolitionist movement, principally in the North, with its leadership of Black and white, male and female.

The great class conflict known as the Civil War finally settled the ascendancy of industrial capitalism by the abolition of slavery. Now the country raced into a period of economic growth, monopolization and trustification. By the end of the nineteenth century U.S. capitalism had entered into its imperialist stage.[4]

With capitalism sweeping triumphantly forward, the labor union movement entered a period of growth, and its prehistory drew to a close. The militant National Labor Union came and went; the Knights of Labor grew into a powerful force, and then faded as the twentieth century loomed.

In 1881, the modern labor movement took the field in the shape of the Federation of Organized Trades and Labor Unions of the United States and Canada. In 1886, this federation merged into the newly formed American Federation of Labor (AFL). So close was the identity of the two federations that the year 1881 has long been considered the founding year of the AFL.[5]

The AFL came into existence in a period when the labor movement stood in need of trade unions capable of challenging monopoly capitalism, with its concentrated industrial giants. It needed a politically advanced, industrially structured unionism which would welcome and unify all workers—skilled and unskilled, male and female, foreign-born and native, Black and white—under the democratic control of its membership.

But the AFL was none of these things. It was a step forward, but too short a step. It started, and remained for almost 40 years, under the autocratic control of one man—Samuel Gompers. Gompers' early radical rhetoric covered up his class-collaborationist essence. The craft-based federation, under his leadership, addressed itself to a small minority of the workers. Blacks, women, foreign-born and the unskilled were largely ignored.

In the very year—1881—which saw the birth of the American Federation of Labor, Elizabeth McLaughlin Foster gave birth to her son William Edward in the small city of Taunton, Massachusetts.[6]

By the year 1900, William E. Foster (the "E" would later become "Z"), the American Federation of Labor, and U.S. imperialism had reached maturity. As it turned out, the shortcomings of the AFL and great evils of monopoly would furnish the framework of struggle and determine the structure of Foster's entire life. There would be twenty years of searching before, at age forty, he found the road—a road neither straight nor narrow—along which that struggle must move. During the forty years of life which remained to him, the organization of the workers and their allies in the struggle against imperialism and for socialism continued to be the objective of his singleminded efforts.

Knowing this, he might have said, as the twentieth century dawned:

> The time is out of joint; O cursed spite,
> That ever I was born to set it right![7]

But he had no such thought. And looking backward in 1949 he said:

My life in the labor, Left-wing and Communist movement has been a very happy one. It has given me the opportunity to do the thing closest to my heart and mind—to fight against reactionary capitalism and for progressive socialism. . . . If I were starting my life all over again, I would take the same course as I have done. . . .[8]

Gus Hall, a colleague and comrade of Foster, says:

Foster became the leading advocate of militant class policies. As the working class matured Foster grew with his class. He was a part of the class, but he marched at its head. . . . Foster was a leader of the trade union movement, but he was a revolutionary. . . .

The struggle against the influence of opportunism in the trade union movement will remain with us until the end of capitalism. . . . Foster was an unremitting and inspiring leader in this struggle.[9]

2

The Philadelphia Story

"Skitereen" is a word with a joyous sound—something like "hootenanny." But actually it was no such thing. Rather it was the name given by residents of a certain especially foul area of Philadelphia's late nineteenth century slums to a stretch of Kater Street.

The vicinity of 17th Street and South Street near Kater became the home of William Z. Foster when he was a skinny, not-quite-seven-year old kid, fresh from the more peaceful precincts of his native Taunton, Massachusetts. He came to Philadelphia "a few months before the famous blizzard of '88."[1]

Foster was born on Weir Street, then—as now—one of Taunton's more important streets. The only streetcar line—horsedrawn, of course—ran on that street. An 1881 map indicates that portions of this street boasted some elegant homes. Other parts were occupied by factories—a mattress factory, a marble works, among others. It was in the vicinity of a stove factory that Bill Foster was born. The city's birth records are of no help in pinpointing the place of his birth. They give it cryptically: "Rear house. Weir Street."

When the Foster family arrived in Philadelphia, Kater Street was "a noisome, narrow side street, made up of several stables, a woodyard, a carpet cleaning works, a few whore-houses and many ramshackle dwellings."[2] Skitereen must have afforded young Foster at least a momentary environmental shock. Taunton, founded as a town in 1639, declared itself a city in 1864. But Taunton was a village compared to Philadelphia, and it could hardly have prepared a child for the rough, sordid and noisy setting into which young Bill Foster had now been dropped.

Philadelphia, where the American centennial was celebrated in grand style in 1876, was (and is) rich in relics of the revolutionary past of the United States. Several of these relics are within walking distance of 17th and Kater.

Taunton too has its page in the revolutionary lore of our country. It claims the distinction of having been the first place to raise the flag of revolution. Not Betsy Ross's Red, White and Blue, but, as Hezekiah Butterworth wrote in 1886, "The red flag of Taunton that flies o'er the green."

When Foster was a kid, playing on Weir Street and keeping out of the way of the horsecars, he took no note of the Taunton Green—which remains today a grassy spot, separating busy lanes of traffic in front of the century city hall.

A flag pole in the Green flies a red flag, with a Union Jack sewn into one corner. Here on "Friday, the 21st of October, 1774, two years before the Declaration of Independence, this Union flag was unfurled with the words Liberty and Union inscribed thereon."[3]

Bill Foster's friend, Elizabeth Gurley Flynn, speculated: "Maybe in the next century, which isn't so far off, the historic 'green' will be renamed for a native-born Irish-American worker, 'a Red' like that early revolutionary flag—William Z. Foster."[4]

It is part of the folklore of American capitalism that out of its slums and hovels have come some of its most "successful" figures. There is just barely sufficient truth in this statement to lend it credibility. But the odds against the slumdwellers always were—and still remain—very high. In the oppressive atmosphere of Skitereen the future—the very life—of a young inhabitant confronted a dubious fate. Elizabeth McLaughlin Foster gave birth to 23 children. Only Bill, his three younger sisters, and an older brother survived to maturity. The midwife and the undertaker were no strangers to the Foster household.

The City of Brotherly Love had a history of riot and violence. In the first half of the nineteenth century racist elements rioted against its Black population in 1833, '34, '35, '42, and '49. In 1838 an abolitionist meeting was attacked and the abolitionist meeting hall burned to the ground. Anti-Catholic riots took place in 1828 and 1844. Thugs and thieves made the city's streets unsafe. About the time of the Civil War the municipal police force was consolidated and centralized and "the gangs of toughs and criminals were penned into small red light districts and civil order maintained."[5] Thus, the solid burghers of the city were spared some of the depredations of the lawless elements. Within the "red light districts" themselves, however, "civil order" was a relative quality.

The Kater Street slum created a set of obstacles for its inhabitants which not all were able to overcome. Many impoverished and unemployed youths adopted an outlaw mode of survival. Many succumbed early to drunkenness and disease.

Neighborhoods had their traditional gangs; in Skitereen and adjacent blocks it was the Bulldogs. Kids smoked, drank, shot crap, and indulged in petty theft. Rowdy behavior, gang fighting, harassing Jewish merchants on nearby South Street, and beating up Blacks who ventured south of the Lombard Street deadline furnished outlets for the underutilized energies of the young Bulldogs. The novelist Charles Dickens would have recognized this scene, and so can we today when slums, no less destructive than those of London, 1850, and Philadelphia, 1890, exist in all our large cities.

But not all the denizens of Skitereen were destroyed. While *lumpen* and *semi-lumpen* elements sank into indolence, criminality and vicious habits, those who found work developed a workingclass consciousness, some of which rubbed off on their defeated neighbors. Trade unionism and strikes were familiar and understood by folks on Kater Street, even by many of those who were sunk in hopelessness.

Foster has painted a grim picture of his home block, and its Bulldogs, in the opening sketch of his *Pages from a Worker's Life.* "Yet," he writes, "there was much real proletarian spirit in our gang. As far as I ever heard, scabs were never recruited in our neighborhood. Indeed, during the fierce streetcar strike of the middle nineties the Bulldogs mobilized in full force and wrecked every car that came through our territory, although each one was manned by several armed policemen."[6]

Bill Foster's formal education lasted only to his tenth year, and by that span it exceeded the education of his father, James. Bill liked to quote his father's remark that "I never went to school but one day— and that day school didn't keep."

James Foster, a brawny, athletic scrapper who worked as a carriage washer and stableman, was indifferent to American politics, though, as an urban Irish Catholic he automatically voted Democratic. His politics were Irish nationalism. His Fenian activities, a response to the harsh British oppression of his native Ireland, made him a political refugee in 1868, when he was 27 years old.

He was born in County Carlow, Ireland, to a peasant family. He became a British soldier in order to advance the struggle for Irish independence. His role was to agitate among the many Irish youths who had enlisted in the army, choosing to accept that harsh life in preference to the crushing poverty which was the alternative. Many poor youths in present-day United States have made a similar choice.

James Foster participated in organizing a proposed revolt of the Irish lads with the intent of seizing Ireland. It was a rash scheme but not without a certain plausibility about it since the British garrison had been weakened through the dispatch of many troops to serve in India. A traitor betrayed the plan, however, and James Foster and many others had to make a quick getaway.

Foster arrived in Boston, a refugee from Queen Victoria's vengeance. His son, William, has described him as "very active and powerful physically." He adds: "He claimed that in his youth he was champion of Great Britain in three sport events: the broad jump; high jump; and hop, skip and jump. . . . His special predilection was to fight Irish policemen."

Jim Foster brought to the New World two possessions which lasted him the rest of his life: his Fenian politics and his fine homespun overcoat.

Bill Foster has said of his father that "as his family grew up in the United States, he fed us on hatred for the oppressor England. It was the intellectual meat and drink of our early lives. I was raised with the burning ambition of one day taking an active part in the liberation of Ireland." And later, Bill adds, "It seemed as natural to hate capitalistic tyranny in the United States as English tyranny in Ireland."

William Z. Foster, though he grew up in a home where Irish nationalism was the principal—sometimes the only—meat and drink, never became an Irish nationalist.

Elizabeth McLaughlin, Bill's mother, was born in Carlisle, England of Scotch-English ancestry. Like generations of her forebears she became a textile worker, a weaver. She came into the factories that, in the preceding generation, had been displacing the hand loom—a change that brought starvation in its wake for many workers. She was a devout Catholic, unlike her husband who was negligent in religious matters.

Elizabeth Foster was slender but sturdy. The years of household drudgery and endless pregnancies nevertheless took their toll. She died in 1901, age 53. Her husband died in the same year, age 60.

Bill Foster followed the practice of Skitereen schoolmates—a practice dictated by economic necessity—of finding casual employment outside of school. In his case it was selling newspapers. He sold the *Star, News, Item,* and *Call*—papers now long defunct. From this Horatio Alger start he might—given his intelligence and drive—have gone the fabled route from rags to riches. But that was not the route Foster sought. From his early years he was committed to work and to the working class. "I wanted to become an industrial worker," he has told us, "and was drawn as if by a magnet to the shops."[7]

Young Foster had to add to the family income. So, at age ten, he was out of school and into his first regular job, and a promising one for a lad of such tender years. He became apprentice to "Old Kretchman," an artist and artisan, a sculptor and painter, a craftsman of many skills and talents. He is listed in nineteenth century business directories as having a studio at 455 Franklin Street at Noble, about a mile and a half from Foster's home. At the time, this was no doubt considered "within easy walking distance" for the average ten-year old.

Edward A. Kretchman had much to teach his new apprentice. In addition to his other gifts, he excelled at modelling, stonecutting, woodcarving, electro-plating, and was an outstanding die-sinker. He had helped the sculptor, Calder, construct the huge statue of William Penn which incongruously perches atop Philadelphia's City Hall.

Kretchman liked young Bill and willingly instructed him in his many skills. But the apprentice "felt no call to a life of art." Besides, at age 13 he had advanced from a starting wage of only $1.50 a week to a hungry $2.00. Bill quit. It was hard times (1894). "Men could find no work," he later wrote, "but there were always places for child slaves."[8] He got a job at $3.00 a week. For three-and-a-half years he learned the type founder's trade at MacKellar, Smith and Jordan's foundry. Lead poisoning was a threat there, and it was an even greater threat at his next job, in the Harrison White Lead Works.

It was as a child laborer, living in a poverty-stricken home, that Bill Foster "felt the iron of the class struggle sink into his heart."[9] The carmen's strike referred to above drove the iron deeper. On a day off from work, the fourteen-year old Foster, already a veteran of four years of wage labor, joined a peaceful parade of striking streetcar employees. As the column passed 15th Street and Market, a hidden troop of mounted police galloped out of the City Hall courtyard and rode down the peaceful procession. In the melee which ensued, a dismounted cop belted Foster in the jaw. Thus was the "iron of the class struggle" driven deeper into the young worker's heart. The blow constituted a declaration of war between him and the capitalist class.

School was finished for Bill, but book-learning continued. The free library of Philadelphia opened on February 22, 1895. From this and other sources came books to feed Bill's hunger for knowledge. (In the year after the big new library opened, William E.B. DuBois came to the city to do research on his landmark study of its Black population. The two Williams, scores of years later, were to become comrades in struggle.)

Young Bill devoured everything he could get on the French Revolution. Moreover, he read Paine's *Age of Reason;* Lecky's *History of European Morals;* Draper's *Conflict Between Science and Religion;* Gibbon's *Decline and Fall of the Roman Empire,* Darwin's *Origin of Species* and *Descent of Man,* and Spencer's *Data of Sociology.* After this siege of secular reading, said Foster, "There was very little, if any, religion left in me. All I needed for a completely materialist outlook on life were the works of Marx and Engels, which I was to read some years later."

Young Foster's reading list comprised books on science, sociology, history and religion. They were all written, as he says, "in the days when capitalism was more honest intellectually than it is now."[10]

His break with religion materially affected the course of his life. "My mother had long wanted to make a priest of me, and her wishes were seconded by Father Joseph O'Connor, a noted orator of St. Theresa's Church in Philadelphia, and a friend of mine. He offered to send me to a Jesuit college to be educated for the priesthood. He and my mother were both disappointed, however, when I let it be known to them that my reading had already taken me far and away beyond the control of the Catholic Church."[11] The future chairman of the Communist Party might otherwise have ended up an archbishop!

The last decade of the nineteenth century was a period of great class struggles as the United States moved inexorably into the imperialist epoch. Class "war" took on literal meaning as strikers confronted, and sometimes routed, armed forces. In 1892 there was a great strike of steel workers in Homestead, Pennsylvania; in 1894, a year of economic crisis, Eugene Victor Debs led a strike against the Pullman Palace Parlor Car Co. The Pullman strike spread to many of the railroads that served the Chicago area. Twenty-five persons were killed and sixty injured in that great struggle. In the Rocky Mountain states, William D. ("Big Bill") Haywood was leading the Western Federation of Miners in a series of historic strikes. Foster knew of these stirring labor battles and followed their course with passionate interest.

He was particularly fascinated by the 1894 movement of the unemployed known as Coxey's Army. He hung around the recruiting office for the "army" at 13th and Filbert, and he was deeply disappointed at the anti-climax of this dramatic movement which ended with Coxey arrested for walking on the Capitol lawn in Washington.

In 1896 Bill was attracted to the populism of William Jennings Bryan's "free silver" campaign for the presidency. Through all his teen years he reacted to the great social events of a turbulent decade. He marched in the Bryan torchlight parades, misjudging (at age 15) Bryan's middleclass program for a "real fight against the great trusts that were oppressing workers and farmers in common."

A series of tough jobs in the fertilizer industry kept Foster lean and hard, and sharpened his anti-capitalist instinct which would soon mature into class consciousness. He was ripe for the appeal of socialism.

This came to him on a summer evening in 1900. He got the message from a socialist soapbox orator at the corner of Broad and South streets. It was his first contact with the socialist movement. In one of those "miraculous conversions," such as are supposed to be merely a cliché of "proletarian literature," he found himself entranced by what the speaker was saying. "His proposals for the workers to take over the government and the industries and to abolish the profit system appealed to me as the only real solution of the workers' problem. . . . " All the further experience of a long lifetime served to confirm him in this opinion.

Of course, in the new world outlook that I had gained so suddenly there was much on my part that was raw and unfinished. Many times since then, in the fight for socialism, I have had to shift my conception of political strategy and tactics, nevertheless the heart of my new viewpoint was as sound as oak and it has persisted with me. Since those far-off days when I became a Socialist, almost half a century ago, I have learned through hard knocks that the capitalists' defense of their system is much more complex and far more stubborn than I even dreamed of and that the struggle for socialism is correspondingly a very difficult one. But my whole experience has gone to justify the correctness of the basic decision I then took to work and fight for socialism.

He says: "Whatever prejudices I had against socialism melted away like snow before a summer sun. The thing was clear at last. . . . I was 'made' that Saturday night in Philadelphia. That's how I became a rebel."[12]

He was nineteen years old. After that it was good-bye to Skitereen!

Thirty years later he went back to the old neighborhood and found "the slums were more horrible even than before." The Black people, formerly barred at Lombard, had moved in as the whites abandoned their shabby turf. "The notorious Bulldogs had vanished," and a "new crop of poverty stricken slum dwellers" now lived along Kater Street.

3

Work, on Land and at Sea

It is probable that the unknown speaker who turned William Z. Foster onto the socialist path in 1900 was a member of the Socialist Labor Party (SLP).

In 1864, in London, the International Workingmen's Association (IWA) was founded, largely on the initiative of Karl Marx who became its political leader. Historically the IWA is known as the First International.

Sections of the IWA were formed in a number of countries; and in the United States, by 1872, the IWA had 30 sections. However, especially in Europe, a bourgeoisie frightened by such events as the Paris Commune (1871) cracked down on the International. Problems within the organization, including a split prompted by anarchists led by the Russian, Michael Bakunin, tended to push the IWA into further decline. Finally, on July 15, 1876, at its convention in Philadelphia, the International Workingmen's Association voted to dissolve itself. (The International was reborn as the Second International in 1889.)

A few days later, in the same city, the U.S. socialist forces formed the Workingmen's Party of America. In 1877, it changed its name to Socialist Labor Party. This party, in which at first the ideas of Ferdinand Lassalle competed with those of Karl Marx, came under the leadership of Daniel De Leon in 1890.

De Leon, a professor of international law at Columbia, has been described as "brilliant, energetic and ruthless." He was a consistent foe of opportunism and class collaboration in the labor movement and an advocate of industrial unionism. He was also hopelessly dogmatic, rigid, domineering and sectarian.

James Connolly, who was executed by the British in the Irish Easter Rebellion in 1916, was a member of the Socialist Labor Party during the years he lived in the United States. He came into sharp collision with De Leon in 1908. "If Connolly had realized the need and the possibility of demolishing De Leon theoretically, American socialism might have saved many lost years and the labors of William Z. Foster, who took up the task in a later epoch, would have been rendered far easier."[1]

A split developed in the SLP which was formalized in January 1900 when a convention representing about half the party membership was held in Rochester, New York. The split-off group also took the name Socialist Labor Party. The "old" SLP became "the tiny, dry-as-dust, backward looking, reactionary sect that it is today."

The "Rochester" SLP, led by Morris Hillquit, a labor lawyer, soon proposed merger with the Social-Democratic Party, led by Victor Berger and Eugene Victor Debs. Berger was a middleclass reformer. Debs, a railroad worker, led the great 1894 strike of Pullman Company workers. This strike was crushed by overwhelming violence. The experience led Debs to become the country's most eloquent advocate of socialism.

Negotiations for the merger of the two socialist groups were slow and complex and frequently stalled by leaders' maneuvering for position. The two factions united on a national ticket for the 1900 elections endorsing Debs for President. On July 29, 1901, a convention achieved the united party the membership had been demanding. The new organization took the name Socialist Party of America (SPA). Sometime in 1900 William Z. Foster became a member of the Party.

During the next 20 years Foster was to join and test most of the available organizational choices. He became part of the workingclass left wing which was never comfortable in the Socialist Party. He became deeply involved with the Industrial Workers of the World (IWW). He studied and theorized syndicalism; he advocated industrial unionism; he deplored dual unionism. When a suitable organization did not exist to implement his ideas he attempted to create one. The third and most successful such attempt was the Trade Union Educational League (TUEL). From 1921 on he found in the Communist Party the proper vehicle for his work. What Lenin called "a party of a new type" served him for his remaining forty years.

By the time Bill Foster was twenty years old he had already accumulated considerable work experience and had held an impressive variety of jobs. His slender frame, an inch or so under six feet, did not appear equal to some of the physical demands his work imposed on it. He was often called "Slim" by fellow workers. He fitted into the cliche of the "lean and wiry" type. His hands, however, were large, dexterous and powerful. During a long lifetime as a public speaker those hands were often used to good effect for gesture and emphasis.

At twenty he had already worked for three years in a type foundry where, he says, "I got myself saturated with lead." He also worked as a fireman in the Harrison White Lead plant in Philadelphia, a place where unsuspecting recent immigrants were put to the killing job of mixing pulverized lead. Of a man working in this "deathhouse," it was said that if he "saved his money diligently he could buy himself a coffin by the time the lead poisoning finished him."[2]

Work in the lead plant was followed, during 1898–1900, by even more foul conditions of work, the worst Foster ever experienced.

The term "environmental protection," which today is a pious phrase and hope, had not yet entered the common vocabulary at the end of the nineteenth century. And "job safety" was a concept which got scant notice.

Foster worked those years in the fertilizer industry as "laborer, steam-fitter, fireman, engineer and skilled fertilizer mixer."[3] His description of the working conditions in the American Reduction Company of West Reading, Pa., and of a similar plant in Wyomissing, Pa., could well serve as a description of hell to scare sinners into mending their ways.

(Readers who wish to read Foster's unsparing and powerful descriptions of the fertilizer plants can find them in his *Pages From A Worker's Life*—but they should not be taken before or after meals!)

At a later date he worked in the Armour and Company fertilizer factory in Jacksonville, Florida. Here the main menace was the dust from the grinding of dry bones. Uncontrolled exposure to the dust-filled, germ-laden air gave him an incipient case of tuberculosis.

Bill's experience in Jacksonville came following a detour during which he left Pennsylvania for the wider world.

First he worked his way to Havana, Cuba, where he found that work opportunities were poor following the recent end of the Spanish-American War. He went to Tampa, Florida, and from there to nearby Turkey Creek where he got a job with a company grading a railroad, but quit when he learned of the virtual peonage the job entailed. He went on a few miles and found work at a sawmill, felling trees. It paid a dollar a day, dawn to dusk, minus three dollars a week for board.

In this lumber camp, six Black workers lived in a sagging shanty while the eight whites lived in the "luxury" of a pine-board shack. Here Foster first witnessed an episode of terrorism of the kind then commonly used in the South to "keep the Blacks in their place." On this occasion the noisy approach of the night riders alerted the Black workers, who fled into the woods where they remained all night. "Slim" Foster, whose mode of speech betrayed his Northern origin, was told by the leader of the racist gang that in that part of Florida "if a Yankee minds his own business he is almost as good as a dog."[3] The mill owner was a buddy of the leader.

After two weeks at the mill Foster decided to move on. His notice to the boss that he was quitting and wanted his pay—a net of about three dollars after deductions—brought a threat of arrest. He slipped out of camp and caught a freight train to Jacksonville, leaving his grubstake behind.

His next memorable job was in New York City where he worked several months as a motorman on a streetcar of the Third Avenue Railway. Standing up on the open platforms of the trolley cars, constantly manipulating the handbrake, exposed ten hours a day, seven days a week, at the mercy of the weather, was rewarded by pay of twenty-two cents an hour.

Bill's route ran from City Hall to a "trolley park" in northern Manhattan at Fort Washington. A "trolley park" was usually a beer garden, open-air in good weather, and operated by the trolley company to furnish a destination to generate fares in off hours. The five-cent ride was taken as a recreational trip. The etiquette of the situation called for the conductor to treat the motorman to a beer during the turn-around of the car, on the theory that the conductor could enhance his income by hanging on to a few company nickels, whereas the motorman did not have this golden opportunity.

The harsh conditions, long hours and pathetic wages on the trolley lines spurred some of the younger workers to attempt organization. Foster got in touch with an AFL organizer who did not stir himself in the matter beyond promising to issue cards to those who were lined up by those on the job. Bill Foster got a card in the Amalgamated Association of Electric and Street Railway Employees. But one day the whole compaign was aborted when the company dismissed Foster and all others who were active in the organization. An informer had blown the whistle.

William Z. Foster's accumulation of industrial experience now took him westward, his first stop being in eastern Texas. From his account, one must believe that eastern Texas was one of the wilder parts of the "Wild West." Holdups, gunplay and knifings were commonplace. Killings were a daily occurrence. In this rough environment Bill Foster found work in a railroad camp where he quickly ascended from "flunkey" (i.e., waiter) to second cook. In later years he was inclined to be a bit boastful of his culinary skill.

Foster's 1901 westward trek eventually brought him to Portland, Oregon, where he was to begin one of the most dramatic periods of his decades as a working stiff. Reference has been made above to the incipient tuberculosis which he acquired in the course of work in the type foundry, the lead works, and in various fertilizer plants. (Evidence that the disease had afflicted him was found many years later when x-ray pictures of his lungs, made in a Moscow clinic, revealed healed TB scars.)

As much in an effort to heal himself as for any other reason, young Foster decided to go to sea. He shipped out, not in one of the steamships which were then driving the sailing ships out of the water, but in some of the remnants of the canvas fleet. Here is the way he summarized his seafaring record:

> The period from 1901 to 1904 I spent going to sea in old square-rigged sailing ships. I sailed one and one-half times around the world, twice doubling Cape Horn and once the Cape of Good Hope. Counting considerable stays on the coasts of Africa, Australia and South America, my journey lasted nearly three years and covered some fifty thousand miles. I sailed in four British merchant ships: the *Pegasus, Black Prince, Alliance* and *County of Cardigan.* I became an able seaman and was qualified to do a sailor's work, from making a ratline on a spinning jenny to stepping a mast.[4]

When Foster went to sea in 1901 he was not yet 21 years old. His strength and capacity for work had been tested under working conditions which can only be called harsh, even considering the brutal norm of that period. His restless quest for work had taken him to broad and varied sections of the country. Now, with the Pacific Northwest as his base, he was about to see the world, or a big piece of it.

Bill's principal vantage points for a view of four of the continents were the "skysail yard," the fo'c's'le, and the tawdry premises where seamen spent their time and pay in port.

The four vessels on which Foster made his voyages were all British owned. If Britannia ruled the waves—and in the early twentieth century she still did—the captain and other officers ruled each individual ship in loyal accord with the rich shipping companies that owned them. The ships were undermanned, paid beggarly wages and served food insufficient in quantity and abominable in quality. Meals corresponded to the minimum standards issued by the British Board of Trade. Most windjammers had the reputation of being "hungry ships." A small twice-weekly ration of lime-juice provided the vitamin C which warded off scurvy, a curse plaguing earlier generations of seafarers. "The lime juice was dosed with saltpeter to check the men's sexual appetites, though it was hardly necessary on such a diet," Foster recalls.[5]

The working day aboard ship was twelve hours, broken up into four-hour shifts or "watches." The mates saw to it that the seamen were kept busy during all their working hours. But the men were never bored, says Foster, even though, for example, a journey from Portland to Capetown might take six months without touching port. On board the English ships, card playing was the principal diversion, with cribbage the favorite game. But gambling was not involved and was not a factor in shipboard activity. Reading was an important time killer and Foster made the most of the limited opportunities for this occupation. In this respect his shipside activities did not differ too much from his shoreside activities except that at sea he had more time for reading, but less of value to read.

Work was hard aboard ship and rations were "hungry." When the Welsh ship *County of Cardigan* reached the small port of Talcahuano at the southern end of Chile to load wheat for Ireland, the crew were fed up. Individual "striking" or refusal of duty was punishable by blacklisting and forfeit of all wages due. This could be up to three years' pay. Men might be goaded beyond endurance by ship owners and officers in a deliberate attempt to justify confiscation of their wages. Sailors were not necessarily paid off until the voyage was over. This left considerable sums in the hands of the captain to be forfeited by the deserter.

Blacklisting led many men to sail under false names; Foster's was Tom Donohoe. The *County of Cardigan* men wanted to be paid off at Talcahuano. They knew if they stayed on till they reached a British port agents for shipowners could seize their wages to "compensate" prior ships they had deserted.

Foster had by that time developed the class consciousness which was almost instinctive with him. He had shown his militancy and leadership in trying to organize on the Third Avenue street railway. Now he was chosen as spokesman to confront the captain with the crew's demand to be paid off in Talcahuano. There were sixteen crew men involved.

Foster's negotiating session with a drunken captain led to the arrest and jailing of all the "mutineers." "Justice" was not administered by the Chilean authorities but by the British. The sailors did not back down under threats and declared a readiness to rot in jail (a fairly rapid process given the character of the local bastille). Their intransigence led to a settlement. But conditions aboard ship did not improve, and the only demand that was fulfilled was the main one: none lost any wages when they returned to England.

Despite all the hardships of the sailor's life, Foster found it attractive. The scenic beauties of nature always appealed to Bill and they, no doubt, had a great deal to do with the fact that while a young man at sea he seriously considered studying navigation and making sailing his career. "But," Foster later said, "I reconsidered the matter, as it took me too far from the acute phases of the class struggle, in which I was deeply interested. So I gave it all up and became a landsman again. But it was a good dozen years before I finally reconciled myself to quitting the sea and its ships and men."[6]

4

Homesteading and Railroading

William Z. Foster was one of the last of the pioneers, literally. Having shaken the sand from his shoes and washed the brine from his hair, he switched from the wide, wide sea to the relatively restricted world of the homesteader.

The Homestead Act, passed in 1862, made millions of acres available to farmers and would-be farmers for no investment beyond a "sweat equity" needed to establish residence on a 160-acre tract and to commence cultivation. By 1904, when Foster started to "prove up" his claim in the foothills of the Cascade Mountains in Oregon, the best of the free land in continental United States had all been claimed.

Bill's claim was located at the juncture of the Indian and Mosier creeks. Homesteaders came in there hoping to duplicate the success others had had in the nearby Hood River Valley, where apple growing had yielded good rewards.

But apples did not prosper in the area along the Mosier, though experts had predicted that they would. Those who put their hopes in apples were generally doomed to failure. Bill had luck, however, growing potatoes which did very well one summer when they were in short supply at the market.

Like many of his neighbors, Bill Foster was not a fulltime farmer. Though the land was free, it was rocky and forested and could cost up to $200 dollars an acre to clear. The poverty stricken homesteaders left their claims for months at a time to find work and accumulate some savings to support them when they went back to clearing the land.

For three years Foster spent the spring and summer improving his claim and building a log cabin. He was helped by the presence on an adjoining claim of Anna and George McVey, his sister and brother-in-law, who were also homesteading.

For the most part Bill, except for his fair-weather farming, earned his keep by working in the lumber camps or on the railroads or, as in the spring of 1907, as a sheepherder, where he hated the sheep and loved the sheep dogs. He was able to prove his claim, and then sell it at a price he estimated at half what he might have earned through an equivalent amount of wage labor. Of his experience as a homesteader, Foster said, it "was the first and last time in my life I ever attempted to gather together property of any kind: money, houses or land."[1] He felt rewarded, however, by the beautiful surroundings and healthful life of his mountain venture. He enjoyed the hunting, the fishing, and the knowledge gained of the woodsman's craft.

From 1901 to 1907 the sea and the mountains gave the youth from Philadelphia's slums a feeling for, and an appreciation of, nature. Most of his life was to be spent in urban settings, but a green thumb remained with him. In the 1950s he often spent the summer months at a semi-rural retreat some fifty miles from New York City. There he enjoyed the labor of gardening a plot of some ten by thirty feet. From this came a creditable quantity and quality of radishes, beans, cucumbers, and tomatoes, sufficient to supply (and impress) his family and some fortunate visitors.

For about twelve years, until 1916, William Z. Foster spent a good deal—probably most—of his working time on and about the railroads. He worked as a gang hand grading the right of way between Spokane and Portland; as a locomotive fireman; railroad brakeman; and, in Chicago, as a car inspector.

When he was not working on the railroad he often was riding the rails as a hobo. In this he was motivated only partly by a quest for employment, or a desire for adventure, or a wish to see the vast variety of the continental landscape. More important was the zeal to spread revolutionary consciousness. This turned him into a sort of mobile missionary. Until 1916 Foster was hopping on and off railroad trains, dodging the railroad police, and taking chances with his life and liberty as he went about the country meeting and agitating his fellow workers, studying conditions at the point of production and, most important, perfecting his organizing technique by a self-study course of on-the-job training.

From 1900 to 1916 he beat his way on the U.S. railroads, by his own estimates, "about thirty-five thousand miles." He says, "Besides many shorter trips, my hoboing consisted of seven runs from coast to coast, and two run-offs from Chicago to the Pacific . . . mostly my hobo travels were for revolutionary agitational purposes, in my work in the Socialist Party, the Industrial Workers of the World, the Syndicalist League of North America and the International Trade Union Educational League."[2]

It was while working as a locomotive fireman that Bill received his introduction to the plays of William Shakespeare. The introduction was made by the engineer in whose cab he worked. The engineer was, to use an elegant word, a devotee of Shakespeare. He quoted him constantly, in and out of context. "Lay on MacDuff," he'd shout to his sweating fireman as the train went up a grade. And the fireman would pile on the coal.

A few days after Bill Foster started work on the locomotive, the engineer brought in one of the plays and loaned it to the new fireman. Foster took it home, read it at one sitting and returned it the next day. The engineer was sullen and silent for a while. Finally he burst out: "You could at least have *tried* to read it!" It was some time before Bill could convince the engine driver that he *had* read it, and not only read it but liked it.

Foster particularly liked to quote the lines of Romeo to the Apothecary in *Romeo and Juliet* (Act V, Scene 1):

Art though so bare, and full of wretchedness
And fearst to die? famine is in thy cheeks,
Need and oppression starveth in thine eyes,
Contempt and beggary hang upon thy back;
The world is not thy friend nor the world's law:
The world affords no law to make thee rich;
Then be not poor, but break it. . . .

Whether hoeing potatoes in the Cascades or shoveling coal on the railroad, William Z. Foster stuck pretty close to the Pacific Northwest from 1904 to 1909, making his base sometimes in Portland, sometimes in Seattle.

He plunged actively into the work of the Portland branch of the Socialist Party. He read and distributed *Appeal to Reason,* a privately owned weekly newspaper which most socialists claimed as their very own. In a style owing much to populism and a content owing much to Marx this crusading paper kept the class-struggle flag flying. During the first 15 years of the twentieth century the *Appeal* generally had a circulation in the hundreds of thousands, and often reached millions with special issues.

The Charles Kerr publishing house, a socialist cooperative, kept people like Bill Foster well supplied with titles. So did the presses of Daniel De Leon's Socialist Labor Party. The works of Paul Lafargue, George Plekhanov, Karl Kautsky and August Bebel were studied. And Foster was fascinated by the writings of the sociologist Lester Ward, a non-Marxist author whose thoughtful works in social science had great appeal for forward-looking people of his time. (Ward published a number of works from 1893 to his death in 1913.)

For persons involved in the labor movement, as Foster was by this time, 1905 was notable for at least two historic events. In Russia the disastrous Russo–Japanese war sparked the attempt of the democratic revolution to curb the autocratic power of the czar and establish a parliament. But soon the reactionary policies of Premier Stolypin reversed the democratic concessions—making necessary the revolutions of February and November 1917. And in the United States a new labor organization came into being (July 1905) which was to be a storm center for the next fifteen years. It was the lusty Industrial Workers of the World (IWW), representing, in its first period, the hopes of those who wanted a militant alternative to the AFL—those who favored industrial, rather than craft, unionism, and admission to membership of the unskilled, the foreign-born, the non-white, the female, the itinerant. This is what the IWW promised and, to some extent, delivered. But it carried with it freight that ultimately bogged it down. Hampering the ultimate success of the IWW was its advocacy, for a time, of sabotage which was treated as a matter of principle. Militant atheism impeded the retention of religious workers, as for example in the Lawerence, Massachusetts, textile strike. And then there was the syndicalist view, which dominated the doctrine of the IWW. This meant the rejection of electoral activity, it meant the belief that the industrial union would replace the state in a socialist society—a version of Daniel De Leon's simplistic notion of simply "locking out the capitalist class."

The IWW brought together at its founding a distinctly mixed political grouping. In it was Daniel De Leon, leader of the Socialist

Labor Party. De Leon, who won respect by such perceptive estimates as his characterization of right-wing union leaders as "labor lieutenants of the capitalist class," also was mockingly referred to as "the Pope" because of his assumption of infallibility in matters of revolutionary doctrine.

Another founder was Eugene Victor Debs, an advocate of industrial unionism, a leading figure in the Socialist Party, but one who refused to assume official positions in the party.

William D. ("Big Bill") Haywood, another of the founders, was a leader of the Western Federation of Miners (WFM), the militant organization of hard rock miners and ore mill workers, an industrial union which had fought memorable battles at Coeur d'Alene, Idaho, and at Telluride and Cripple Creek in Colorado. From the WFM also came Vincent St. John, William Trautman and the maverick priest, Father Thomas J. Hagerty.

Also present was "Mother" Mary Jones, 75 years old and with 25 fighting years left her. "Mother" Jones had been a coal miners' organizer since 1867. (In 1919 she was "loaned" by the United Mine Workers to work in the great steel strike under William Z. Foster's leadership.)

Compared with its predecessors in the U.S. socialist movement, the Socialist Party was a success. In its first decade its membership went from 10,000 to almost 120,000. Debs polled 400,000 votes for president in 1904 (and about a million in 1912). In 1910 Victor Berger of Milwaukee, the most prominent of the gradualists of the Socialist Party, was elected to Congress. When he took office there were SP mayors, or similar office holders, in some 32 cities. The SP forces had clout in a dozen AFL internationals. By 1912 the party had over 300 publications daily, weekly, monthly, in English and in many foreign languages. And, of course, there was the *Appeal* and the volunteer "Army" which circulated it. William Z. Foster wrote: "I was an ardent supporter of the *Appeal to Reason,* a member of its famous 'Army'."[3]

Foster did not immediately turn to the IWW, though its advocacy of industrial unionism appealed to him. On the other hand, it derogated electoral work and participation in parliaments. The young railroader stuck with the SP.

After the economic crisis of 1907, Bill tended to examine the general scene and his own party more critically. The huge army of unemployed which seemed to be created almost instantly as a result of the crisis, was what he had come to expect of the insanity of capitalism. But the program of the SP, in which articulate, radicalized elements of the middle class had taken over leadership, diluted its Marxism with a pallid, nineteenth century brand of populism. As he saw it: "Their maximum program was a thin gruel of government-owned industries, duly bought from the capitalists and called 'socialism' . . . they systematically cultivated illusions of a gradual and peaceful transition from capitalism to Socialism."[4]

From 1907 (when he lost his job on the railroad) to 1909, Foster worked in Seattle, principally as a building laborer and sawmill employee. He transferred his Socialist Party activity to the Seattle branch. The opportunism of the Socialist Party caused some of the militant, workingclass members to leave the party and join the IWW. But Foster remained in the party and involved himself in the inner-party struggle—a phase, he has noted, "of the general class struggle."

The inner-party struggle during 1907–1909 became particularly sharp on the Pacific coast. The SP leadership in the state of Washington was held by a group of intellectuals in which right-wing opportunists predominated. The majority of the membership favored the Left. But the right wing used its bureaucratic control to pack the 1909 state convention at Everett with a majority of the delegates.

The left-wing opposition was led by Dr. Herman F. Titus, editor of the *Seattle Socialist*. He was a gifted speaker, writer, and agitator—and hopelessly "leftist."

Though outnumbered at the convention, the left wing, in Foster's judgment, should have hung in there and fought the matter out locally and nationally. But Dr. Titus impulsively pulled his forces out of the convention. They held their own convention and laid claim to being the Washington Socialist Party. Resolute action by the National Executive Committee of the SP soon placed most of the Titus-led rebels outside of the party. Foster was among them.

The sequel to this was the founding, in February 1910, of a new party—the Wage Workers Party. It was "a sort of hybrid between the SLP and the IWW"[5] It solved the problem of the tug of war between proletarian and petty bourgeois members, which had wrecked the Washington state SP, by decreeing that only wage workers could join the party. Dr. Titus was consistent and logical with respect to this provision: he forsook the practice of medicine and for the rest of his life was an elevator operator. He died in 1931.

But the Wage Workers Party died in its infancy, almost stillborn. It was significant mainly as a symptom of the developing split in the SP between a revolutionary left wing and a reformist right wing. This came sharply to the fore in 1912, and in 1919 it manifested itself in the organizational split which gave rise to the Communist Party of the United States.

But in 1909 Foster and a large group of others in Seattle, (including his future son-in-law, Joseph Manley), turned to the IWW. This was probably consistent with the fact that, like Dr. Titus, they had for some time been strongly influenced by De Leonism, although they were repelled by the SLP's sectarianism. In joining the IWW Bill Foster now took a giant step into the camp of syndicalism. He was still a dozen years away from finding his true political home.

5

A Syndicalist in the Making

William Z. Foster joined the IWW while in a Spokane jail. He had gone to Spokane to report the IWW free speech fight for Dr. Titus's *Workingman's Paper,* formerly the *Seattle Socialist.*

The free speech fight in Spokane followed a similar fight in Missoula, Montana. It was a prolonged struggle, doggedly fought by the Wobblies (as the IWW were called), and their supporters. It was brutally repressed by the police and the courts.

The IWW had been successful in organizing the migratory workers who worked in the forests, sawmills, and lumber fabricating plants in the Northwest. Hiring for the jobs was done through "crimps," that is, employment agencies which fleeced the workers unscrupulously in a variety of ways.

The IWW sought a union hiring hall and declared a boycott of the crimps. It held frequent meetings in the vicinity of the crooked hiring halls. A city ordinance was then passed banning meetings from the area.

The IWW defied the ban. On November 2, 1909, the gage was thrown down when James P. Johnson, local organizer for the IWW, was pulled down from the speakers' stand and hauled off to jail on a disorderly conduct rap.[1]

One hundred and fifty persons followed Johnson on the stand and all followed him to jail on the same charge that evening, one after another.

In the days, weeks, months that followed thousands of Wobblies from across the country came into Spokane to climb the stand and fill the jails. They were beaten, frozen and starved in prison. Representatives of the Spokane AFL and of the Socialist Party urged the city council to reverse its ban and thus end the conflict. The council stood pat.

The undaunted Wobblies paid in misery for daring to challenge Spokane's unconstitutional anti-free speech ordinance. Three of them died as a result of their treatment in jail. In one two-month period over 1,000 prisoners had to be hospitalized.

In December Bill Foster was covering the free speech scene for his paper. One night not long after his arrival, he was grabbed in the crowd and thrown into the clink, where he spent most of the next two months. He wrote his next few weekly dispatches from his cell.

It was in the Spokane free speech struggle that Bill Foster first met Elizabeth Gurley Flynn, who was by then already a well-known orator and agitator. Their paths were to cross frequently in future years. Gurley Flynn was then 19 years old and married to an active Wobbly, J.A. Jones. She was in midterm of pregnancy at the time. The local all-male committee in charge of the free-speech fight forbade her to speak at street meetings. It was considered unseemly because of her "condition." She spoke at indoor events, however, and for a while edited the IWW paper, *Industrial Worker.* But one night she was arrested nevertheless, charged with "conspiracy to incite men to violate the law." She spent only that one night in jail, being released on bail. But her writings about this brief, sordid and sexist experience brought about reforms in the county lockups, including the employment of matrons in the women's sections.[2]

Foster, who had his feet frozen while in jail, became head of the committee which negotiated with the city authorities for a settlement of the free speech issue. Spokane was sick and tired of the struggle; it faced a dogged foe, was incurring unbearable expense, and faced an IWW damage suit for $150,000. The settlement, which came in March 1910, was a great victory. Among other things it restored the streets to the workers. Soon after, the city council revoked the licenses of most of the offending employment agencies, whose rapacious methods had precipitated the hard-fought battle.

William Z. Foster had now come to syndicalism, a tendency in the labor movement which was to structure his activity for most of the next ten years.

Syndicalism has been subject to various definitions. It is often associated—especially in dictionary definitions—with forms of violence. In the repressive legislation employed against the labor movement in the United States there appears the ill-defined charge known as "criminal syndicalism."

Perhaps Foster can be safely quoted to explain what syndicalism is: after all, he wrote the book on it. (*Syndicalism* by William Z. Foster and Earl Ford, 1912). Here is how he put it in an article in 1935 (by which time he had long ceased to be a syndicalist):

> In its basic aspects, Syndicalism, or more properly, Anarcho-Syndicalism, may be defined very briefly as that tendency in the labor movement to confine the revolutionary class struggle of the workers to the economic field, to practically ignore the state, and to reduce the whole fight of the working class to simply a question of trade union action. Its fighting organization is the trade union; its basic method of class warfare is the strike, with the general strike as the revolutionary weapon; and its revolutionary goal is the setting up of a trade union "state" to conduct industry and all other social activities.[3]

Foster points out in *From Bryan to Stalin* that "the left wing's most outstanding leaders over a period of 30 years—De Leon, Debs, Haywood—could do no better than help it lose itself in the syndicalist swamp." And he remarks in a footnote: "I did my share to help increase the syndicalist confusion."[4]

The syndicalist Industrial Workers of the World was a leftist response to the reformism prevalent in the American Federation of Labor and the Socialist Party. Foster, in joining the IWW, was making his own personal response to the same stimuli.

He was attracted by the success of the French General Confederation of Labor (CGT). The CGT in 1910 had great prestige among Left forces internationally. Using the weapon of local and national general strikes, reinforced by militant action and sabotage, the Confederation had won impressive gains for its membership. The revolutionary forces within the CGT, starting in the 1890's, had worked within the existing unions, challenging the reformist Socialist leadership and, so to speak, capturing the trade union movement for syndicalism. The revolutionaries had started as anarchists, but in the course of practical activity had dropped the anarchist inclination to individual action in favor of trade unionism and mass action. They now thought that sabotage and the general strike could even put an end to capitalism itself, which would give way to a society based on and managed by the trade unions.[5]

Not yet thirty years old, Bill Foster set out to study the successful French movement—and the French language too. (As needed for his study and work he eventually added German, Russian and Spanish to his stock of languages.)

He left the state of Washington with a grubstake of one hundred dollars and made his way via New York to Paris. During a six months' stay in France he had access to every level of the French labor movement. He met its leaders and studied its literature. He was in touch daily with Jouhaux, Yvetot, Monatte, Merheim and other prominent leaders. These were the "great revolutionaries" of the day, some of whom, when World War I broke out a few years later, became "great patriots" and leading jingoists. (In this respect the IWW syndicalists had a much better record than the French!)

Foster's bad experience in the Socialist Party predisposed him to accept the French syndicalists' rejection of political action and their sharp antagonism to the SP. Along with this he absorbed anarchist notions of spontaneous action and decentralization of organization. This he assumed was the proper remedy for the pernicious control of labor unions by bureaucratic reactionaries. "In short," he wrote later, "I became a thorough syndicalist."

In France he studied the policy of boring-from-within, an idea based on the concept of a militant minority within the existing trade unions. Such disciplined groups of revolutionaries gave the syndicalists control of the CGT. The boring-from-within tactic departed from the theoretical position of the IWW in two important respects: It departed from the idea that left wing dual unionism could be defended as a principle; and it rejected the IWW idea that there should be no leaders—i.e., that all members are leaders.

After six months in France, Foster went to Germany for a similar period, again studying both the labor movement and the language. In Germany he lived at the home of the leader of the syndicalist union.

As in France, he made the acquaintance of leading figures in the SP and the unions, including Karl Kautsky and Karl Liebknecht. (Kautsky, who had been a colleague of Frederick Engels and had made important intellectual contributions to the socialist movement, later became a centrist who defended "the fatherland" in World War I. Karl Liebknecht, whose father had been a friend of Marx and Engels, opposed the war and was assassinated by ultra-reactionaries in collusion with the Social Democrat regime soon after the Armistice.)

Foster wrote articles in Germany for the IWW press in which he took a dim view of the German Socialist leadership of the party and unions. When the war broke out his opinion of the German reformists was confirmed. But he has acknowledged that his criticism of Kautsky, Liebknecht and Luxemburg for not withdrawing from the Social Democratic Party was wrong; and he passed the same judgment on his own (1909) withdrawal from the SP. Boring-from-within was the thing.

Foster had started a cram course in the languages of Italy and Spain in the hope of spending six months in each of those countries. But this intention was aborted when Bill received a cable from Vincent St. John, general secretary of the IWW. The "Saint," as St. John was called, asked Foster to represent the IWW at the meeting of the International Trade Union Secretariat.

St. John provided the sum of ten dollars for travel expenses. Travel involved getting from Berlin to Budapest, where the meeting was to be held on August 10 to 12, 1911. The distance was 600 miles. Foster started out with $15.00.

The first stage of the journey to Nuremberg was made by rail in fourth class, something like a cattlecar. The next 150 miles were done on foot. In all seriousness Foster has called this "a lovely hike through Bavaria and Saxony," which brought him to Dresden where he attended the German trade union congress. He arrived in beautiful Budapest after another fourth class rail ride with $1.50 in his pocket.

At the conference he duly challenged James Duncan, vice-president of the AFL, for the right to represent the U.S. labor movement. This bit of IWW chutzpah led to a day-long debate, at the end of which the IWW's nervy representative mustered only two votes—those of the French CGT.

The challenge by the obscure William Z. Foster for the seat given to

James Duncan, the AFL delegate at Budapest, was noted by Samuel Gompers at the AFL convention in November of that year. Without naming him, he referred to "the would-be delegate for the corporal's guard that composes the Industrial Workers of the World." Duncan also reported on the incident, in more detail, and referred to a "misguided man, named Foster, from Chicago, claiming to represent an alleged organization of labor in America, called the International (sic) Workers of the World."[6] (Statistics will show that the IWW was, and is, miscalled *International* almost as often as it is called by its correct name *Industrial!*)

As for Bill Foster, the man who had crossed middle Europe to challenge the powerful AFL at an international meeting, he found himself without the price of a bed that summer night in Budapest and made his bunk in a parked moving van, only to be awakened and arrested for the Hungarian equivalent of vagrancy.

He spent a foul night in a foul jail and faced a six-months sentence from which he was rescued by the head of the Hungarian trade unions. The CGT delegates, Jouhaux and Yvetot, treated him to a good dinner and lent him ten dollars, with which he took in the sights of Budapest for a couple of days. Then came a letter from St. John calling him back to the States for the IWW convention. Fifty dollars was enclosed for the trip.

Ten dollars went to repay the loan. A fourth class railroad ticket to Hamburg took another bite out of his slender fortune. He next paid fifteen dollars for a steerage ticket on a steamer. When he presented himself in Vincent St. John's office in Chicago he still had four dollars in his pocket.

This was travel—Wobbly style, 1911 model.[7]

Foster arrived in Chicago in time to attend the IWW Sixth Convention in September 1911. He had sent correspondence during his year of absence reporting on his observations abroad. But he had not broached his advocacy of "boring-from-within." He thought the convention would be the suitable forum for springing this idea.

The 1911 convention did not appear to represent a movement with a future. The Industrial Workers of the World which, in 1905, represented the hopes of all militants in the labor movement, had reached a peak of 55,000 members and was now down to 6,000. The convention was attended by 31 delegates.

Bill Foster's proposal was that the IWW cease to be a union and, instead, convert itself into a propaganda league to organize militant minorities within the old unions. These groups would defeat the entrenched reactionary leaderships and revolutionize the unions. But Foster found he could count on only five or six votes—his own, Jack Johnstone's, Earl Ford's and a few others. He therefore did not put forward his plan as a resolution. His agitation for a propagandist IWW got no encouragement from the controlling leaders such as St. John, Joe Ettor, William Trautman and "Big Bill" Haywood.

The Foster group decided to agitate first among the membership. They got this opportunity when Foster was nominated by a Western group to be editor of the Spokane *Industrial Worker*. This was a post to be filled by referendum following a campaign in the paper. Thus Bill got a forum for his ideas.

With the IWW at a low point in membership and influence, the agitation was around the question of "Why doesn't the IWW grow?" The debate which began on November 2 in the columns of the *Industrial Worker* and *Solidarity* was concluded by order of the editors late in December. Foster was not elected editor (the administration had padded the vote against him). And most of the letters generated by his initial articles were opposed to his position. (The selection of the letters, of course, was made by the editors.)[8]

But soon—starting in January 1912—all arguments about "why doesn't the IWW grow?" became moot, for suddenly the IWW grew like Jack's beanstalk. This came about as the result of the great textile strike in Lawrence, Mass. The strike came under leadership of the IWW and brought out all that was best in that remarkable organization and exposed some of its inherent weaknesses as well.

A law limiting hours of labor for women and children to 54 hours per week was put into effect by the American Woolen Company in Lawrence on January 1, 1912. The new hours were extended to adult males as well. So far, so good.

But the company also reduced wages by two hours per week, equivalent—as the workers saw it—to four loaves of bread. The workers were not apprised of this until they opened their pay envelopes on January 12. The response of the workers, already on the edge of starvation, was furious and spontaneous. Within thirty minutes a strike had started in the Washington Mills and spread within a week to all sections of the sprawling plant until 32,000 workers were on strike.

A score of nationalities and languages were represented among the strikers. The IWW was called in by a few Italian workers to give guidance. Bill Haywood, Joseph Ettor, and Elizabeth Gurley Flynn were among the top leaders who immediately responded and organized rank and file control of the strike.

Mass picketing was introduced; marching and singing released the pent-up spirit of the workers; the workers put on debates, shows, entertainment. What had appeared as a tired, crushed, gray mass found gaiety, voice, and spirit—and became unbeatable.

Public support was organized. The workers were fed, the children cared for, the framed-up defended. And finally, on March 14, the boss gave in. Wage increases of 5 to 20 percent, and other benefits, were conceded, with the higher percentages going to the lowest paid. Soon textile mills throughout New England gave similar benefits to their workers as a direct sequel to the Lawrence victory.

A scholarly authority on the IWW called the strike a small social revolution. "It showed what latent power is in the great mass of semi-skilled and unskilled workers."[9]

Ten thousand of the Lawrence workers joined the IWW. The Wobblies' prestige grew throughout the Northeast as it once had in the Northwest. By 1916 the IWW had 130,000 members.

It was a poor time for William Z. Foster to be asking: "Why doesn't the IWW grow?" But he asked it anyhow. With the IWW press closed to him he turned to the pages of *The Agitator,* Jay Fox's semimonthly anarcho-syndicalist paper. It was published at Home, Washington, from November 1910 to November 1912, after which it continued under the name *The Syndicalist* and was published in Chicago under the editorship of Jay Fox and Bill Foster. Its final number was in September 1913.

Jay Fox, who was an anarchist and then a syndicalist and finally a Communist, became a colleague of Bill Foster and was a friend over a long lifetime.

Fox was sixteen years old in 1886 when the Haymarket tragedy occurred. The day before the explosion in Chicago's Haymarket Square, young Fox had a finger shot off during the May 3 attack by the police on the McCormick Reaper plant. Together with Albert Parsons' widow, Lucy, he addressed a memorial meeting for the Haymarket martyrs at Waldheim Cemetery in 1900.

Fox was associated with Emma Goldman's circle of anarchists and was arrested in a police roundup of "suspects" following the assassination of President McKinley by Leon Czolgosz. The police used this as a pretext to smash the paper, *Free Society,* which the anarchist group had published.

Jay Fox and William Z. Foster were friends and comrades of Lucy Parsons until her death in 1942. (For a while Lucy ran a boarding house in Chicago and Bill boarded there.)

Between April and July 1912 a series of articles by Foster appeared in *The Agitator* on "Revolutionary Tactics," answering the question "Why doesn't the IWW grow?"[10]

But after the brilliant success in Lawrence the IWW was not listening. The Wobblies led well-fought strikes in Paterson, Akron and Detroit (among others) in 1913. These were "lost" strikes which, nevertheless, won some concessions.

The 10,000 members in Lawrence dwindled away to 700. However, the IWW membership was growing across the country until it peaked at 130,000 on the eve of United States' entry into World War I, after which it went into catastrophic decline (partly as a result of ruthless government persecution).

But if Bill Foster was failing to impress his IWW comrades in general, he did succeed in gathering around him a militant cadre of non-dual union syndicalists, many of whom were later to work with him in the Communist Party.

Little has been said in the present volume of William Foster's private life, and little will be. He himself rarely mentioned family matters in his writings. On one of the few occasions when he did so he paid tribute to the woman he lived with happily from 1912 to the end of his life forty-nine years later.

Esther Abramowitz Foster was one of the anarchists who rallied around Bill's syndicalist banner in 1912. She was one of a group which included Jay Fox, Joe Manley, and Samuel Hammersmark (who, in 1886, at age 14, was so shocked by the Haymarket affair that he became an anarchist).

Esther Foster came from Russia to the United States in her early girlhood. She worked in sweatshops under harsh conditions which soon led her to turn to anarchism. Like her husband, she joined the Communist Party in 1921. Bill said of her in 1937: "An intelligent and devoted comrade, she has been my constant companion and a tower of strength to me in all my labor activities for these many years."[11] And this remained so for the years to come as well. Most of Foster's books are dedicated: "To Esther."

Esther presented Bill with a ready-made family; she had three children (Rebecca, Sylvia and David) by previous marriage. Bill's own early view, borrowed from the French syndicalists, was that workers should have as few children as possible—preferably none— to restrict the available labor supply and thus improve the bargaining position of the working class. By the time his great grandson Joseph was born, Bill had retreated from this austere position.

The borers-from-within determined on a campaign to win the IWW for their policies. This campaign was called off when the dual-union euphoria, engendered by the Lawrence victory, made the Wobblies deaf to the Foster message.

Before the hopelessness of the campaign was realized, Bill had started on a "lecture tour" to agitate IWW locals with the boring-from-within gospel. It was a hobo trip which carried him 6,000 miles through the West in freezing weather. Riding the rods he froze his face and hands, and on several occasions almost lost his life under the wheels.

The syndicalists now formed themselves into syndicalist leagues and dropped out of the IWW. They joined the AFL in a score of cities in the West and Midwest. Bill, who held a job as a railroader, joined the Brotherhood of Railway Carmen of America, in Chicago, in February 1912. About this time he started on his 6,000-mile freight-hopping tour.

Foster chose to make his base in Chicago. Chicago was the hub of the nation's railroads and a rail job brought him in contact with a highly mobile communication network, namely the railroad workers.

Without the formality of a convention, the local leagues formed the Syndicalist League of North America (SLNA). They also had groups in Canada and hoped to form some in Mexico. Foster was named National Secretary. Meetings were held in Lucy Parsons' home, which served as the League's address.

Following the broad lines of the French syndicalist program, the SLNA aimed to overthrow the capitalist class and confiscate the industries. But it also had an immediate program of higher wages, a six-hour day, and better working conditions. Strikes were to be used, and sabotage was part of the syndicalist advocacy. In fact, the SLNA journal, *The Syndicalist,* carried a column called "Society Notes" which instructed workers on how to sabotage their jobs and industries. The League was anti-political and anti-parliamentary. It did not meet craft unionism head-on, but advocated industrial unionism through amalgamation of unions in related crafts.

The cardinal organizational principle of the SLNA was stated as follows: "The militant minority is the thinking and acting part of the working class. It works out the fighting programs and takes the lead in putting them into effect." As Foster explains: "The organized militants were the little leaven that leaveneth the whole lump." (Bill knew his Bible as well as his Shakespeare!)[12]

Though William Z. Foster generally accepted the thought of Karl Marx and Frederick Engels at this time, it came to him through an eclectic lens which yielded an anarcho-syndicalist image.

During the two years of existence of the SLNA, all branches of the labor movement seemed to be making gains. The AFL grew rapidly; the IWW was in its heyday; and the SP garnered a million votes for Debs.

The SLNA, too, had promising success and creditable activities in a number of cities and unions. It carried on a vigorous campaign for the freedom of J.J. and J.B. McNamara who were serving long sentences after being induced to plead guilty to the dynamiting of the Los Angeles *Times* Building.[13] With Tom Mooney, Foster attended the Molders union convention in 1912 to bring forward the League program.

In 1913 the SLNA sponsored a tour of the United States by the prestigious British syndicalist, Tom Mann. Mann's participation in the labor movement bridged the period from Karl Marx's lifetime to the early years of World War II. (He died, age 85, in 1941.) Like Foster he became a Communist.

Mann arrived in the United States in 1913 with fresh credit for having led recent great strikes of miners, dockworkers, and rail-roaders in Britain. He was invited to the United States by the left-wing Socialists. But they were turned off and withdrew their sponsorship when they became aware of his endorsement of boring-from-within. The League then took over his tour.

Despite considerable activities, the Syndicalist League of North America never grew to a membership of more than 2,000. These were mostly native-born skilled workers. Its failure to grow rapidly led to its liquidation by the summer of 1914.

The Syndicalist League of North America, like the Industrial Workers of the World and other well-intended leftist organizations, led by dedicated, self-sacrificing leaders, was grounded in an over-simplified—and hence flawed—theory. In this theory the question of the state is ignored. Consequently the need for a revolutionary political party, capable of flexible forms of varied action, is ignored. The class struggle is then to be fought out almost entirely on the trade union front. A few years after the demise of the SLNA, the Russian Revolution of November 1917 took place. The defeated classes then mounted counter-revolution in every mode, on every front, military and political.

It took a revolutionary state guided by a Leninist party to defeat the counter-revolution. The state represented the power of the productive classes, first of all the working class. The trade unions were quite incapable of "locking out" the capitalists as the syndicalists and anarchists had dreamed.

This negation of the state and politics was not the only weakness of syndicalism. But a listing of all its theoretical weaknesses would still not explain its failure to fly. The fact is that, in its vast majority, at the time we are discussing, the left wing was repelled by the boring-from-within policy (despite its essential correctness) and beguiled by dual-unionism (despite its incorrectness). The Syndicalist League just couldn't reach that constituency of "militant minorities" it had planned to attract.

Historically the SLNA deserves credit for having been "the first organized effort of revolutionary workers to wrest the leadership of the trade unions away from their reactionary leaders."[14] This was a first for William Z. Foster too. As a continuing effort it was to constitute a major part of his life work.

The present writer once asked Bill Foster: "What was Earl Ford's contribution to *Syndicalism?*" And Bill answered with a smile: "Well, mostly, he contributed the money to pay the printer."

Foster wrote *Syndicalism* during the summer of 1912 while employed as canvasman with a traveling tent show, a theatrical repertory company which moved by wagon from small town to small town across southern Indiana and Illinois.

The touring show was owned by a cousin of Earl Ford. Ford, an actor, was associated with Foster in the founding of the SLNA. The three months of touring gave Bill sufficient leisure to complete the pamphlet, and it was the kind of experience he always enjoyed—a trip through beautiful countryside.

6

Foster's Militant Minority

The Syndicalist League of North America (SLNA) did not last long but it deserves a place in U.S. labor history as the first organized effort of revolutionary-minded workers to supplant the reactionaries in the leadership of the trade unions.

The second such effort followed soon after. William Z. Foster's restless revolutionary energy was again applied to the creation of an organizational format to further the boring-from-within tactic in pursuit of the syndicalist goal. On January 17, 1915, about half a year after the end of the SLNA, a dozen militants assembled for a conference in St. Louis. Out of this meeting came the International Trade Union Educational League (ITUEL). (Foster remarked on one occasion that it sometimes seemed that the smallest organizations had the largest names.) In any event, the ITUEL did not grow and prosper and was soon reduced essentially to its Chicago group. This, as we shall see, led to some very important results.

An attempt was made to extend the organization nationally and, once again, in the middle of winter, Bill Foster set out to ride the rails on a hobo tour of the West. This time he covered 7,000 miles, but failed to build the organization. It was his last such trip.

The ITUEL had at least one important theoretical departure from the SLNA doctrine. This made the *Syndicalism* pamphlet obsolete for the new organization, which directed Bill to write a new document. It appeared as a booklet: *Trade Unionism: The Road to Freedom,* published by the weekly, *Chicago Labor News.*

In the next to the last paragraph of this booklet, Foster declares:

> In spite of its faults the Trade Union movement is the greatest libertarian movement this planet has ever known. It is fighting the last battle between master and slave. Its inevitable triumph will mean the ... final overthrow of tyranny and the eternal ascendancy of liberty and justice.[1]

This rosy view of the revolutionary power and future of trade unionism assumed the eventual spontaneous development of the strength of the unions in a manner which left no need for a specifically revolutionary theory or party. It laid only minor stress on the importance of developing class consciousness among the workers. The building of mass unions was the principal task of revolutionaries, almost the only task.

In proposing this theory, Foster was moving further away from the IWW's leftist sectarianism. In fact, as he later acknowledged, he had moved too far to the right. His theory, he says, "had in it . . . traces of Bernsteinism, which erroneously concludes that trade unions can permanently improve the workers' conditions under capitalism."[2]

Foster's self-criticism here is harsher than he deserved, in invoking comparison with Edouard Bernstein, or even "traces" of him. Bernstein developed, in 1898, the entire system of "revisionism"—the transformation of Marxism from a revolutionary theory to a reformist one. Bernstein, the intellectual petit-bourgeois, never led a class struggle. Foster, the quintessential American proletarian, was born into the struggle and remained there always.

The writings of V.I. Lenin were largely unknown in the Western Hemisphere in the pre-1918 period. They were certainly unknown to William Z. Foster. A few years later he was to encounter Lenin's work—and Lenin himself—and embrace Lenin's system of thought, which is to say the Marxism of the epoch of imperialism.

As far back as 1906 Lenin had pointed out that Marxism does not bind "the movement to any one particular form of struggle." It does not "concoct" them but merely "gives conscious expression to those forms of struggle . . . which arise of themselves in the course of the movement. Absolutely hostile to all abstract formulas and to all doctrinaire recipes, Marxism demands an attentive attitude to the *mass* struggle in progress. . . ." [Lenin's emphasis.] Further: "Marxism, therefore, positively does not reject any form of struggle."[3]

Despite the ITUEL's theoretical flaws its active Chicago group was destined to play a historic role in the U.S. labor movement. This role was ordained by the major valid points in its program—its boring-from-within policy and its rejection of leftist dual unionism.

Much has been written over the years both for and against dual unionism. With the founding of the IWW in 1905 support of dual unionism was elevated to the level of principle. For almost twenty years thereafter the left wing of the U.S. labor movement—inside and outside the IWW—was strongly in favor of dual unionism. This was true of the Left in the Socialist Party, notably Debs, and of the SLP official position antedating the IWW by a decade.

Such dual-unionism mandated the withdrawal of revolutionary workers from existing (mainly AFL) unions and the organization of new unions with a revolutionary perspective. Against such a sectarian view William Z. Foster led the fight.

It should not be thought that all "dual" unions were and are of necessity beyond the pale. A case in point is the history of the Amalgamated Clothing Workers (now the Amalgamated Clothing and Textile Workers.)

The ACW was once a "dual" union. It was formed in a revolt against the conservative leaders of the United Garment Workers (AFL) in 1914 and soon became the "mainstream" union of the men's clothing industry. Incidentally, the United Garment Workers were also once a dual union. They had split away from the Knights of Labor in 1891 and a year later became part of the AFL.[4]

As a generalization then, it may be said that dual unionism as a *principle* of revolutionary tactics is unacceptable but as a means of advancing the organization of the working class it is not always to be spurned. Otherwise how would the American workers have activated their largest single historic advance—the organization in the 1930s of the Congress of Industrial Organizations!

During the short life of the ITUEL, which corresponded to the early years of World War I, the major policies of the organization had no appeal for most of labor's left wing. In this period the spreading corruption within the AFL and its conspicuous inability and unwillingness to tackle the great monopoly-controlled industries alienated the Left. Even so popular a figure as Eugene V. Debs would have nothing to do with the AFL. Foster and his group must have seemed like mavericks to their old IWW and SP buddies.

The Chicago group of which Foster was the conspicuous leader included a number of men of outstanding militancy, influence, and incorruptibility. Included among them were Jack Johnstone, Joe Manley, and J.A. Jones. The group was rooted in the Painters, Railway Carmen, Carpenters, Machinists, Barbers, Retail Clerks, Tailors, Ladies Garment Workers, Metal Polishers and Iron Molders.

Bill Foster, late in 1915, was a car inspector at the Swift car shops in the Stockyards. He was elected business agent of the Chicago District Council of the Railway Carmen by referendum vote of the council's 13 locals.

The ITUEL group in the Chicago Federation of Labor developed excellent working relations with the leadership of the federation. John

Fitzpatrick, a horseshoer by trade, was president of the federation, and Edward N. Nockels was secretary.

Fitzpatrick's politics at this time were hardly distinguishable from those of Samuel Gompers and he did not challenge the two-party system. But he and Nockels were outstanding in the AFL for their honesty and courage and their commitment to the welfare of the workers they represented. Within the Chicago labor movement the Fitzpatrick forces had defeated the gangster clique in the building trades department led by the unscrupulous "Skinny" Madden. Fitzpatrick's principled and courageous activities carried him into sharp confrontations with Gompers on more than one occasion.

The ITUEL group was active in local strikes. Their militant and honest unionism brought them into collision with such pre-Prohibition Era labor racketeers as the Murphy and O'Donnell gangs— specimens of a social phenomenon for which Chicago was to become notorious in the twenties.

In 1916 a proposal by the Socialist Party for a national 8-hour day law found Foster and Fitzpatrick on opposite sides of that question. Foster and his group strongly advocated a general strike to win the 8-hour day while Fitzpatrick, who took a dim view of strikes, thought it could only be won by legislative fiat. Both sides were, it would appear, too unilateral on the question. In any case, Fitzpatrick gained new respect for Foster when, two years later, he backed Foster in a great, mass struggle which won the 8-hour day in the meat-packing industry throughout the country—without a new law, and almost without a strike.

After Upton Sinclair's famous novel, *The Jungle,* was published in 1906 it became common knowledge that the highly-trustified meat-packing industry, centered in Chicago, was one of the worst for its employees, who were paid the lowest of wages for the longest of hours and exposed to wretchedly dangerous and unwholesome working conditions.[5]

Shortly before the start of World War I, a group of steamfitters in the Armour and Company plant, though used to the general misery of working in a packing plant, felt they had a particularly oppressive grievance. They chose a committee and a spokesman and sought an interview with the company to discuss it.

To their surprise the interview was granted and they were ushered into the luxurious office of an Armour vice-president. The spokesman presented the workers' grievance and outlined an inexpensive method of correcting it. But the V.P. replied in a deliberate, provocative, contemptuous tone, with irrelevant remarks on the pleasant weather then prevailing.

The indignant workers asked if the V.P.'s sneer was Armour's answer. The V.P. shouted: "Yes! Tell your union friends that organized labor will never get anything from this company that it hasn't the power to take."[6]

This offensive reply, which merely paraphrases a commonplace axiom of international diplomacy, was a succinct statement of one of the basic principles of industrial relations. Sophisticated public relations methods now generally tend to inhibit company executives from expressing themselves so grossly. (Nevertheless, Charles E. Wilson, president of General Motors, did say to a Senate committee in 1952: "What's good for the country is good for General Motors and vice versa." The Senate then proceeded to confirm him as Secretary of Defense.)

The remark of the Armour vice-president rankled William Z. Foster when he heard it and, as he says, "I never forgot those cold, cynical words, nor did I fail to draw the full class-struggle logic from them." A few years later the same V.P. had to face a union committee representing 200,000 organized packinghouse workers. He did not on that occasion talk about the weather.

Foster refused nomination for a second one-year term as business agent for the carmen. He went back to work as a car inspector on the Soo line in Chicago. His working day of twelve hours and his working week of seven days made it impossible even to attend meetings of the Chicago Federation of Labor to which he was a carmen's delegate.

Bill's preoccupation, even as he inspected freight cars, was with how to get some meaningful organization work started. One day, as he walked to work—a one-hour walk—the idea came to him that a start should be made by organizing the workers of that bastion of the open shop, the Chicago meat-packing plants. The day was July 11, 1917. He never fogot that date. It proved to be a day which shaped the course of all his days to come. The sequel earned him a reputation as the foremost labor organizer in the country.

Bill did not lose a moment in putting his idea into action. On the evening of July 11 he went before a meeting of the Chicago District Council of Railroad Carmen. The Council was dominated by a group of his comrades from the defunct ITUEL. They promptly endorsed his proposal. Two days later Foster joined a committee which went before the weak Local 87 of the Butcher Workmen, where the idea got a reluctant endorsement. On July 15 the Butcher Workmen, jointly with the Railroad Carmen, proposed a resolution to the Chicago Federation of Labor requesting the Federation to call a meeting for a joint campaign of all Chicago locals related to the meat-packing industry. Carried unanimously. The drive was on.

By July 23, twelve local unions ranging from butcher workmen to office workers, from machinists to steam fitters, had been federated by Foster into a Stockyards Labor Council. The council gave industrial structure to the dozen assorted crafts by placing the council under a single executive board and a single set of business agents. The movement was infused with the spirit of industrial unionism.

The first meeting of the Council decided to place primary stress on signing up the unskilled, who were the majority of the 60,000 packinghouse workers in Chicago. Among the unskilled, some 12,000 were Blacks. The rest were mostly foreign-born. Almost all the Blacks were barred from membership in craft locals. But they found a welcome in the evolving large locals of the Butcher Workmen. The result was the largest Black trade union membership of any U.S. city.

Money and organizers were needed to get the drive on the way. But the AFL was cool and skeptical about "Foster's folly." Bill, Jack Johnstone and some other former ITUEL militants worked on a voluntary basis at first. Then Bill was made a paid organizer for a 90-day trial period. Once the drive took hold Jack Johnstone, two Black organizers from the Illinois Federation of Labor, and others were added. Fitzpatrick was supportive from the start. But he shared the prevailing opinion that packinghouse workers just could not be organized.

After a slow start, the campaign did take hold. But by the time half of Bill's trial period had elapsed only 500 workers had been organized. Fitzpatrick thought this was excellent! But Bill knew that the scores of thousands of packinghouse workers would never be organized unless they could be brought in *en masse*.

Foster devised a careful plan whereby the 500 already signed up, together with militants from other unions, could be used to bring most of Chicago's 60,000 meat-packers out on strike and into the unions.

But this tactic was abandoned when the situation took an unpremeditated turn: locals west of Chicago, stimulated by reports from that city, began to shape up strikes in a number of centers. Foster's group then called a national conference to draft a set of demands and, at the same time, gave a story to the press that this conference would probably endorse a nationwide packinghouse strike.

This hint had sensational effect. Banner headlines the next day proclaimed: "Strike Looms at Yards."

The discontented workers reacted immediately to this promise of action and flooded into the Chicago locals. The feeble Local 87 signed up 1400 workers at its first meeting following the strike prediction. And across the country in Sioux City, St. Louis, Fort Worth, Omaha, Kansas City, St. Paul, St. Joseph, Oklahoma City, Denver and other packing centers tens of thousands joined. A seemingly hopeless task had been performed! Then a dozen national unions joined in a loose national committee with John Fitzpatrick as chairman and William Z. Foster as secretary.

The packers prepared to strike back and tried various dirty tricks. One Swift and Co. subsidiary, Libby, McNeil and Libby, fired some fifty union members at its Chicago plant.

The answer of the organizational committee was to take a national strike referendum which brought an almost 100 percent "yes" vote. A wartime strike in the crucial meat industry seemed inevitable. However, at the climactic moment, the American Federation of Labor intruded into the situation and maneuvered the militant movement into the dubious course of government mediation.

Foster and his associates had limited options. Although they were in operative charge of the movement, an actual strike would require the approval of the AFL and the conservative leaders of the dozen unions in the national committee. The militants reluctantly yielded to the array of superior forces—the packers, the government, and the leaders of the AFL. Now, deprived of the strike weapon, they would have to rely for victory on their movement's strength and militancy and ingenuity.

In December an agreement was reached with the Federal Mediation Commission in Chicago which yielded a number of concessions to the workers: the right to organize and set up shop committees, to present grievances, to attend union conventions. A 10 per cent wage increase was granted. The principle of seniority in employment was recognized and discrimination because of creed, color, or nationality was banned. Arbitrary dismissal was abolished and proper facilities for dressing rooms, lunchrooms, and washrooms were to be provided.

Early in 1918, arbitration proceedings were held in Chicago before Federal Judge S. Altschuler. The parties involved were the Big Five of the packing monopoly on one side and the workers in their plants on the other. John Fitzpatrick and the prominent lawyer Frank P. Walsh represented the workers. For three and a half weeks Foster mustered a parade of witnesses to the stand—workers, economists, labor leaders (including Sam Gompers himself). The testimony exposed the miserable working and living conditions of the employees and the vast profits of the packers. The head of Armour and Company admitted on the stand to a $40,000,000 wartime profit in 1917.

Perhaps one of the most effective witnesses for the labor side was a witness called by the packers. He was a coal shoveller, a native-born worker by the name of Grump. He had been called to refute the charge that the plants were flooded with immigrant workers who were poorly equipped to defend themselves.

> Worn and twisted and bent from excessive drudgery, he [Grump] said that for many years he had worked from twelve to seventeen hours daily, Sundays included, unloading coal from railroad cars. His age was unguessable, he was so warped and deformed from years of grueling labor. His arms hung down loosely and his hands were hooked from grasping the shovel. . . .

> A gasp went through the crowded courtroom as this pitiful example of exploited humanity took the stand. Grump cut a sorry figure as a witness. Feebly he tried to tell how good his job and bosses were.

> With tact and gentleness, Walsh questioned Grump. His mere appearance was a powerful argument for us. He was a living example of how the packinghouse exploiters were sucking the life out of their worker victims. As Grump left the stand and shambled towards the door we could hear the packers' attorneys angrily quarreling among themselves over the responsibility for fishing up this shocking specimen from the depths of the packinghouse jungle.[7]

The award was handed down by Judge Altschuler on March 30, 1918. The expose of the avaricious and tyrannical rule of the meat bosses and the inhuman conditions under which the workers and their families subsisted had been overwhelming; and 200,000 workers, ready to strike, were watching the outcome.

The demands which had been drafted by the unions were granted almost totally. Another 10 percent to 25 percent wage increase was provided by the award. There was to be a basic eight-hour day with ten hours' pay and extra pay for overtime. The judge ordered equal pay for men and women, a guarantee of five days' work per week in slack seasons, and time off with pay for lunch periods in eight-hour shifts.

Across the country packing industry workers hailed the victory and flocked into the unions. Foster's forces had the job of mopping up. Besides the Big Five, hundreds of small packers were obliged to sign the Altschuler award. Then the ancillary sections of the industry were brought in: retail butcher shops, soap makers, glue, fertilizer, cooperage, and other such works. Machine shops, car works and other plants caught the union fever and were organized.·

One short strike was needed to make victory complete, and it showed dramatically the reserve power the workers possessed, which could have been called upon had the judge's award gone against justice and reason.

The Union Stockyards and Transit Company (UST), the facility which shunted cattle around, fed them in pens, drove them to the killing beds, and served as a market place for the industry, refused to sign the Altschuler award. The stockyards manager claimed the yards were not part of the industry but merely "a hotel for cattle." When warned that his attitude would lead to a strike, he said the union was bluffing.

A mass meeting of stockyard workers was held that very night. Foster reported on his session with the UST boss. When he finished there were a dozen calls for a strike vote. The vote was taken, the motion approved, and the workers streamed out of the hall onto the picket line.

Within a few days the strike cut off the flow of animals into the plants. Foster and Johnstone were taken in to the Department of Justice and threatened as saboteurs. But on the fourth day, the big packers, the real owners of the UST, realized that they had been checkmated and ordered the stockyards manager to sign.

Less than a year had passed since Bill Foster got the bright idea to organize packinghouse. Now, for the first time in U.S. labor history, an entire mass production industry had been organized; and in a single great drive 25,000 Black workers had become union members. Foster's prestige was tremendous. In his first real try he had proved himself to be the greatest labor organizer in the country.[8]

7

Steel: Organization and Strike

The United States appeared to be a nation of pacifists led by a pacifist president during the first part of the European War. Generally speaking the U.S. people wanted no part of it. When President Woodrow Wilson made his bid for re-election in November 1916, he was returned to office under the slogan: "He kept us out of the war."

But on April 2, 1917, he asked the Congress to declare war, which it did on April 6. In his message he said our war aim was to make the world "safe for democracy." The European War was now the World War.

The war ended with an armistice on November 11, 1918. Less than a year later, September 5, 1919, Wilson said in a speech: "Who does not know that the seed of war in the modern world is industrial and commercial rivalry? . . . This war was a commercial and industrial war."

Most Socialists and Wobblies and the left wing of the labor movement had understood, with varying depths of profundity, the truth which Wilson spread on the record after the war was safely over.

When the United States entered the war the right-wing Socialists bolted the SP and joined in the patriotic hoopla. The left wing fought against the war and a number of them went to prison for their temerity. (Eugene Debs was one such victim. Charles Ruthenberg and Alfred Wagenknecht, among the founders in 1919 of the Communist Party USA, served time in Ohio for opposing the War.)

The Socialist Propaganda League of Boston, a left-wing group within the Socialist Party, issued a four-page anti-war leaflet in October 1915 that was basically so sound that it caught the attention of V.I. Lenin, who was then living in Switzerland.

The IWW, in accord with its abstention from politics, did not take an official stand against U.S. participation in the war. Each member was free to take his or her own position. Some wanted militant action against the war; some even took such action. But the leadership was generally cautious. Bill Haywood probably stated its attitude when he said: "the world war is of small importance compared to the great class war."[1]

Nevertheless, the IWW was persecuted viciously as an anti-war, anti-patriotic entity. Its members were physically assaulted and some were murdered; and the federal government destroyed the organization's viability by prosecutions resulting in long sentences.

William Z. Foster, with his anti-political, syndicalist ideas, "was convinced that capitalism was shooting itself to pieces in the war." He saw the two Russian revolutions in 1917 "as the beginning of the end of capitalism."[2] Nevertheless, his underestimation of the role of class consciousness in the struggle led to a belief that the trade unions— even those of the conservative type—were the only force that could defeat capitalism. He saw the necessity, therefore, of taking advantage of the war situation to build the trade unions. In the previous chapter we have seen how this belief led to the uniquely successful drive in the meat-packing industry. "Food Will Win the War" was a government slogan. Foster's strategy made the fullest use of the critical importance of the meat industry to advance the cause of labor.

Bill Foster emerged from the packinghouse drive with great prominence and prestige in the AFL. He had the option then of choosing a well-paid, comfortable career as an AFL hack in the packing industry; but this did not tempt him for a moment.

At the time that Judge Altschuler handed down his award, Foster already had in his pocket the plan for his next campaign—an amalgamated drive by all unions claiming jurisdiction in the steel industry—a storming of the citadel of the open shop. If it was true that "Food Will Win the War" could not, at the very least, the same be said of Steel?

The principal union of the steel industry was the Amalgamated Association of Iron, Steel and Tin Workers (AA). The AA took in only skilled workers in the rolling mills and puddling furnaces. The majority of steel workers were not even eligible for membership.[3]

The Amalgamated Association, a craft union older than the AFL itself, was badly crushed in a strike in Carnegie Steel at Homestead, Pennsylvania, in 1892. In 1901 the United States Steel Corporation was formed with about half the steel industry, including Carnegie, becoming part of a giant monopoly.[4]

In 1901 a strike against U.S. Steel resulted in a defeat which further reduced the ranks of the Amalgamated. In 1909 another strike was lost and the union was eliminated from Big Steel. The trust ruled its labor force from then on with the absolutism of an unchallenged

tyrant. One result was that while the workweek in unionized industries ran generally from 44 to 53 hours a week, half the labor force in
steel worked 72 to 78 hours, based on a 12-hour day. To get a day off,
many workers had to pull a 24-hour shift every other week. Fewer
than 25 percent of the work force put in less than 60 hours per week.

Most of those who worked over 60 hours were immigrants from
Southern and Eastern Europe. They were the common laborers and
the semi-skilled. The hourly wages of such workers were so low that
it took a 12-hour day to earn a subsistence wage.

In 1910, not long after the lost strike which eliminated the union
from the mills, a study by J.A. Fitch noted that "repressive measures
have been introduced designed to enable the companies to retain for
themselves the advantages which they gained for themselves when
they eliminated the unions. These measures . . . have resulted in a
thorough-going and far-reaching censorship that curtails free speech
and the free activity of citizens."[5]

The National War Labor Board, which came into existence when
the United States entered the war, mandated that "The right of
workers to organize in trade Unions and to bargain collectively
through chosen representatives is recognized and affirmed. This right
shall not be denied, abridged, or interfered with by the employers in
any manner whatsoever."[6]

The great United States Steel Corporation—and the rest of the
mighty steel industry—paid exactly no attention to these pretty
words. Why should they when, having suppressed "free speech and
free activity," no one was capable of compelling them?

The plan which William Z. Foster had in his pocket in March 1918
was designed to change all this.

"No one can realize the might of steel unless he has been in the steel
towns and traveled along the rivers on whose banks steel is made, past
the mills where night and day a process akin to creation goes on.

"For mile after mile the chimneys of the mills are like pipes of giant
organs. A pall of smoke forever hangs over these towns, and at night
the darkness is perpetually shattered by the nightly hallelujah of the
blast furnaces."

So wrote Mary Heaton Vorse in 1935.[7]

One evening, early in 1918, Bill Foster and John Fitzpatrick were
aboard a B & O train returning from a meeting in Washington, D.C.
After nightfall the route ran through the steel producing district in the

Pittsburgh area. The mighty spectacle of the steel mills by night was on display in the near distance. Lincoln Steffens had called it "Hell with the lid off." Foster pointed to the hellish scene and said to Fitzpatrick, "John, after packinghouse, that's what we're tackling next." "Bill," said Fitzpatrick simply, "you're crazy."

But later, when Foster showed Fitzpatrick the plan he had devised for bringing unionism to the steel industry, the spunky leader of the Chicago Federation of Labor pledged his full support.

The campaign was to be an amalgamated one, achieving an industrial impact while respecting the jurisdiction of existing unions which were in any way connected with Steel. If it came to a strike, such a federation could shut down the whole industry at once.

In this plan the elements of speed and surprise were essential. "The idea," Foster wrote, "was to make a hurricane drive simultaneously in all steel centers that would catch the workers' imagination and sweep them into the unions *en masse*."[8] He had in mind the fact that many steel workers toiled in the sprawling plants with little close contact with their fellows. When, as followed, they were brought together in huge mass organizing meetings they were astounded by their own numbers and potential strength.

Bill's first move was to introduce a resolution into the Chicago Federation of Labor (where he was a representative from the Carmen) on April 7, 1918, calling for a nation-wide AFL campaign to be waged jointly by all unions claiming jurisdiction in Steel. The country had been at war for one year and the AFL top leadership had made no move to organize the basic industries despite the War Labor Board's pious permission to do so. "Social peace" summed up their wartime policy.

The CF of L adopted Foster's resolution unanimously in April but Gompers sought to quash the idea by referring the resolution to the convention of the Amalgamated Association of Iron, Steel and Tin Workers. In Foster's words, "He might as well have sent it to the United States Steel Corporation."[9]

The AA ducked the question and Bill reintroduced the proposal into the CF of L. It was adopted and he was sent as a delegate to the AFL convention in June.

Gompers was too clever to engineer the resolution's defeat. He let it pass and then attempted to nullify it by delay—a delay of six weeks in calling a conference of steel union delegates. Foster protested that the delay was counter to the language of the resolution. A meeting was then called during a lunch break at the convention. A few curious onlookers stopped to listen. Bill hastily adjourned this farcical meeting and announced the meeting to reconvene the following night. Gompers was then roped into being present and a good attendance of union officers therefore showed up. There a formal conference was scheduled for Chicago, six weeks later, August 1 and 2. Four crucial months had been wasted.

At the August conference fifteen steel industry unions were represented. Gompers was present but had no proposals to offer. Foster, however, was ready with his own. He called for a whirlwind campaign to start at once, simultaneously in all important steel centers and to be carried on jointly by all the steel industry unions, closely federated in a national committee headed by an AFL representative.

Foster proposed a six-week drive to sweep the workers, who were ripe and ready for organization, into the unions. A proposed 25 cents per capita assessment based on the membership of the 24 unions which affiliated to the national committee would have provided nearly $500,000. Bill estimated $50,000 would pay for the six-week drive.

But the unenthusiastic bureaucrats at the Chicago conference rejected all proposals except the important one of a federated campaign. This took the form of the National Committee for Organizing Iron and Steel Workers. The 24 unions comprised by the Committee had few members in the steel industry at the start, but their jurisdictions, at any rate, covered all the workers, from the producers of raw materials to those who delivered the finished products to the railroads.

Samuel Gompers was chairman of the National Committee and William Z. Foster, the actual leader of the campaign, had the unsalaried job of secretary. (He was then an organizer for the Carmen's brotherhood which continued to pay his wages.)

At the founding conference the bloodless bureaucrats of the AFL voted down the plan for a huge, simultaneous, national drive, proposing instead a single locality—even a single mill—for a starter. The bid for a 25-cent assessment was ignored. The 15 unions present pledged a mere $100 each and the AFL did not pledge a nickle. The next day Gompers withdrew with some of his cronies for some socializing in a nearby hotel, leaving John Fitzpatrick to preside. This, at least, served Foster's aim of involving Fitzpatrick in the campaign.

"I was deeply dismayed by the results of the Chicago conference," Foster says. "The final defeat of the steel workers sixteen months later was directly traceable to the rejection of my plan by the Gompers leadership at the Chicago conference."[10]

With only $2400 to finance the drive, and only a half-dozen organizers assigned from the 24 federated unions, a decision was made to limit the initial drive to the Chicago steel area. In September, mass meetings were held in Chicago, Gary, Hammond, and Joliet and the limited drive met with instant success.

United States Steel was a dictatorship over the lives of hundreds of thousands of people. The individual tyrant who wielded its power was "Judge" Elbert H. Gary who (fronting for J.P. Morgan) ruled the corporation from its founding in 1901 until his death in 1927. His pose as a *benevolent* despot seems to have fooled some people, including the authors of *Webster's American Biographies.* Here we read that his attitude toward labor "was in some respects remarkably advanced for the time. He saw to it that working conditions at U.S. Steel were conducive to health and safety, introduced a profit-sharing plan for employees, and maintained a high wage scale. In response to public opinion, he abolished the 12-hour day and the 7-day week in U.S. Steel's mills."[11]

The "public opinion" referred to here was nothing other than the initial success of the steel organizing drive. His gesture, meant to defuse the drive, established a basic eight-hour day, with overtime to be paid at time-and-a-half. This did not end the long hours but it did raise the pay slightly. It was first blood for the National Committee and prompted the spreading of the drive.

Pittsburgh, the heart of the industry, was by-passed and then encircled by campaigns in Youngstown, Cleveland, Buffalo, Sharon, Johnstown, and Wheeling. Efforts in these areas were met with success despite lack of funds and foot-dragging by the bureaucratic hacks. Even the difficulties created by a multi-lingual work force of over 40 nationalities were surmounted.

The war ended in November 1918, depriving the drive of one of its main pressure points, but Foster's committee pressed on. In the spring of 1919 they were ready to tackle Pittsburgh.

On May 25 a conference was held in Pittsburgh of almost 600 delegates representing 80,000 new union members from Colorado to Alabama to Pennsylvania. In June there were 100,000 members and efforts were made to induce Judge Gary to negotiate.

Gary ignored Gompers' invitation to the negotiating table, so a strike vote, which took a month to complete, was taken. Ninety-eight per cent voted for a strike and a list of 12 demands was drawn up—with the right of collective bargaining at the top. Further requests for meetings with Gary were rebuffed. Gompers appealed to President Wilson to arrange a conference with the steel czar but got no assurance from the President. A local strike took place at the Standard Steel Car Company at Hammond, Indiana, and, on September 9, police killed three strikers and wounded many more.

The presidents of the 24 steel unions were meeting in Washington when this happened and they again appealed to Wilson to arrange a conference; but Wilson stalled (apparently inferior in power to the chairman of U.S. Steel). The national strike date was then set for September 22.

It had come to the point where postponement of the strike would have lead to a rash of wildcat strikes, doomed to failure and meaning the end of the union. A national strike had a fighting chance. If lost, it would be lost under honorable conditions and the workers' confidence in and respect for the union would be maintained.

Immediately President Wilson, seconded by Gompers, asked for a postponement until after an industrial conference in Washington on October 6. But the momentum of the strike call could no longer be stopped and 200,000 copies of the call were distributed.

It was about this time that the *Chicago Tribune* (which would soon portray Foster as a wild-eyed advocate of sabotage and soviets in industry) reported Judge Altschuler's observation of Foster that "in his representation of employees in various controversies before me in which he participated, he impressed me as being particularly intelligent, honorable, moderate, tactful and fair."[12]

On September 22, 275,000 workers were out on strike. By the end of the month the number had grown to 365,000. In the Chicago district and in Youngstown, Canton and Massillon, and many other towns, the workers' response was almost total. Nationally the strike was 90 percent effective. Philip Taft calls it "One of the greatest organizing feats in American labor history."[13]

Of those who remained at work, the majority were American-born skilled workers. Among the unskilled and semi-skilled, who were the bulk of the steel force, the strike was solid. These were preponderantly the immigrants—the despised "hunkies." Chauvinism and jingoism, fanned by the recent war, were rampant in the country. The Bolshevik revolution was surviving in Russia after two years of challenge; the Boston police struck in September 1919; the Communist Party, USA, was founded in Chicago three weeks before steel walked out. The red scare and charges of "un-Americanism" were spread by press and pulpit.

As the strike date approached, a reporter from *Iron Age*, the leading trade journal of the steel industry, went snooping around Pittsburgh looking for dirt that might discredit the organizers. He found what he considered damning evidence when he came upon a copy of Foster's (and Earl Ford's) *Syndicalism*, published in 1912.

Ten days before the strike deadline the *Iron Age* man confronted Foster in his tiny office in the McGee Building in Pittsburgh.

During the drive, about six months earlier, Foster had been "exposed" as a syndicalist by the *Labor World*, a phony labor paper in the service of the employers. Bill then offered his resignation to the national organizing committee but received a vote of confidence. For a while his "sinister" past was forgotten.

Now it rose to plague him again in the form of his obsolete pamphlet. Bill told the reporter that his past was unimportant. What mattered now was that he had Samuel Gompers' full confidence. When *Iron Age* showed Gompers a copy of *Syndicalism* with the suggestion that it justified calling off the strike, the old man spurned the idea. (Gompers would gladly have averted the strike but he hoped that President Wilson would find the way out for him.)

Gompers was a pragmatist who judged by results. Foster had gotten brilliant results in Packinghouse and had brought most of Steel into the AFL. As for the pamphlet, he regarded that as the work of a young man who had "dogmatically laid down the phantasies of his brain." But *Iron Age* (September 18, 1919) cried that the strike "proposed by a small band of agitators would be a crime against civilization."

Thus, for a while, *Syndicalism* took front stage on the scene. The day after the strike started, Representative John G. Cooper, a congressman from the steel area, stood on the floor of the House and declared that Foster's words "disqualify him from the name of an American citizen or the protection of the American flag!"

"Mr. Speaker," the Congressman exclaimed, "can it be possible that in this critical time of our nation's history such men as William Z. Foster are spokesmen for the working classes of the country?" Cooper demanded that the AFL fire Foster from his leadership post in the steel organizing committee, and he favored prosecution of persons who "advocate revolution in the United States."[14]

The Senate was not to be outdone by the Congressman from Pennsylvania. Commenting on Foster, the Committee on Education and Labor said vituperatively: "Such men are dangerous to the country and they are dangerous to the cause of union labor. . . . The American Federation of Labor should purge itself of such leadership in order to sustain the confidence which the country has had in it under the leadership of Mr. Gompers."[15]

The New York Times intoned about the "ulterior and actual designs of the radical and revolutionary agitators." A Federal judge at a naturalization proceeding in Delaware denounced Foster and warned new citizens "to beware of him and his kind."[16]

The Pittsburgh printing firm of John Mellor and Sons printed a facsimile edition of *Syndicalism,* identical in all respects with the original (except that the original bore a union label while the facsimile did not).

The printer circularized businessmen with sample copies accompanied by a letter that explained, "A well known manufacturer had paid for the compilation and typesetting of the enclosed booklet." The printer offered copies at a scale of prices ranging from $7 for a hundred to $750 for 50 thousand. It is probable that Foster's pamphlet received a larger circulation in the facsimile edition than it ever had in the original!

Rev. P. Molyneux, a priest in the steel town of Braddock, Pennsylvania, said in a sermon: "This strike is not being brought about by intelligent or English-speaking workmen. . . . We dare those outsiders to start a little gun music on our streets, and they will quickly see how long we will stand it . . . "[17]

(Father Molyneux possibly was the prototype of the character "Rev. Salvation" in Marc Blitzstein's music drama *The Cradle Will Rock,* which deals with a 1930s steel organizing drive.)

A U.S. Senate committee immediately "investigated" the strike and found "that behind this strike there is massed a considerable element of I.W.W.'s, anarchists, revolutionists, and Russian soviets" (sic!) and it recommended the deportation of non-citizen strikers.[18]

The Senate investigation (need it be said?) was clearly hostile to the strike. It began just after the strike started. Foster was called before the committee. He was gravely conscious of his responsibility to the 365,000 workers he had led onto the bricks and the one million members of the families whose lives and well-being were affected.

Revolutionary rhetoric was out for the duration. He carefully turned aside questions which were meant to provoke him; he masked his true feelings about the imperialist war, and he acknowledged that he had purchased Liberty Bonds to a value of "$450 to $500."

For this admission he later drew flak from "leftists," who had made no effort to help the strike. An amusing footnote to this episode was provided in 1962 by Elizabeth Gurley Flynn when she told a group of students and faculty at Northern Illinois University:

> . . . [Y]ears later I learned something from my friend, Vincent St. John, who had been secretary of the IWW for years and a personal friend of Foster's, that he went in there in 1919, to the steel workers' headquarters where they had all bought Liberty Bonds, all the organizers, Foster, all of them, and he said, "Now, look here Bill, what are you doing with those Liberty Bonds—just putting them in a safe place? Give them to me and we will use it for bail for the IWW." And that was done. The AFL organizers all turned over their bonds, their Liberty Bonds, to the IWW Defense Committee and many an IWW was bailed out as a result, although that was not known for many, many years.[19]

The "un-Americanism" attributed to the strike was used to justify the widespread denial of free speech and assembly throughout the strike areas. Hundreds were arrested for attempting to hold meetings. Jail terms and fines for "offenses" like "refusing to obey orders" and "laughing at the police" were handed out with a minimum of due process. The Interchurch Commission found that "men were arrested without warrants, imprisoned without charges, their homes invaded without legal process, magistrates' verdicts were rendered frankly on the basis of whether the striker would go back to work or not."[20]

The denial of civil liberties to the steel strikers was accompanied by the physical violence of police, deputy sheriffs, strikebreakers, mill guards, vigilantes and hired thugs. Twenty-two were killed, hundreds wounded. In Gary, Indiana, federal troops enforced martial law; state troops were sent to East Chicago. The mayor of Duquesne, Pa., declared that "Jesus Christ himself could not speak in Duquesne for the AF of L."

Within ten days after the start of the strike fourteen persons, all strikers, were killed. Fannie Sellins had already been murdered a few weeks before the strike started. She was an organizer for the United Mine Workers who had been lent to the steel organizing committee. She had earned the hatred of the employers in the Black Valley district where she had brought thousands of workers into the unions. She was 49 years old, a grandmother; one of her children had been killed in the War.

On August 26, 1919, during a strike of miners at West Natrona, a mine official and twelve drunken deputies attacked the picket line with guns and clubs. As Mrs. Sellins tried to get some children out of the way she was clubbed to the ground by the official. Then four lethal shots were fired into the prostrate woman. As her dead body was dragged to a truck, a deputy crushed her skull with a cudgel.

A close-up photo of the pathetic corpse is printed in Foster's book, *The Great Steel Strike,* a ghastly reminder of the cruelty and vindictiveness of the steel bosses.[21]

The violence and denial of civil liberties which hobbled the strikers, plus the "Red" and "un-American" charges were abetted by a systematic attempt to divide them on nationality lines. For example, Sherman Service, Inc., a strikebreaking agency in South Chicago, instructed its agents: "We want you to stir up as much bad feeling as you possibly can between the Serbians and Italians. Spread data among the Serbians that the Italians are going back to work. Call up every question you can in reference to racial hatred between these two nationalities."[22]

But probably the most effective propaganda of the employers was the spreading of false rumors that the strike had failed and workers were flocking back to the mills. Two days after the strike started the *Pittsburgh Leader* headlined the lie: "Pittsburgh Mills Running Full." On September 30, when the strike was at its height, *The New York Times* spoke editorially of "The Dying Steel Strike."[23]

Black workers, without industrial experience, were brought from the South to break the strike and to break the strikers' morale. The bitter use of the color line penalized the unions for their racist exclusion of Blacks which now played overtly into the hands of the steel trust.

Foster said: "The need for action looking towards better relations between whites and blacks in the industrial field should be instantly patent."[24]

On the eve of the strike Sam Gompers resigned as chairman of the National Committee and appointed John Fitzpatrick to replace him. Fitzpatrick did not have the power and prestige of a Gompers but Foster, with Fitzpatrick at his side, gained a committed activist in place of a prestigious figurehead with no confidence in workers' power. Foster later wrote that "official pessimism, bred of thirty-years of trade-union failure in the steel industry hung like a millstone about the neck of the movement in all its stages." This pessimism showed itself in lack of support especially among the 24 unions directly involved. Financial assistance from "outside" was much more generous. The Ladies Garment Workers gave $60,000 for strike relief; Amalgamated Clothing Workers contributed $100,000. Gompers didn't raise a dollar, and never spoke at a steel workers' meeting.

Beaten, starved, misled, and even betrayed by officers of participating unions—some of these officers were paid company agents—the strike began to break up. Attempts at mediation failed as Elbert Gary maintained that what the strikers demanded were "the closed shop, Soviets and the forcible distribution of property." This was Gary's translation of their actual demand for collective bargaining, a living wage, shorter hours and better working conditions.

To protect the goals of the strike Foster often had to parry thrusts based on his syndicalist writings. Once, asked by a Pittsburgh churchman, the Rev. Daniel L. Marsh, whether he advocated taking property without compensation, he answered "No." But he went on to point out that many owners of large fortunes had no more title to them "than the Southern planters had to their black slaves."

He also told Rev. Marsh: "The present strike is one of the most important moves for liberty ever undertaken by workingmen in this country. It is aimed to secure fundamental justice from one of the most heartless and unscrupulous aggregations of predatory wealth upon the face of the globe."[25]

On January 8, 1920, when the number of strikers was down to 100,000 (though steel production was no more than 60 percent) it was decided to call off the strike and have an orderly and honorable return to work—after three-and-a-half months of painful struggle against the pillars of industrial monopoly. The steel trust had won this round but, though Judge Gary would not live to see it, the stage was set for its defeat in the next one.

Mary Heaton Vorse, a prominent journalist, came to Pittsburgh to handle publicity for the National Committee for Organizing Iron and Steel Workers. "Within two days after I arrived in Pittsburgh," she says, "the huge strike had wiped out my personal life. I could not think of anything during the next months but the workers and the strike." Mrs. Vorse has left us a valuable word picture of the strike's 38-year old leader:

> Foster's office was in the McGee Building opposite the post office. There was never a leader of a big strike more accessible than Foster. Anyone

could see him by walking in at the door. His office was a room in a business block. On the walls was one of the war posters, "Americans All." There was a picture of murdered Fanny Sellins. Mrs. Foster and Foster's stepdaughter, Mrs. Manley, worked here, and there was one stenographer. There was also Edwin Newdick who directed publicity. All day long strikers came to ask advice and tell their troubles. . . .

Foster gave the appearance of the calmest man in the world. He was a tall, blond man with a high intellectual forehead. . . . No matter what happened he did not lose his appearance of judicial calm. As one came to know him, one realized that this calmness was because of the high tension under which he worked.

He never faltered, never was at a loss but worked with tireless precision, taking up one problem after another and finishing with it. Everything in the office was in perfect order always. In the immense complexity of the strike there were no loose ends. He held in his hand the threads of all the vast detail of strike strategy, relief, commissary, publicity. He knew everything and attended to everything. Yet he could delegate responsibility. . . .

He attended to too many details himself. He personally acknowledged every penny sent in for relief whether it was a dollar from some individual worker or a donation of thousands from some union. . . .

He was one of the few public characters I have ever known who had no *figura*, no pretense. He did not dress his shop window. He spoke extremely well but without rhetorical tricks. He had neither vanity nor egotism. I do not think he ever thought about Foster. He was probably the ablest labor organizer this country has ever known. He had the strategic sense of a great general. Yet when the stupid reactionary attitude of others prevented him from carrying out his first brilliant plan of organization of the steelworkers, he worked with the material at hand. He had a comprehensive grasp of the labor movement abroad and in this country, for he was a ceaseless student.[26]

The William Z. Foster Mary Vorse described, for all his soft-spoken control, was tough as a steel bar and as flexible as a steel ruler. In his book *The Great Steel Strike* he asks:

Was the steel strike, then, worth the great suffering and effort that it cost the steel workers? . . . I say yes; even though it failed to accomplish the immediate objects it had in view. No strike is ever wholly lost. . . . Better by far a losing fight than none at all. An unresisting working class would soon find itself on a rice diet. But the steel strike has done more. . . . it has given the steel workers a confidence in their ability to organize and to fight effectively, which will eventually inspire them on to victory. This precious result alone is well worth all the hardships the strike cost them.[27]

Mrs. Vorse pronounced this autopsy on the strike:

"The strike died of a slow bleeding. Neither terror nor violence could stamp it out, nor could silence smother it. The indifference and treachery of instituted labor knifed it, and the formidable forces against it overwhelmed it."[28]

8

From Syndicalist to Communist

Foster's strategy had called for a victory in steel to touch off an organizing drive in all the basic industries. Over a period of three years 565,000 workers had been brought into the unions on the initiative of Bill Foster and his tiny cadre of syndicalists.

The grandeur of this achievement was dazzling but among the AFL brass who had been drawn into the drive in spite of themselves, it caused tension and anxiety. The AFL craft bureaucrats, generally content to organize a barber shop here, a small tool and die shop there, were not comfortable in the mass organizing business and found it distinctly unpleasant to be part of a movement which flouted government restraints and rocked the boat of monopoly interest.

With the loss of the steel strike, Samuel Gompers was not about to let Foster try again. Added to this was the fact that the employers had gone over to the offensive. An open-shop drive had started, political repression was rampant, and unionism was on the defensive.

For Foster two lessons learned in the recent organizing campaign stood out: one was that the boring-from-within policy was correct; the other was that this policy called for the existence of a left wing, organized, militant minority. Again Bill Foster set out to build one.

First he resigned his business agent job with the Brotherhood of Railroad Carmen. Then he spent a few months writing his classic labor work, *The Great Steel Strike*—a brilliant critical analysis of the history of the strike and the campaign which preceded it. This book,

Foster's first full-length work, was the first time a strike's leader had troubled to set it all down—a lesson-book for other leaders and for the rank and file. It was unsparing in self-criticism and irrepressible in confidence for the future. It was also extremely readable.

Next he tried to find a railroad job. There was none to be had for him in Chicago—he was blacklisted. Briefly, he worked on the official organ of the Chicago Federation of Labor. When he quit this he became one of the unemployed.

But Foster and Jack Johnstone and Joe Manley and the other stalwarts who had gone through so much, and achieved so much, in the past few years were not giving up their goals. (One of the stalwarts had been missing since 1916. He was Tom Mooney of the Molders Union who had been framed up—together with Warren K. Billings—and sent to prison where he would remain until 1939.)

With two dozen members, all in Chicago, a new organization was started in November 1920. It was called the Trade Union Educational League (TUEL).

One of the casualties of World War I was the Socialist Party of America. It never recovered from the trauma it experienced after the United States entered the war and after the Bolshevik Revolution took place about seven months later.

The left elements of the SP bravely resisted the jingoism which pervaded the country during this first world imperialist war. When the Revolution came in November 1917, the event was hailed by the left elements in the United States—those in the SP, the SLP, the IWW and the former SLNA—and by working people generally. The joy and love with which the first Socialist state was welcomed by its supporters were equalled by the fear and hatred it aroused among its enemies in conservative ranks.

During the first part of 1919, while Foster was building unions in the steel areas, the Socialist left wing gained overwhelming ascendancy within the SP. A referendum calling for the party to join the new Communist International carried by a better than ten to one vote. In a referendum to elect a new National Executive Committee, the left won 12 seats to 3 for the right. But the right threw out the results and hung on to its posts. A convention was set for Chicago, August 30, 1919.

The SP majority, that is the left wing, did not arrive at the convention united. A majority group spurned the convention and met on September 1 to found the Communist Party.

Meanwhile a smaller group had gone to participate—if possible—in the SP conclave on August 30. They felt they had won this right by winning the referendum.

But it was not possible. As a matter of fact they were ejected from the convention hall by the police at the behest of the rightwing officers. They met, therefore, on Sunday evening August 31, and constituted themselves the Communist Labor Party. An attempt, made on September 2, to unite the two newly-fledged parties foundered on account of disagreements unrelated to truly important principles. Two years would pass before organizational unity was achieved.

The two new parties (which came to be viewed historically as the joint initiators of the present Communist Party, USA) were in the midst of the complex task of organization, inevitable to such an important movement in the early period of formation. This task was soon rendered more complex by government intervention.

An opening shot was fired by a New York State legislative committee, headed by Sen. Clayton R. Lusk. The committee was assigned to investigate "seditious activities." On November 8 a coordinated series of raids by hundreds of police and federal agents resulted in the confiscation of tons of "evidence"—papers and literature—and hundreds of arrests. Many were prosecuted and convicted including the foremost Communist leader at the time, Charles E. Ruthenberg. Two hundred and forty-nine persons, including the prominent anarchists, Emma Goldman and Alexander Berkman, were promptly deported to Russia. Thus, while still in its infancy, the CPUSA was confronted with the beginning of what would become a long history of persecutions which reached their height in the 1950s.

Early in January 1920 over 5000 persons were rounded up and jailed in a series of raids planned by the U.S. Attorney General, A. Mitchell Palmer. They were under the command of young J. Edgar Hoover. Hundreds were prosecuted and convicted.[1]

As the result of this "legal" terrorism the young Communist Party was driven underground and its membership was drastically reduced.

William Z. Foster and the Communist Party had to find each other. Initially there was an estrangement between them, the result of Foster's anti-politicalism and the CP's pro-dual-unionism.

The Communist line on trade unionism was in need of sharp correction. The left wing of the socialist movement had taken a giant step toward achieving its historically necessary form and structure when it organized as the Communist Party. But it brought along with it an accumulation of sectarian baggage picked up from the IWW and the Socialist Labor Party. This impedimenta had kept those who became the first leaders of the Party from being leaders in the trade union movement, especially the AFL. Sectarian notions held them aloof from support of the 1919 steel strike—a 100 percent AFL struggle.

Soon after the TUEL was formally established in November 1920, signals began to reach Foster that the most experienced revolutionary leaders in the world—the highly political leaders of the new Soviet state—were by no means dual unionists.

Toward the end of 1920, the text of V.I. Lenin's extraordinarily influential pamphlet, *Left-Wing Communism: An Infantile Disorder,* reached the United States.[2] Foster, who welcomed and admired the Bolshevik Revolution and wondered only whether it could survive the powerful forces thrown against it, read the pamphlet. He says: "Here to my joy and amazement, I found revolutionary dual unionism condemned and the boring-from-within policy endorsed much more clearly and forcefully than we had ever expressed it."[3]

Lenin scolded those who thought "that it is necessary to leave the trade unions, to refuse to work in them, to create new *fantastic* [Lenin's emphasis] forms of labor organization . . . To refuse to work in the reactionary trade unions means leaving the insufficiently developed or backward working masses under the influence of reactionary leaders . . . "[4]

Soon after receiving this encouragement from a uniquely authoritative source, Foster was pleased to receive an invitation to observe the first congress of the Red International of Labor Unions (known best as the Profintern, a term derived from the RILU's Russian name). He went to Russia in the spring of 1921 as correspondent for the Federated Press, a labor news service, to which he sent articles dealing with the congress. But his primary interest was his self-education. The congress was held in July.

Foster's first observation of Lenin occurred during this trip. Evidence became available a few years ago that the two men had seen each other's work before this time. We know that Foster read *Left-Wing Communism* in late 1920. Now we know that Lenin received Foster's *The Great Steel Strike* in the fall of 1920.

The book was sent to Lenin in September by John Reed, the great

American journalist, who had helped to found the Communist Party just a year before. Reed was then living in Moscow, where he contracted cholera and died a month later.

The story is told in a volume on "Lenin as Reader", by a Russian writer, published in Moscow in 1977. The author states:

> A book, *The Great Steel Strike and Its Lessons,* written by William Foster was published in New York in 1920 and is listed as #7747 in the catalog of Lenin's library. How did this book happen to come to Lenin's attention? In the middle of September 1920, John Reed decided to send Foster's book to Lenin.

> With the book went a concise message describing the book and its author. Reed did not conceal from Lenin all the contradictions in Foster's life, attraction to syndicalism in particular.

> Apart from this, Reed praised Foster as the best informed leader of the American working class. "You see," Reed wrote to Lenin, "that he has original ideas, a number of which are very valuable. I know him personally. Moreover, the book is the most accurate and interesting analysis of the great strike. . . ."

> Foster wrote many years later, "My interest in Lenin was so great because he exerted such a profound influence on my ideology and on my entire life. . . . I was grateful to Lenin because, after more than 20 years of groping on my part, it was he who finally put me on firm revolutionary ground."[5]

Some 220 delegates representing labor movements around the world attended the RILU congress and at its start it claimed an affiliated membership of two-fifths of the organized workers of the world. As an international body the Profintern opposed splitting the unions—that is to say, it opposed "revolutionary" dual unionism.

But splitting of another kind did take place in the years which followed. It was accomplished by a policy of expulsion of large numbers of militants who dared oppose class collaboration in the "standard" unions. Such expulsions took place in a number of countries, the United States and Canada included. They were generally engineered by social-democrats, though in the United States a "pure-and-simple" trade unionist like John L. Lewis of the Coal Miners showed particular ruthlessness in expelling members. Many other unions showed a similar unrestrained hostility to their left wing.

In Moscow, Bill Foster again met "Big Bill" Haywood, who was living in Soviet Russia. Haywood, in poor health and facing a 20-year term in federal prison, had accepted asylum in the first socialist country and remained there until his death in 1928. He joined the Communist Party and gave up the syndicalist ideas he had espoused in the IWW. But the IWW itself, which had other representatives at the Moscow congress, had a new set of leaders who were pulling the Wobblies into the sectarian desert where the organization soon became a tiny, dusty sect (as it remains to this day).

Haywood's exile in Russia deprived the young Communist Party of the participation of one of the great figures of the early twentieth century labor movement. He came out of the rugged metal mining areas of the West and built a deserved reputation as a dogged fighter against the tyranny of exploiters and the opportunism of labor fakers. We once asked Foster: "Why was Haywood called 'Big Bill'? Just how big was he?" Foster answered: "Oh, he was a big guy all right. But that's not why we called him 'Big Bill.' It was the way he did things. Everything about him was *big!*"

Other Americans attended the RILU congress. One of them was Earl Browder, who had joined the CP in New York and was to play a prominent, and ultimately destructive, role in the Party. "Mother" Ella Reeve Bloor was also there. She was a veteran activist from the Socialist Party and helped to found the CPUSA. "Mother" Bloor, who was 59 years old at the time, continued to be one of the leading figures in the Communist Party for the next thirty years.

While in Moscow, in 1921, Bill Foster had a chance to renew acquaintance with the prominent anarchists, Emma Goldman and her friend Alexander Berkman. After being deported during the 1919 "anti-red" raids, the couple took up residence in Moscow, where they flew the black flag of anarchism from their apartment window.

One evening Foster, accompanied by Browder, was invited to visit them. While he chatted with Berkman, Goldman prepared the dinner—a sumptuous spread which surprised Bill because the country was then on semi-starvation rations. Soon after the RILU congress, at which they played an anti-Soviet game, Goldman and Berkman left the Soviet Union where they had been constantly hostile to the development of the organs of state power. They spent the rest of their lives villifying the Soviet Union. This made them the favorite "revolutionaries" of the bourgeoisie.

Foster had friends among the anarchists and ex-anarchists—Jay Fox, Lucy Parsons, Esther Foster, to mention a few. These later joined the Communist Party. But Goldman, in Foster's estimate, "was a petty bourgeois political adventuress, never a revolutionist."

Moreover he found her to be "an insufferable bureaucrat and petty tyrant."[6]

In Moscow, Bill Foster was able to observe the Third Congress of the Communist International also known as the CI, the Comintern, and/or the Third International. The congress met June 22 to July 12 in what had been the great throne room of the palace of the deposed czar. This congress, where Bill first saw Lenin in action, and the Profintern congress, and wide and intensive reading of Communist political literature—all these—transformed him into a convinced Communist.

This transformation was registered emphatically in the book he wrote on his return to the States: *The Russian Revolution.*

In this book Foster undertook to describe "in a general way the evolution, present status, achievements, and problems of the various important social institutions of the new society, such as the state, the political parties, the trade unions, the industries, the army, etc. It is a brief worker's history of the revolution."

Later he would acquire a working knowledge of the Russian language but on this first trip he found that his English, French and German took him over most language hurdles. But, he noted, because "the social disorganization is very great and everything is changing with unbelievable rapidity, it is exceedingly difficult for even native investigators to get exact data on the situation."

In 1921, even as today, the commercial media (which then did not include the radio and television news channels) were ever-ready to discredit reporting favorable to the Soviets. Foster, anticipating this, included in the introduction to his book a long paragraph describing his freedom of access to information. He concluded: "From what I could learn, once a correspondent gets into Russia he is free to do pretty much as he pleases . . . the tales of the 'stuffing' of foreigners with propaganda is a joke among Russians." The next 150 pages of this book are vivid pictures, complete with all the blemishes, of the struggling new society.[7]

Bill Foster came home from Moscow—"home" was Chicago—and joined the Communist Party. In it he no longer found resistance to his anti-dual-unionism line and, for his part, he had come to know and recognise the need for a revolutionary vanguard party to lead the revolutionary movement, to be its "general staff."

The fact is that Foster's highly educational stay in the Soviet capital did not *begin* his abandonment of the syndicalist fallacy of rejecting political action. His own experiences in the packinghouse and steel campaigns had begun to change his view. Were not the proceedings before Judge Altschuler part of the political process? Had not President Wilson maneuvered to defeat the steel strike? Had Bill not found himself one day at the White House with Gompers and Fitzpatrick, trying—in vain—to make the political process work for the workers' side?

During 1920, no doubt as a consequence of the same deep stirrings in the labor movement which had produced the strike movements of the year before, there began to be considerable interest in the idea of a labor party—a political movement independent of the two traditional parties in the same way that Britain's Labor Party was independent of the Liberals and the Conservatives.

The year 1919 had not only seen the great steel strike and the strike of the Boston police, but a nationwide coal strike, the Lawrence textile strike and the February general strike in Seattle. Another 15 years would pass before the number of workers on strike in a single year surpassed the record of 1919.

All the strikes had encountered the intervention of a hostile government. The labor party idea sought to achieve a government sympathetic to labor's immediate aims.

John Fitzpatrick, president of the Chicago Federation of Labor, was enthusiastic about the Labor Party idea at the same time that he was aiding Foster in the steel campaign and strike. He ran for mayor of Chicago in 1919 on the ticket of the Cook County Labor Party and got 60,000 votes—better than ten percent of all votes cast.

In 1921, when Foster returned to Chicago and to the Trade Union Educational League, the revolutionary wave which had swept Europe after World War I and the Bolshevik Revolution was receding. The Social Democratic party of Germany had collaborated with reaction in the murder of Rosa Luxemburg and Karl Liebknecht, curbed the advance of the German workers, and restored full power to the capitalists; in Italy in 1920 a series of strikes which had revolutionary potential were settled for a few minor concessions, and the way was paved for Mussolini's fascist state; in Hungary power was attained by the workers and then recovered by the counter-revolution.

Before the first imperialist war, left-wing socialists distinguished themselves by their opposition to the reformist theories of Edouard Bernstein which, in the United States, had their counterpart in the reformism of Morris Hillquit, Victor Berger and the Socialist Party right wing. After the war the Left—now organized in the Communist Parties—had to fight the reformist *practices* of the right-wing socialist leaders which had such counter-revolutionary consequences for the workers of the world. No wonder that the history of the twenties and after is marked by sharp antagonism between the Socialists and Communists. In this period the world view of Marxism as developed by V.I. Lenin, a revolutionary genius in action and theory, became the guide to workingclass revolutionaries. This view was adopted by Foster under the impact of events and as a result of his close study of the Soviet scene. It was a view which remained his guide to action for the rest of his life. In this view, the present epoch is the epoch of imperialism—the stage of capitalism in decay—and of the centrality of struggle for peace and socialism. Lenin foresaw a period of wars and revolutions—and his foresight was confirmed by subsequent history.

Foster's three-and-a-half month stay in Soviet Russia coincided with one of the most difficult periods in the Revolution's history. In the seven years of war and revolution the country "had passed through a thousand Valley Forges." Famine, cholera, and typhus plagued the land. Wreckage and ruin were everywhere. But what he saw and learned was that "the brave Russian working class, led by the indomitable Communist Party with the great Lenin at its head [was] ready to begin the ten times 'impossible' task of Socialist reconstruction in the backward, ruined country."[8]

In his 155 page book, *The Russian Revolution,* while describing the bitter situation faced by the revolution, he stated his judgment that "the Russian Revolution will live and accomplish its task of setting up the world's first free commonwealth."[9] He never had occasion to change that judgment.

Part of Foster's political education, stemming from his firsthand observations of the functioning of the Soviet government, was a thorough understanding of the role of the state in socialist society. Already, in 1920, when he had taken part in Fitzpatrick's early steps to build a labor party, he had dropped his opposition to political workingclass action in capitalist society; in Russia—and from Lenin's writings on the state—he became convinced that a strong workers' state is indispensable for the building of socialism during the long transition to a classless, stateless Communist society. This bit of knowledge banished the last remnants of syndicalism from his ideological makeup.

"Only after . . . considering Communism, not alone with regard to the Russian Revolution, but especially as to the applicability of its program to the United States," Foster has said, "did I declare myself a Communist."[10]

9

The TUEL: With the Tide

The Trade Union Educational League, which was formally launched in November 1920, had not really gotten off the ground when Bill Foster returned to Chicago in the fall of 1921 after three and a half months in Soviet Russia. But soon after, in a matter of months, it was flying.

The adherence of Foster and his formerly syndicalist colleagues to the Communist Party was a boon to both the League and the Party. For the Party it meant the healthy infusion of a corps of tested, experienced, proletarian labor leaders. The Party was not short of proletarians, but it lacked persons who had led labor struggles. For the League it meant access to the cadres, the organizational connections and important international exchanges which helped orient the fledgling organizations.

The first few years of the TUEL were impressively successful.

In its first year it set up groups in many cities and established its monthly organ, the *Labor Herald*, edited by Foster. In August 1922 the League held its first national conference. This was in Chicago, attended by 45 delegates who came from 22 cities of the United States and four in Canada.

In the months prior to the conference Foster produced ample evidence of his ability to combine a prolific writing schedule with an active leadership role.

In March 1921, before he left for Soviet Russia, he wrote *The Railroaders' Next Step,* a 48-page pamphlet; in November he finished

The Russian Revolution, a 155-page book; by mid-December he wrote *The Revolutionary Crisis in Germany, Italy and France,* a 64-page pamphlet.

By the time Foster was seventy years old he had written ten books, and in the next five years he wrote four more. Each of the four was over 500 pages. He also wrote about 80 pamphlets and some 1200 magazine and newspaper articles during his lifetime. Almost all of his books bore the simple dedication: To Esther.

When Bill joined the Communist Party it was still in its formative period.

Efforts to create a single unified Party did not succeed until May 1921. The united organization took the name Communist Party of America (CPA).

The Party had not only suffered the handicaps consequent to its split condition. Its functioning was further complicated by the fact that, within a few months of its founding, it had been driven underground by such repressive measures as the Lusk Committee in New York, the Palmer Raids nationally, and the "deportation delirium."

When Foster came into the Party it had been essentially unified and, not long after, a major move was made to end the "illegal" phase. This was the formation of the open Workers Party (WP) at a convention in New York City on December 24, 1921. (This has become known as the First Convention in the CPUSA system of numbering its conventions.) However, the underground CPA continued to coexist with the WP until the Second Convention of the WP a year later. In fact, it lingered on until April 1923, when it formally dissolved.[1]

The first issue of *Labor Herald* is dated March 1922. It opens with a lengthy statement of "The Principles and Program of the Trade Union Educational League." But a more succinct statement of the program may be derived from the resolutions of the League's first national conference (August 26-27, 1922). The program may be summarized as follows:

1. Rejection of dual unionism.
2. Rejection of AFL class collaboration policy and adoption of class struggle principle.
3. Industrial unionism through amalgamation of existing unions.
4. Organization of the unorganized.
5. Advocacy of unemployment insurance.
6. For a Labor Party.

7. For the shop delegate system.
8. For affiliation of the American labor movement to the RILU.
9. Support of the Russian Revolution.
10. Abolition of the capitalist system and establishment of a workers' republic.

To achieve this list of goals the TUEL sought to establish a left-progressive bloc in the trade unions.

A glance at the program will suggest that more than a few years would be needed to achieve it. It also appears that the program was a bit heavier than a rank-and-file movement could hope to sustain, given the state of development of the labor movement as a whole in 1922. One may even question whether points 8, 9, and 10 belonged in such a program. Their presence suggests a certain blurring of the lines between a revolutionary party and a left-progressive trade union bloc. (The TUEL itself was the United States section of the RILU.)

In practice, of course, some of the points received more attention and met with greater acceptance than others. Soon three slogans achieved truly mass support. They were: "For Amalgamation," "For a Labor Party," and "For Recognition of the Soviet Union."

In order to avoid being stigmatized as a dual union, the TUEL charged its members no dues beyond a voluntary $1 per year sustainer. It met its expenses mainly by selling its journal and its literature and through collections at meetings.

In the early decades of the twentieth century, amalgamation of craft unions within a given industry may have seemed the logical course leading to the establishment of industrial unionism. But as matters developed, the main surge toward industrial unionism came when the CIO cut the Gordian knot in the thirties.

Even the term, amalgamation, had long been out of favor. Nevertheless, the idea proved to be highly popular in the first half of the 1920s when the TUEL proposed it. To vote for it was to vote for industrial unionism. Consider the International Typographical Union (subject of the lead article in the August 1922 *Labor Herald).* The ITU's 1921 convention in Quebec resolved "that this convention favors the amalgamation of the various printing trades, to the end that there be but one union in the printing industry."[2]

There is no doubt that the printers really wanted this, but, sixty years later, there are still multiple unions in the graphic arts industry.

However, among the dozen or so unions in that industry there have been several mergers in the last decade, and further merging is in process. So "amalgamation," at long last, may be taking place!

The railroads were a special concentration in the TUEL amalgamation drive; and in the 18 months following March 1922—when the movement got an overwhelming vote of 114 to 37 in the Chicago Federation of Labor—3,377 local unions in the railroad industry gave formal endorsement to the amalgamation slogan.[3]

Nevertheless when, in December 1979, a strike was called on the Long Island Rail Road, seventeen unions were involved. The railroads, seemingly a natural for industrial unionization, have not gone that route.

With 16 international unions, 17 big state federations, and thousands of locals (besides those in railroad) endorsing amalgamation in an 18-month period, the TUEL was able to claim that the majority of United States and Canadian labor were on record for the amalgamation slogan.

The slogan was "amalgamation" but the goal was industrial unionism. The generation of leaders which campaigned—seemingly in vain—for amalgamation in the 1920s was the same generation which helped bring about industrial unionization in the 1930s—in auto and steel, in maritime and chemical, in electrical and communications, right down the line.

Bill Foster might have remarked of this outcome: "Well, that just shows that theory [amalgamation] is gray but life [industrial unionism: the CIO] is green." This was an apothegm he had picked up from Lenin who had quoted it from Goethe's *Faust:* Theory my friend, is gray, but green is the eternal tree of life."[4]

Bill could cite other examples of the "gray and the green." There was the matter of the labor party, for instance, which between 1922 and 1924 took on the form of LaFollette's Progressive Party—a form so changed that advocates of the labor party did not recognize this farmer-labor-petty-bourgeois movement as the real-life crystalization of their slogan.

Another example was the Bolshevik Revolution, so painful and harsh in its actuality that some who had worked to bring it about said: "No, this can't be it" because it was not all a matter of sunrises and banners.

But the TUEL was so in tune with the times in 1922 and 1923 that almost all of the Left in this country lined up to support it. For the Communist Party, the building of it was a central task. The left wing of the IWW joined it and the Proletarian Party endorsed it. But the Socialist Labor Party, committed for eternity to dual unionism, held aloof, as did the right wing of the SP. However, Eugene Victor Debs, the Socialist Party's leading figure, wrote an article for the *Labor Herald* in which he said:

> The Trade Union Educational League, under the direction and inspiration of Wm. Z. Foster, is in my opinion the one rightly-directed movement for the industrial unification of the American workers. I thoroughly believe in its plan and its methods and I feel very confident of its steady progress and the ultimate achievment of its ends.[5]

This statement by Debs came from a man who had advocated dual unionism for more years than Foster had opposed it.

Debs wrote this friendly article toward the end of his life. He died in 1926. In the years following the Russian Revolution in 1917 Debs frequently aligned himself with its supporters. He resolutely opposed U.S. participation in World War I. When Alfred Wagenknecht, Charles Ruthenberg and Charles Baker were in prison in Canton, Ohio, in 1918 for anti-war activity, Debs addressed a meeting outside the prison in their support. When Wagenknecht and Ruthenberg helped to found the Communist Party in 1919, Debs was in prison as a consequence of his Canton speech.

Eugene Victor Debs was an unsurpassed orator and agitator for industrial unionism and socialism. Though he often sided with the Communists he sometimes took opposing positions and never forsook his basic loyalty to his Socialist Party comrades. "Debs is a revolutionary but without a clear theory, not a Marxist," wrote Lenin in 1914—an observation which aptly sums up both the principal strength and major weakness of the great proletarian fighter Debs.

Much of the support referred to above was rendered relatively ineffective by the fact that the Left, by reason of its traditional dual-unionism, was not rooted in the AFL and Railroad Brotherhoods. And that is where the TUEL's work was being done. Meanwhile Sam Gompers was muttering that "Foster wants to become the Lenin of America."[6]

The campaign for a labor party picked up the pieces of a spontaneous movement which started in 1918 and then bogged down in 1920. The Fitzpatrick forces in Chicago had sparked the establishment of a National Labor Party which later became the National Farmer-Labor Party (NFLP). The word "National" was based more on aspiration than reality.

But in 1922, the TUEL, the Workers Party and the Fitzpatrick group jointly took up the farmer-labor party issue and found extensive interest in the trade union movement. The TUEL canvassed 25,000 locals with a referendum on the question. Of those which took the trouble to reply over 7,000 endorsed the idea.

In December 1922 the Conference for Progressive Political Action held a conference which invited the Socialist Party and, among others, the National Farmer-Labor Party (with Nockels and Fitzpatrick), but did not invite Ruthenberg, Foster and the Workers Party. The conference voted down the NFLP resolution to found an independent party. Whereupon the NFLP, against the advice of the WP, withdrew from the conference.

The third principal slogan of the TUEL—Recognition of Soviet Russia—tied in with the relief drive of the Friends of Soviet Russia and of the Trade Union National Committee for Russian Famine Relief. The slogan, like the others, registered extensive support.

"These were prosperous times for the TUEL," Foster wrote. " . . . It had fairly leaped from a small sect to a real power in the labor movement." In fact, it had been so successful that the AFL bureaucrats and the federal government joined forces to try to destroy it.[7]

The hostility of its enemies was not provoked merely by the League's programatic successes. The League had also played a role on some of the active fronts of labor struggle. Notable was the coal strike of 1922 when the TUEL forces in Southern Illinois mobilized the miners to defeat the moves of the treacherous president of the Illinois UMWA, Frank Farrington, and saved the strike nationally.

In the same year such TUEL militants as Charles Krumbein, Neils Kjar, and Jack Johnstone played a big role in the Chicago building trades strike, while in New York TUEL groups played an important role in the big needle trades strikes of this period.

It was during a vigorous drive to assist the national strike of 400,000 railroad shopmen that Foster was kidnaped in Denver by Colorado State Rangers.

Bill Foster had worked at many jobs but he thought of himself first of all as a railroad man and always paid special attention to the railroad industry. In March 1922, he wrote *The Railroaders' Next Step*, a plea for amalgamation, based on an analytical and historical study of the United States railroads and their unions. In the summer of 1922 he was one of several speakers sent out into the field by the TUEL to work among the striking railroaders.

Foster was slated to speak in Denver on August 6. About an hour before the start of the meeting he was resting in his room in the Oxford Hotel when three State Rangers seized him without warrant and drove to Brighton, about 20 miles north, where he was jailed overnight and prevented from communicating with anyone. In the morning he was taken first to Greeley and then to Cheyenne, Wyoming. He was handed over to a Cheyenne County sheriff who drove him for hours to Torrington, Nebraska, where Bill caught a train and arrived in time for a speaking date in Omaha, poised and ready.

The kidnaping created a sensation. It was made a central issue by the Democratic candidate for governor of Colorado in November. The Democrat won, and during his term in office the State Rangers were abolished—only to be restored by a later governor.[8]

The Denver incident was the second kidnaping experience for Foster. He had been seized by a vigilante gang during the steel strike in 1919 to prevent his speaking in Johnstown, Pa. The gang put him on a train and deported him to Altoona. Several steel organizers were driven out of Johnstown at the same time, causing serious complications for the handling of the strike.

The conservative clique in the AFL were made to feel that, for the first time in their history, they might lose control of the situation. Not only the TUEL but rivals of Sam Gompers, not quite left of center, were making the AFL president uneasy. At a meeting of 1500 union officers in a Chicago hotel Gompers lost his cool and challenged Foster, who was present, to debate him on the amalgamation question in public. Foster, of course, accepted the challenge immediately and, for months afterwards, kept needling Gompers to set the date. No more was ever heard from Gompers on the matter.

A student of the situation wrote:

> . . . [T]he potential rise of new leaders . . . is a constant menace to the machine. Mr. Samuel Gompers and the bulk of the Federation's present officialdom must keep their eyes on Mr. William Z. Foster. . . . Mr. Gompers has had his opponents since he first attained leadership. . . . Yet Foster's challenge today is more formidable than these others in the eyes of the leaders because the idea of change has been hurled at labor by the Russian Revolution and the postwar upheaval and all that underlie them.[9]

But despite all its efforts and successes, at the end of 1922 the TUEL slowed down as if it were a train whose emergency brake had been pulled. The TUEL was stopped by the long boom phase of the economic cycle, lasting from 1923 to 1929, which came to be called the Coolidge prosperity period.

The post-war depression had been marked by the employers' union-smashing, wage-cutting drives. The following years were marked by speed-up, increased productivity, squeezing more profits out of each worker.

The entrenched labor leadership fell willingly into the drive for increased profit-per-worker. They helped to cultivate prosperity illusions in the working class and consciously made war against the left-wing's class struggle program.

Leaders who had been classified as Progressive (from their support of the Conference for Progressive Political Action) now yielded to the outright reactionaries in the AFL and Railroad Brotherhoods and adopted, even improved upon, their ideas and their language for misleading the workers. Johnson of the Machinists, Stone of the Locomotive Engineers and Hillman of the Clothing Workers were among the first to make the sharp turn to the right and to lower the Labor Party flag. These represented the right wing of the CPPA.

The TUEL still preserved its alliance with the Chicago Federation forces but the latter were feeling pressure from the AFL and from the super-heated prosperity atmosphere. In June 1923, with a new Labor Party convention set for July 3, the AFL cut the CFL's monthly subsidy by 50 percent and threatened it with intervention if it didn't break with the Communists and drop the TUEL slogans.

The break came at the Labor Party convention when Fitzpatrick's group moved to exclude the Workers Party. Although the convention voted this down, 500 to 40, the split was final and fatal. The Chicago split severed TUEL ties with militants across the country and shattered the united front which had shown such great promise.

The Socialist leaders of the needle trades unions gave the oldtime right-wing leaders of the AFL advanced lessons in how to beat the Reds, physically as well as organizationally. They expelled militants from the locals and brought in gangsters to enforce their dictatorial control.

The support the TUEL had won in the needle trades is acknowledged in an official history of the International Ladies' Garment Workers Union (ILGWU) written by Professor Louis Levine, and published in 1924. Dr. Levine notes: "The industrial depression of 1920-21 created a favorable opportunity for the 'Lefts' in the International . . . the 'Lefts' succeeded in electing many of their followers and in several instances gained a majority in the executive boards during the elections of 1922."

But in 1923, the General Executive Board of the ILGWU declared "the Trade Union Educational League a dual union . . . Some of the most persistent 'Lefts' were excluded from the International, while many more were deprived of the right to hold office . . . Two local unions were dissolved . . . to eliminate the 'Lefts' that were in control."[10]

How far the reactionaries in the ILG were ready to go in order to tame their rebellious members was shown by an incident in Chicago's Carmen's Hall on the night of August 25, 1923. Eleven militants had been expelled earlier in the month and 3,000 garment workers had gathered in the hall to voice their protest. Some ILGWU officials were also present to heckle the speakers and cause commotion. Late in the meeting it was Bill Foster's turn to speak when a thug entered the hall from a door near the platform and promptly fired three shots from a revolver in Bill's direction. They lodged in the ceiling over his head. The gangster was recognized but escaped and was never prosecuted.[11]

Expulsions were the style now. The 1923 Portland convention of the AFL picked up the dual-unionist charge and declared war on Communists in the unions. Expulsions became the official weapon to reinforce the suppression of union democracy. The Brotherhood of Railway Carmen expelled Foster by first refusing to accept his dues and then dropping him for non-payment.

The right wing was not only riding a prosperity bandwagon, they had the reins in their hands.

10

The TUEL: Bucking the Tide

There was no public announcement of William Z. Foster's joining the Communist Party when he became a member in 1921. The Party was still underground at that time and the identity of its members was kept as secret as possible.

"Those were the days," wrote Frederick Lewis Allen in his book, *Only Yesterday,* "when column after column of the front pages of the newspapers shouted the news of strikes and anti-Bolshevist riots; . . . and when the Vice-President of the United States cited as a dangerous manifestation of radicalism in the women's colleges the fact that the girl debaters of Radcliffe had upheld the affirmative in an intercollegiate debate on the subject: 'Resolved, that the recognition of labor unions is essential to successful collective bargaining.' It was an era of lawless and disorderly defense of law and order, of unconstitutional defense of the Constitution, of suspicion and civil conflict—in a very literal sense, a reign of terror."[1]

Attorney General A. Mitchell Palmer, the man responsible for organizing the "reign of terror," claimed in justification: "Like a prairie fire, the blaze of revolution was sweeping over every American institution of law and order a year ago. It was eating its way into the homes of the American workman, its sharp tongues of revolutionary heat were licking the altars of churches, leaping into the belfry of the school bell, crawling into the sacred corners of American homes, seeking to replace marriage vows with libertine laws, burning up the foundations of society."[2] This shows, at any rate, that the "reds" were not the only ones who overestimated the tempo of revolutionary advance.

And as one final sample of the grotesque anti-radicalism which proliferated in the post World War I period, we may cite the words of General Henry J. Reilly who predicted "if things continue to go as they have recently in Washington we can expect to see Jane Addams President and William Z. Foster, Secretary of War." (Jane Addams, of course, was a prominent pacifist and the country's best known settlement house worker. In 1912 she seconded the nomination of Theodore Roosevelt and in 1928 and 1932 she would endorse Herbert Hoover for President.)[3]

Foster's membership in the Party became public knowledge in August 1922, after a raid on the C.P. convention which was held in the small resort village of Bridgman, Michigan.

At that time the underground stage of Party existence was already being phased out, superseded by the open Workers Party. This process was completed in April, 1923.

The careful preparations of the 1922 convention were thwarted through the presence of one Francis A. Morrow, who happened to be Special Agent K-97, a part-time informer of the Department of Justice. Morrow, described by Foster as "a little, ferret-eyed sneak of a man,"[4] in turn called in Jacob Spolansky, a full-time bloodhound of the Bureau of Investigation. Spolansky called in the local sheriff.

Thirty-two persons were arrested in the Bridgman raid but only two persons were ever tried. They were Charles E. Ruthenberg, the Party chairman, and William Z. Foster. The proceedings were brought under Michigan's criminal syndicalism law. The offense was unlawful assembly and the penalty was five to ten years in Jackson penitentiary.

The first to be tried was Foster who went on trial March 12, 1923, at St. Joseph, following a nation-wide mass defense campaign. Bill's chief defense attorney was Frank P. Walsh, the distinguished lawyer who had handled the workers' side of the meat-packing hearings before Judge Altschuler in 1918.

The jury panel was a seemingly bottomless pool of businessmen, professionals and farmers. The defense soon exhausted its peremptory challenges.

Then Mrs. Minerva Olson was called. The prosecution was pleased; the defense was not. Mrs. Olson seemed the kind of person the defense should have saved a challenge for. She was active in patriotic movements, a member of the Daughters of the American Revolution, and a Gold Star Mother, having lost two sons killed in action in the World War. When asked her definition of a "red" she replied, "An ignorant foreigner." Walsh tried his best to disqualify her but failed. Only Esther Foster judged Mrs. Olson more favorably and—though Bill had great respect for Esther's judgment of people—the defense group considered the woman juror a sure guilty vote. The twelve people in the jury box sat there looking cold and hostile, with Mrs. Olson as cold and hostile as any.

But the trial did not end with the quick verdict of guilty for which the prosecution hoped and which the defendant expected. Instead, on April 6, after thirty-six hours, the jury reported itself hopelessly hung—split six to six, right down the middle, with Minerva Olson voting for acquittal.

In fact, from the outset of the jury's deliberation, Mrs. Olson had led the "not guilty" faction. Bill and Esther found this out when they visited her next day to thank her. Mrs. Olson, they learned, believed in old-fashioned freedom of speech. She did not think Communists should be excluded from First Amendment protection. And besides she was convinced that her two sons had died fighting for just this kind of democracy.[5]

The disappointment of the redbaiters in the performance of strong-minded Mrs. Olson is shown by the analysis of her conduct printed in *Reds in America,* an early "expose" of the Communist Party, written by R.M. Whitney (Harvard, Class of 1897). Mr. Whitney, in the course of trying to explain how Foster got a hung jury, complains irritably:

> Then again there was a woman on the jury . . . she was evidently more or less emotional. Her sympathies were successfully aroused. She was made to believe that Foster was a highminded person, working at great personal sacrifice, to aid the "struggling masses." . . . [S]he was unable to grasp from the mass of testimony that Foster was heading a great conspiracy against civilization and Christianity. Because of her high-mindedness, she was wholly incapable of grasping the fact that there could be such a conspiracy.[6]

The newly-launched *Time* magazine reported: "William Z. Foster received an ovation of several minutes when he stepped upon the stage of a New York hall to address an audience of 600 ardent radicals. He reviewed the trial and likened himself and his colleagues to Christ, whom he called 'the original Communist. He ran the capitalists out of the temple and they hated him for it.' "[7]

Foster, and all the others accused by the State of Michigan, with the exception of Charles E. Ruthenberg, remained under heavy bail until 1933 without being brought to trial. The cases were then dismissed. But a carefully screened jury convicted Ruthenberg, who died while his case was under appeal.

As was indicated in the previous chapter the "good times" of the era of Coolidge prosperity proved to be hard times for the TUEL in its three-pronged campaign for amalgamation, a labor party and recognition of the Soviet Union. Prosperity illusions, expulsions, and terrorism combined to cost the League a loss of mass contacts and mass influence.

When the prosperity bubble burst in 1929 and the Great Depression of the thirties cast its pall, the years of 1923-1929 were looked back upon by some as the Golden Age. Tricky bonus and piece-work schemes, "welfare" systems, illusionary retirement plans and employee stock-purchasing offers were used to bait the speedup trap. Output per worker increased by 29 percent and profits doubled and tripled, while real wages advanced by only 4.5 percent.

The trade union bureaucrats threw themselves vigorously into the exploitation schemes. They purchased recognition and tolerance for their unions in exchange for expediting the profitmaking schemes at the point of production.

One of the best known of class-collaboration devices was the B & O Plan, so-called from its original introduction on the Baltimore and Ohio Railroad. And one of the most corrupting of the products of this period was the proliferation of labor banks, insurance companies and real estate enterprises, a movement to which Bill Foster gave the name "trade union capitalism." Since most of these enterprises were milked to the profit of the corrupt union leaders, the end of the process was foreseeable—and Foster has described it in such works as *Wrecking the Labor Banks* (1927), and *Misleaders of Labor* (1927).[8] The latter is a book of more than 300 pages in which Foster describes, in fascinating detail, the process by which the workers were robbed and the leadership enriched by "trade union capitalism."

In 1924 Samuel Gompers died and was succeeded by William Green. But in the AFL nothing changed, except that a colorful bureaucrat was replaced by a drab one.

Of course, in order to carry through the crass deception of the workers which was taking place, the opposition had to be squelched. And this meant, in the first instance, the TUEL. Hence the violence, the expulsions, the lies, and the dirty tricks which were used against it.

The TUEL's relative isolation in the period we are discussing was aggravated by its own sectarian errors. Most glaring of these was its too-close identity with the Communist Party, whose program it practically adopted whole. This being the case, it must have seemed quite logical to merge its official organ, *Labor Herald,* with that of the Party, the *Workers Monthly,* which it did in November 1924. The TUEL, intended as a broad rank-and-file mass opposition movement, became too politically restrictive.

But despite its sectarian errors—and despite all the stuff that was thrown at it by its exuberant enemies—the TUEL managed to carry on several broadly-based struggles in this same period. One of these was in the Carpenters Union where the usual expulsion policy was used against the militants by a corrupt and autocratic leadership. In 1925 a Communist, Morris Rosen, ran for president against the incumbent, William L. Hutcheson, and received 9,014 votes against 77,985 for the latter. Not a bad showing when we consider who counted the votes! (Ten years later Hutcheson was to receive an historic punch in the jaw from John L. Lewis, a blow which started the CIO on its way to glory.)

In the Machinists Union the TUEL fight was led by Andrew Overgaard, a Communist, who in the McCarthy period of the fifties was deported to his native Denmark. Here the fight was directed against William H. Johnston, the union's head, who was the first to sponsor the B & O Plan. Overgaard and many others were expelled. In a united front, the TUEL supported the progressive John Frederick Anderson in the union election of 1925. The election was won—no, stolen—by Johnston, claiming 18,021 votes to Anderson's 17,076.

Even the Coolidge economic boom did not help the coal industry, which went into chronic depression several years before the 1929 crisis. The Communist Party and the Trade Union Educational League were in a constant state of mobilization to counter John L. Lewis's dictatorship in the United Mine Workers. His class collaborationist policies and his reckless use of his power as president were the focus of a "Save the Union" campaign in which Foster guided the setting up of a national, united front Save the Union Committee. In this period Bill spent five months on the road organizing the fight.

In 1927–1928 the left-progressive bloc worked valiantly to save the general strike of the coal miners. Mass picketing and a relief system were organized by Alfred Wagenknecht, but the strike, which lasted more than a year, was lost. The UMWA was practically wiped out in the bituminous fields.

Margaret Cowl, Tom Myerscough and Pat Toohey were among the militants who tried to save the miners union during its crisis years of the twenties.

In the textile industry, which, like coal, could be described as "sick," the TUEL scored a success in organizing the unorganized, and did it while skirting the perils of dual unionism.

In October 1925, despite the supposedly prevailing affluence, the textile manufacturers in Passaic, New Jersey, decreed a 10 percent wage cut. The average wage for women in the woolen mills was $17 a week; for the men it was $24. For the employers, earnings on investment were as high as 93 percent. The "affluence" was a one-sided proposition.[9]

The United Textile Workers (UTW) of the AFL should have carried the ball against the wage cut but it did not enter the picture. Instead the TUEL set up a United Front Committee of Textile Workers, and the Communists assigned young Albert Weisbord to organize the resistance.

When, on January 25, 1926, a committee of 45 workers presented the United Front Committee's demands to the Botany Mills, the company response was to fire the entire committee. Then a strike started which involved Botany's 5,000 workers, and soon spread to almost 16,000 workers, tying up the entire Passaic textile industry (and that included Garfield and Lodi as well).

The hard-fought strike lasted to the end of the year and every day the picketlines faced police brutality and intimidation. With a fine lack of discrimination, the police smashed not only the heads of workers but the cameras of newspaper and newsreel cameramen, who came out next day in armored cars to get their pictures.

Weisbord, a law school graduate, had a gift for oratory but was a poor strategist. The Communists reinforced his frail leadership with fighters like Will Weinstone, John Ballam and Alfred Wagenknecht. Elizabeth Gurley Flynn (not then a CP member) brought to the strike experience she had gained in the textile wars of Lawrence and Paterson.

The left-wing forces had no wish to preserve a dual union. In order to facilitate a settlement they withdrew and turned the organization over to the UTW. Botany rescinded the wage cut and agreed to recognize grievance committees; the other mills accepted the same terms. But the UTW permitted the union to disintegrate and militants to be blacklisted.

This caused Foster and the TUEL and the Communist Party to review the wisdom of a rigid anti-dual unionist policy, when this could lead to the unfortunate result of Passaic. In time this review led to a different approach to the organization of the unorganized.

The needle trades—fur, women's garments, men's clothing, millinery—were generally under the control of Socialist leaders. And no section of union leadership participated more whole-heartedly and expertly in the application of class-collaboration policies and in the implementation of the "higher strategy of labor."

More than 100,000 needle trades workers accepted the leadership of the TUEL and many more were influenced by it. The internal fight developed most sharply in the New York locals of the fur workers and the ILGWU.

The struggle developed to a considerable extent as a political contest between the Communist Party and the Socialist Party. For many years the bitterness engendered by contention on the needle trades front poisoned the relationship between the two parties. The social-democrats of the unions were emulating, within the limits of their power, the treachery which their counterparts in Europe had used to stifle revolution in central Europe and Italy. Relationships between the two workingclass parties went through various stages over the years. Eventually the Socialist Party disintegrated into a number of splinters. Today, a leadership cadre of social-democratic union bureaucrats remains entrenched in the U.S. labor movement. Its largest segment is its right wing, which is unsurpassed in anti-Communism and anti-Sovietism and is an ever-willing supporter of U.S. imperialism.

To the left wing's struggle to preserve a living wage, decent conditions, and union democracy in the needle trades in 1925 to 1927, the union leadership's ultimate answer was expulsion. Thus some 50,000 furriers and garment workers were thrown out of their unions. Expulsion also took place in textile (only five percent organized), and in coal mining, where the UMWA was falling apart.

Nevertheless, when TUEL's Third National Conference took place in New York on December 3 and 4, 1927, the main orientation was still toward working in the AFL. Reinstatement of the expelled workers was a goal, and the central slogan was "Save the Trade Unions." However in the program adopted at the Conference (actually a convention) something new was added which soon was to take on increased importance: "Wherever possible, the unorganized must be brought into the existing unions; where no unions exist or where the existing unions refuse to organize the masses, the progressive workers must organize new unions and struggle for admission into the general labor movement, as well as fight the immediate battles of their members."[10]

In March 1928 the Fourth Congress of the RILU was held and the situation of the American unions received the close study of this world body which pooled the experience of unionists around the world.

Foster attended the RILU congress and he came away convinced that the TUEL had erred for some time in not paying more attention to organizing the unorganized directly in the basic industries. Opposition to dual unions had deterred it from organizing new industrial unions where this gave the only hope for bringing workers into, or back into, the organized fold.

At the Fourth RILU Congress the new policy was strongly advocated by A. Lozovsky, who was the head of the Red International of Labor Unions. It generated animated discussion in the ranks of the TUEL and CP and resulted in agreement that, where the AFL failed to function, an effort should be made to organize independent unions. The TUEL lost no time in orienting itself toward the new policy.

At the same time the CP Central Committee pointed out that the AFL still had about 3,000,000 members. The Committee said: "These we cannot surrender to the leadership of the reactionary bureaucrats. We must continue and extend our work among these organizations. . . ."[11]

This caveat was a timely one and Foster later had occasion to remark "that the TUEL and CP would have done well had they borne it clearly in mind during the next few years."[12]

11

Toward a Labor Party

Fascism, a new word and a qualitatively new form of capitalist state power, came into prominence in 1922 when Benito Mussolini, a former right-wing social-democrat, seized power in Italy. In the same year the nazi movement was organized in Germany.

By mid-1921 it was evident that the revolutionary wave that surged in 1917 was now receding. This prompted Lenin to initiate the concept of the united front of the working class in order to spur it into action against the capitalist class. The focus of the united front's activities would be immediate issues, economic and political. The effect would be to heighten the workers' class consciousness and to strengthen their organization and, hopefully, to revive the revolutionary trend.

The question of the united front received full attention at the Fourth Congress of the Communist International, November 7 to December 3, 1922. This was just after Mussolini's so-called March on Rome. The judgment of the Comintern congress was that the electoral expression of the united front in the United States should be a labor party. The Workers Party had come to the same conclusion six months before.

In the early years of the Communist Party—its "formative years" from 1919 to 1929—it had to overcome a tendency to left sectarianism, a tendency which sometimes led to the relative isolation of the Party from the major mass movements.

The Party suffered from some holdovers and hangovers of certain traditional positions of the pre-Party Left. It had to learn that immediate political demands were not necessarily reformist; that both a minimum and maximum program were required; that anti-parliamentarism was not, in all cases, revolutionary; that it was necessary to have a positive attitude toward American democratic traditions and culture; and that it was important to build alliances with organizations of the Black people and of the agricultural poor.

The Communists' early efforts to assist in the creation of an independent labor party were hampered by sectarian modes of thinking and lack of experience in such broad political work. After all, part of the heritage of the Left was the anarcho-syndicalist rejection of political activity and the Socialist Party belief that *it* was the labor party.

Following Henry George's campaign for mayor of the City of New York in 1886, Frederick Engels made the observation that "A million or two workingmen's votes next November for a *bona fide* workingmen's party is worth infinitely more at present than a hundred thousand votes for a doctrinally perfect platform."[1]

It does not appear that the Communists of the early twenties were familiar with Engels' remark.[2] In any case they labored mightily to found a labor party based on a "doctrinally perfect platform." Meanwhile an independent movement grew up around Senator Robert M. LaFollette's ambition to be president of the United States. His Progressive ticket did not grow into a bona fide workingmen's party to be sure, but it grew into an American-style electoral movement that united, if only for the moment, a major part of the trade unions, plus farm organizations and sections of the middle class. The Socialist Party and the American Federation of Labor backed LaFollette, a new departure for both of them. Even the National Association for the Advancement of Colored People was part of this electoral coalition. But while one out of every six voters cast a vote for the Progressives in November 1924, the Communists were in the opposition. Moreover, they had lost their valuable alliance with Fitzpatrick and the Chicago Federation of Labor.

One unforeseen result of the whole situation—and not a negative one—was that William Z. Foster became candidate for president.

It has been mentioned above (Chapter 8) that a farmer-labor party was formed in 1920 under Fitzpatrick's leadership. It polled 250,000 votes that year.

Of greater impact was the Conference for Progressive Political Action (CPPA). It was led by the railroad unions and included, besides other labor unions, farm organizations and some middle-class groups. The CPPA, with some 3,000,000 persons behind it, evolved into the movement which sponsored the LaFollette campaign.

But the CPPA did not favor a labor party and in its 1922 conference adhered to the non-partisan policy of the AFL. It barred delegates from the Workers Party and thereby aroused the indignation of Fitzpatrick, who insisted on building a farmer-labor party with Communist participation.

In agreement with the Workers Party, the Fitzpatrick group called a convention for July 3, 1923, to form a federated farmer-labor party. But, on the road to the convention, changed circumstances made Fitzpatrick change his mind. He too, like the bulk of the conventional labor movement, was being softened up by the Coolidge economic boom. Moreover, his friendly relations with the Communists had incurred the wrath of Gompers to the point where the AFL had withdrawn its subsidy to the Chicago Federation. And, besides, the mainstream of the labor movement was now moving into the CPPA.

The break came as a surprise at the July convention to form the Federated Farmer-Labor Party (FFLP). Fitzpatrick, who had planned the event with the Workers Party, now wanted the WP excluded. When he was voted down he pulled out his troops. The new party was born nevertheless but, as Foster has said, it was "a baby on our doorstep." It did not survive its infancy.[3]

In a last ditch effort to keep the FFLP alive the Workers Party brought about a convention in June 1924 based on such progressive contacts as it had retained. The National Farmer-Labor Party was formed. But it did not have a chance. By this time LaFollette had gathered in the component parts of his coalition and was ready to announce his candidacy.

The newly-born National Farmer-Labor Party then retired from the field and the Workers Party, for the first time, nominated its own Communist candidates, William Z. Foster for president and Benjamin Gitlow for vice-president.

Little need be said here of Foster's running mate. He came into the Communist Party out of the Socialist Party, a young firebrand. His ardor was soon quenched and he spent the rest of his life as a professional anti-Communist and FBI informer.

The Workers Party saw the LaFollette ticket as "petty bourgeois and dominated by labor aristocrats, millionaire liberals, and reformist Socialists."[4] But in 1952, Foster wrote in his *History of the CPUSA*, expressing the wisdom of hindsight: "The LaFollette movement represented a united front of workers, petty bourgeoisie, and farmers in the struggle against monopoly capital, with the petty bourgeoisie and labor leaders in control . . . The Party should have gone along in critical support of the LaFollette movement . . . "[5]

The Communist Party national ticket succeeded in getting on the ballot in thirteen states and 33,076 votes were counted for it.

The year 1924 is notable in Communist Party history for a number of events which marked the development of the Party as it entered and passed its fifth year. For one thing, on January 13, 1924, the *Daily Worker* began publication in a Chicago building for which the Party had raised the funds. (The newspaper is continued today as the *Daily World.*) In the same year publication of the *Workers Monthly* commenced (this continues today as *Political Affairs*) and the Workers School was founded in New York. Nineteen twenty-four was also the year in which Alexander Trachtenberg founded International Publishers and began the first systematic publication of Marxist-Leninist works in the United States.

Mention may also be made here of the Young Workers League which was founded in 1922. It later became the Young Communist League (YCL) and was particularly prominent in the 1930s under such leaders as Gil Green, Henry Winston and Dave Doran. The YWL was open to students and workers. It had hundreds of members among young workers in coal, iron, and textile who supported the TUEL activities. The YWL opposed militarism and campaigned against the Ku Klux Klan and similar racist organizations.

Foster has noted in his *Negro People in American History* that it was about this time that the Communists began to show active interest in Afro-American liberation as a special question, a major aspect of the Party's work ever since.

Until the formation of the Communist Party in 1919, the U.S. Left had not grasped the character of Black liberation as a special question, that it required a program of special demands within the general struggle of the working class and all working people for liberation. Indeed, initially the Communist Party program, while addressing itself to the struggles of the Black people, did not achieve an advanced position on the question.

When the Workers Party was formed in 1921, the Communists had become familiar with Lenin's theses regarding oppressed peoples. The Party adopted a resolution in 1922 which stated it would help the Blacks "in their struggle for liberation, and will help them in their fight for economic, political, and social equality."[6] This resolution had the merit of singling out the question as a special one.

Typically, the TUEL demanded that "Negroes be given the same social, political, and industrial rights as whites, including the right to work in all trades, equal wages, admission into all unions . . . "[7]

The Universal Negro Improvement Association (UNIA)—better

known as the Garvey Movement—was the largest mass movement of the Black people during the twenties. The Party took a friendly but critical attitude toward this confused but well-intended organization. In June 1924, the WP Central Committee sent a letter to the UNIA offering support and cooperation.

The Workers Party was the only multi-racial organization invited to the "All Race Congress or Sanhedrin," held in Chicago in 1924. The Sanhedrin, which was attended by such prominent Blacks as W.E.B. DuBois, Monroe Trotter, Dr. Alain L. Locke, and Ida B. Wells Barnett, was addressed by such leading Communists as Robert Minor and Lovett Fort-Whiteman. (Fort-Whiteman became national organizer of the American Negro Labor Congress which was formed in 1925 following a conference convened by the Communist Party.)

During the course of the labor party campaign 1922-24, a factional division developed in the Workers Party which rapidly resolved itself into a formal division within the organization.

In November 1924 there were majority and minority theses issued by the respective factions dealing with the political situation and immediate tasks of the Party. There was nothing reprehensible at the time in belonging to a faction. Rather it was an accepted thing.

In 1924 William Z. Foster was chairman of the Workers Party and, with Alex Bittelman, headed the majority group. Charles E. Ruthenberg, the Party secretary, with John Pepper, headed the minority.

With some changing of sides and internal positions, factions persisted until 1929. Eventually the factional situation became a critical matter resulting in expulsions in 1928 and 1929. This will be dealt with later.

But, because of the conditions of the Party's twin birth and its complex course of development, there was a certain inevitability in the factional situation. The membership had been derived from a number of left-wing tributary sources—the Socialist Party, the Socialist Labor Party, the IWW, anarchists, syndicalists, and others. The resolution of the internal fight slowly led to the welding of the Party into a united Marxist-Leninist entity.

But, while they lasted, the factions frequently developed a bitterness which was harmful to the Party's work. At the 1925 Fourth Convention of the WP, the Foster-Bittelman group controlled a majority of delegates. However, it agreed to a Central Committee on which the two groups had parity. But the parity did not last and the Ruthenberg-Pepper group soon became the new "majority."

At the 1925 convention, the decision was made to change the Party name to Workers (Communist) Party. At the Seventh Convention in 1930 the name was changed to Communist Party, and in the following pages we shall refer to it by that name—as consistently as possible.

12

The Trade Union Unity League

The final pages of Chapter 10 reported the decision to orient the Trade Union Educational League toward a major emphasis on independent industrial unionism. We have also mentioned some of the actions in which the TUEL participated, particularly in Textile, Needle Trades and Coal Mining, which prepared the way for the new orientation.

About a year after the Communist Party and the TUEL had opted for independent unionism the fourth convention of the League was held in Cleveland, Ohio, on August 31 and September 1, 1929. On this occasion the TUEL was reorganized as the Trade Union Unity League (TUUL).

In the months preceding the founding of the TUUL there had been an intensification of the circumstances which made the new orientation necessary.

The expulsion policy of the Socialist trade union leaders in the needle trades was especially ruthless. The contest between left wing and right wing in the needle trades had one of its most decisive collisions in the Fur Workers Union.

By 1925, the Furriers Section of the TUEL had become a mass movement which, more truly than the union leaders, represented the interests of the fur workers.

Ben Gold was the unchallenged leader of the militant majority of the fur workers. As head of the Furriers' Section of the TUEL from its inception in 1923 he led a constant fight against the official union leadership which collaborated with the employers and which hired gangster support to enforce its rule. If a worker was bold enough or naive enough to stand up at a local meeting and complain about some aspect of union service, a gangster was sure to yell: "Shut up! Sit down or we'll knock you down." Gold's refusal to "shut up" had cost him a broken head in 1923. He was known, and respected, as a Communist.[1]

A close associate of Ben Gold from 1925 on was Irving Potash, who was 23 years old when Gold recognized his usefulness in the fur workers union. Together with such stalwarts as Jack Schneider, Joseph Winogradsky, and Sam Burt, Potash was one of the Foster-trained TUEL forces who built the union of fur and leather workers in the face of employer intransigence, government intimidation, right-wing betrayal, and gangster violence.

Potash, who at 16 was a Socialist Party member, became a charter member of the Communist Party. He was one of the Party's political committee when its members were arrested and tried under the Smith Act in 1949. After serving a term in prison he was deported in 1955 to Poland from which his parents had brought him in 1912. Determined to rejoin his family, he returned to the United States, served another prison term, and spent the rest of his life active in trade union work.

He is probably best remembered for the courage he showed in the fight to drive the gangster element out of the fur industry. Together with Sam Burt, he gave the testimony which finally placed the notorious gangsters, Lepke and Gurrah, behind bars.

Under the leadership of the TUEL forces the New York City fur workers held fast in a general strike that lasted from February to June 1926. The key demand was for an unprecedented 40-hour week. Victory brought the left wing into leadership in New York and in a number of other locals in other cities.

By 1928, it was evident that the AFL top brass and the right-wing leaders in the fur unions would wage continuous war to bar the fur workers from a democratic choice of officers as long as those officers were of the Left. They wrecked the union rather than permit such a choice.[2]

This made necessary the establishment of an independent Needle Trades Workers Industrial Union consisting basically of the furriers and of the cloak and dressmakers, who were also victimized by the AFL expulsion policy. Thus, in December 1928, the TUEL took another step toward independent industrial unionism.

In Textile, the catalysts for independent left-led unionism were two long, hard-fought strikes in which the Party and the TUEL played the decisive roles.

The first involved 26,000 cotton mill workers in New Bedford, Massachusetts, in April 1928. That strike led to others in the surrounding textile area—at Fall River, Woonsocket and elsewhere. The strike lasted six months but ended with an AFL sell-out. As a result the National Textile Workers Union was formed, affiliated to the TUEL.

In February 1929, the National Textile Workers Union (NTW) boldly advanced into the South, a region of the country that the AFL seldom seemed able to find on the map.

Unlike textile workers in the North, the workers in the southern mills were almost all native-born, of "old American stock." Their low wages and speed-up conditions made them ripe for organization. The Communist Party sent many organizers into the field. They helped bring 25,000 textile workers of the Gastonia area into the union fold.

On April 2 a strike started at the Loray mills and 2,500 workers walked out. They were later joined by 1,700 others.

The governor of North Carolina lost no time in sending several companies of militia to break the strike. They had the willing help of vigilantes, organized by the American Legion, and of deputized thugs led by the Chief of Police, Orville F. Aderholt. On June 7 these worthies made an armed raid on the union's modest headquarters. They were repelled by the strikers, and Chief Aderholt was killed in the melee. One hundred workers were arrested in connection with the chief's death. Seven strike leaders were found guilty and given sentences of up to 20 years.

The strike was finally beaten but the mills were obliged to make concessions to the workers' demands.

As has been previously stated, the TUEL was active in the coalfields almost from its inception. In June 1923 it organized the Progressive International Committee within the UMWA, a left-progressive coalition. The committee's program called for a six-hour day, five-day week, unemployment insurance, organization of the unorganized, and nationalization of the mines, as well as other demands necessary to the miners' well-being. The left-progressives ran a slate in the UMWA elections on which a Communist rank-and-file miner, George Voyzey, ran against John L. Lewis. Lewis counted 66,000 votes for Voyzey and gave himself 136,000.[3]

In the Save-the-Union campaign of 1926 the progressive forces nominated John Brophy, president of District 2, for UMWA president. But again Lewis counted himself in despite Brophy's allegations of gross fraud.

In September 1928, with the UMWA crumbling, following Lewis's abysmal handling of the long 1927-8 strike in the bituminous fields, the National Miners Union was founded.

Delegations from the new independent unions—the National Miners Union, the National Textile Workers Union, and the Needle Trades Workers Industrial Union—numbered 322 delegates of the 690 who met to found the Trade Union Unity League. William Z. Foster was elected general secretary. *Labor Unity* became the official organ of the TUUL, as it had been for the TUEL since February 1927. The headquarters were established in New York City.

The program of the TUUL differed from that of the TUEL in only one major respect: the TUEL had put its main emphasis on rank-and-file work within the established unions; the new league emphasized the organization of the unorganized into industrial unions. It already had three affiliated unions (see above) based on the principle of "one factory, one industry, one union."

Eventually the organization of the unorganized took place, on a mass scale, under quite different circumstances and auspices than those existing in 1929. Millions of workers came into the Congress of Industrial Organizations (CIO) and, in spite of everything, into the American Federation of Labor, in the thirties. But in 1929 the existing labor movement had lost its prerogative to organize—lost it by default.

The situation in the giant automobile industry is a good illustration of this fact. In 1926 the industry was producing vehicles at the rate of four-and-a-half million per year. The AFL held its 1926 convention in Detroit and created a brief flurry in the press by adopting a resolution to organize the auto industry.

But nothing came of this. Instead of using sound organizing techniques, the necessary painstaking, manifold approaches to the workers, the AFL was content to have its president, William Green, approach the employers "to negotiate an understanding." But the employers spurned these overtures. After two years, with 19 unions claiming jurisdiction, the AFL had to admit that "up to the present we are not in a position to even report progress." At the 1928 AFL convention nothing was said about plans to organize auto.[4]

The message of the AFL to the manufacturers had been: "Recognize us or the reds will get you." The manufacturers had replied: "We can handle it."

The key craft union having nominal jurisdiction in the auto plants was the Machinists Union. But, by 1928, after organizing about 2,700 units out of 150,000 garages, repair shops and service stations then existing, the union had still made no progress in the manufacturing end and, indeed, had stopped talking about it.

This outcome might have been foretold as early as 1925 when P.J. Conlon, head of the Machinists national organization department, was reported as saying: "Let Foster do it." (See page 3.)

Certainly Foster was ready to "do it." The Auto Workers Union affiliated to the TUUL in 1929. It had gone through many changes since starting out in 1893 as the Carriage and Wagon Workers International Union of North America, affiliated to the Knights of Labor. After two years, it switched its affiliation to the AFL. In 1911, apparently convinced that the horseless carriage was here to stay, it became the Carriage, Wagon and Automobile Workers' International Union (CWAWIU). But in 1916 the AFL, finding that the union's industrial scope impinged on the jurisdiction of some craft unions, ordered the CWAWIU to drop the "A" from its title. But by this time the union was solidly in the auto industry. It had 23,000 members in 1918 when the AFL lifted its charter. It reached 45,000 in 1920. After that it declined but still retained a nucleus of militant supporters in ten or more important Detroit shops.

In 1928 this union was known as the Automobile, Aircraft and Vehicle Workers Union. Its Detroit Local 127 issued a call for a conference to take preliminary steps to organize 300,000 auto workers. It was held on January 13, 1929 in Detroit. Bill Foster attended representing the TUEL. This support by the League advanced the Communists toward the strategic role they played in the eventual organization of auto. The isolated Detroit local became the Auto Workers Union, affiliated to the TUUL.

The Communists had Party clubs ("nuclei") in a number of auto shops. Robert W. Dunn in *Labor and Automobiles* tells of this and of the many four-page shop papers issued by the Party:

> Some of those published in Michigan are *The Ford Worker, The Fisher Body Worker, The Dodge Worker, The Packard Worker, The Hudson Worker, The Chrysler Worker,* and the *Buick Worker.* These little four-page papers, which range in circulation from 1,000 to 20,000 (Ford has the largest), . . .

constantly urge the workers to join a union. Even the most conservative workers will buy these papers, sold for a penny at the gates of the plant by volunteers.[5]

The Communists, as this shows, were early on the job in the organization of auto workers. Their TUUL union of automobile workers never brought in the great mass of workers that later became the United Automobile Workers of today. But when the victories began to be won in GM, Chrysler, and later, in Ford, the Communists were there and ready, and played a key role.

Bill Foster was again his party's candidate for president in 1928 (and again Gitlow was his running mate). The Party was on the ballot in 32 states and polled 48,228 votes.

Foster carried the campaign deep into the South where Art Shields, veteran political reporter, "heard him lashing disfranchisement, lynchings and peonage in a hall in Atlanta, Ga., in 1928 while racist cops stood at the door."

It was in the 1928 election campaign that the Communist Party put forward the necessity for a government system of unemployment insurance. This had never before in the country's history been raised as a political demand.

Though the labor party slogan was in the Communist program for the 1928 elections it was not a live issue. LaFollette died in 1925 and the third party idea died with him—though it would be resurrected, under quite different circumstances, years later.

Within the Communist Party the question of a labor party was no longer a factional matter after 1925. But factions persisted. There was much good will on both sides. Both the Ruthenberg-Pepper group and the Foster-Bittelman group made efforts to resolve their differences. However, before the factional problem got better it got very bad—so bad in fact that it just had to be concluded.

Charles E. Ruthenberg's death on March 2, 1927, at the age of 45, was a serious loss and a terrible shock to the Party which he headed as general secretary. He had helped consolidate the Party and steer it out of its "illegal" stage into open, mass struggle. His courage in self-defense and in defense of the Party, displayed in trials in 1917, 1920, and 1922, were a model to be emulated by all his comrades. And, though he was head of a faction, he was trusted by his Party adversaries.

One of the leading members of the Foster-Bittelman faction was James P. Cannon. He came into the Communist Party out of the Socialist Party (and, before that, the IWW).

On the international scene, manifested by developments in the Comintern, 1928 was the year when it became necessary to eliminate the counter-revolutionary ideological tendency known as Trotskyism, and to neutralize it as an organizational opposition.

The tendency took its name from Leon Trotsky who had come into prominence in the Bolshevik revolution after a checkered pre-revolutionary past. In 1903, at the time of the split which gave rise to the Menshevik and Bolshevik tendencies in Russia, Trotsky sided with the Mensheviks, the reformists. Until July 1917 he generally opposed the Bolsheviks and Lenin. He and his centrist group then came over to the Bolshevik Party and he was given responsible posts. In 1923 he resumed his opposition. He and the contemporary movement which takes his name have been characterized by a reformist essence disguised by super-revolutionary phrases.

Foster, summarizing the Trotsky position, says: "Trotsky's central argument was that socialism could not be built in one country and that, consequently, an immediate European revolution was indispensable. His policies to force such an artificial revolution would have been fatal to the Russian Revolution and would have brought about the restoration of capitalism in Russia."[6]

Trotsky, who was in exile in 1928, had rallied an international coterie about him—one of whose secret members was Cannon.

Cannon returned from the Sixth Congress of the CI and began agitation against Party work in existing unions and against the united front. He also began organization of a new faction. Foster and his group brought charges which resulted in the expulsion of Cannon and his lieutenants, Max Schachtman and Martin Abern. Before long some 100 adherents of the Cannon-Trotsky position were ousted from the Party. From them came the nucleus of the present-day Socialist Workers Party which, in turn, has spawned mounting numbers of Trotskyite splinter groups.

Following Ruthenberg's death Jay Lovestone, who had been a leader in the Ruthenberg-Pepper faction, gained the post of executive-secretary.

He remained as secretary for two years during which the vaunted Coolidge prosperity reached its peak and the stock exchange created dizzying billions of paper profits.

The Sixth World Congress of the CI in 1928 viewed capitalism's sparkling performance with a cool eye. It regarded its apparent stabilization as partial, temporary and relative and it identified right opportunism as the main danger in the field of inner-Party policy.

Lovestone was a skilled and relentless factionalist. He surrounded himself with a corps of some 200 adherents who advocated his particular brand of right opportunism. He was ready to accept the Sixth Congress view that capitalism was moving toward economic crisis, but he was not ready to accept it for the United States. Under a cover of Marxist phraseology he presented a thesis of "American exceptionalism," maintaining that this country possessed a superior variety of capitalism which made it exempt from the internal contradictions of capitalism generally. Relying on the superficial differences between features of U.S. capitalism and features in other capitalist countries, he advocated positions based on such differences rather than the basic sameness.[7]

The result of Lovestone's position would have been to disarm the working class, ignore the impending crisis and conclude that the manifest glories of U.S. capitalism made a sharpening of the class struggle improbable. He was upheld in this view by such of his factional cronies as John Pepper, Bertram Wolfe and Benjamin Gitlow. His right-wing position and his pre-occupation with the niceties of inner-Party control were a drag on the functioning of the Communists during the period of his tenure.

The Foster group challenged the entire line of Lovestone's policies and the struggle reached a critical point at the CP Sixth Convention in March 1929. The majority of the delegates were behind the Lovestone group. Discussion proved futile and a unanimous decision was made to ask the Communist International to help solve the problem.

The American Party's factional situation attracted the attention of a number of leading Marxists from several affiliates of the CI. Joseph Stalin was a delegate and spoke critically of both groups for their narrow factional conduct. Speaking in support of a view which expressed the general opinion of the participants in the discussions, Stalin found that both sides tended to overestimate the strength of American imperialism. Speaking on May 6, 1929, when most non-Marxist theoreticians were still dazzled and blinded by the flashy successes of the U.S. economy, he said: "The three million now unemployed in America are the first swallows indicating the ripening of the economic crisis in America."[8]

Along with this observation, and a judgment that factionalism was the "fundamental evil" of the U.S. Party, the CI condemned "American exceptionalism."

The Lovestone group rejected this view and, after they had failed in an attempt to seize physical possession of the Party's assets, they were expelled.

Lovestone soon made the dubious transition from communism to capitalism and began a life term of service to anti-communism.

The six-year ordeal of factionalism, 1923–29, was now over. The Communists had cleaned house and girded themselves for the tasks which devolved upon them when the bottom fell out of the stock market on October 29, 1929—announcing the arrival of the great economic crisis whose "first swallows" had been counted in May.

A secretariat of Max Bedacht, William Z. Foster, Robert Minor and Will Weinstone was named to direct the Party, pending selection of permanent leadership.

13

Facing the Crisis

It was a brand new ballgame after October 29, 1929. The crash had shocked the country into an awareness of reality. If it had been possible to ignore the significance of three million unemployed in May, it was impossible to do so in November. The index of industrial production which reached 119 in 1929 went to 96 in 1930, to 81 in 1931, and in 1932 it went to an abysmal 64.[1]

The economic crisis which now squeezed the working people of the United States in its torturing grip was not a result of the stock market crash. Rather, the crash was caused by the crisis which, in turn, was a cyclical product of the anarchy of capitalist production, aggravated by the fact that it occurred within the on-going general crisis of capitalism. And, making it worse, the crisis spread until it was world-wide within the orbit of the profit system.

But *only* within the orbit of the profit system! In the sixth of the world which was socialist—which is to say, in the Soviet Union—

production growth continued and, while millions joined the expanding army of unemployed in the capitalist countries, the Soviet Union issued the last unemployment insurance payment to the last of its unemployed.

In October 1931, *Business Week* reported: "Amtorg Gets 100,000 Bids For Russia's 6,000 Skilled Jobs." The story read, "New Yorkers dominate the flow of Americans who have decided, at least for the time being, to cast their lot with the Russians. . . . More than 100,000 applications have been received at the Amtorg's New York office for the 6,000 jobs. . . . Three principal reasons are advanced for wanting the positions: (1) unemployment; (2) disgust with conditions here; (3) interest in the Soviet experiment."[3]

If in its early days the Communist Party was sometimes inclined to overestimate the imminence of the socialist revolution, now it was the demoralized spokesmen of capitalism who were haunted by this spectre. Prof. Irving Fisher of Yale, a leading economist, saw danger of the United States being "devoured by some form of socialism." Congressman Rainey stood on the floor of the House and said the country was "right up against Communism." Though Republican politicians cheerfully claimed to see prosperity right around the corner, an air of gloom and doom quite rightly pervaded reports in the press.

With the onset of the crisis, with the beginning of what was to be known historically as The Great Depression, the Communist Party had its work cut out for it. It was a small party—less than 10,000 members in 1929 and only 18,000 four years later.[4] Workers by the hundreds of thousands followed the leadership of the Party in militant actions. The Party showed the way to the unemployed, struggling for work or relief; to the unorganized workers seeking the protection of union membership; to Blacks fighting for equality. Capitalism still held a grip on the minds of these workers. But the Party's immediate program in the years of the Depression had great appeal. Workers followed it, encouraged by the occasional taste of victory and the inspiration of active struggle. Fortunately for the Communists they were a united Party as the storm broke. With the end of the factional fight they were ready to shape up and ship out.

In the absence of a specific organization of the unemployed—and in the absence of leadership from the American Federation of Labor and a floundering Socialist Party—the Trade Union Unity League, backed by the Communist Party, undertook to lead a national unemployment demonstration to take place on March 6, 1930.

With hunger stalking the land, President Herbert Hoover acted as if the economic depression was just a storm which would blow itself out and go away. The president's only serious measure to meet the critical situation was one for the benefit of the railroad companies, the banks, and industrial corporations. He set up a Reconstruction Finance Corporation which poured two billion dollars into business at the top, asserting that this would "trickle down" into the hands of the workers. But it didn't.

In numerous meetings, preparing for the March 6th demonstration, a list of demands was formulated: "unemployment relief and insurance, with stress upon demands for the Negro people, against wage cuts, and against fascism and war." Prominent among the slogans were: "Work or Wages!" and "Don't Starve—Fight!"[5]

The demonstrations on March 6th began the national phase of the organized fightback. They launched a 10-year battle against the consequences of the Great Depression.

This great kickoff of the long struggle was the kind of event that suited William Z. Foster's talents. It had the sweep and magnitude and strategic importance of the kind of campaigns that were his hallmark.

On March 6th, in major cities across the country, the people responded to the call of the TUUL and the CP. One hundred thousand massed in Detroit; 50,000 turned out in Chicago and the same number in Pittsburgh. There were more tens of thousands in Cleveland, Milwaukee, San Francisco, Los Angeles, Seattle, Denver, Washington, Philadelphia and smaller cities. There were, all told, some 1,250,000 people demonstrating that March day.

The largest crowd was the one which jammed into New York's historic Union Square. Five speaker's platforms were arranged about the square from which as many speakers addressed the crowd. (There was no sound system that could have reached them all.) Five speakers at a time spoke under the watchful eyes and menacing force of an army of police. This army was under the command of Police Commissioner Grover Whalen, the dandified former manager of Wanamaker's department store, ineffable with a white carnation in his lapel.

Foster was the principal speaker. He denounced the array of force mobilized to preserve "law and order" and he dismissed Whalen as that "floor walker from Wanamaker's." Foster and a small committee, as the meeting was drawing to a close, went to Whalen's command post and asked, not for the first time, for a permit to march down Broadway to City Hall to present a petition to the mayor. Whalen said "no." Foster returned to the platform to report. When he asked the crowd whether they accepted the police commissioner's answer the crowd roared its own "no!" and began to form a column for the march. The committee entered the subway to head for City Hall. The committee got there, but the marchers never made it.

No sooner did the people begin to move from the Square toward the distant City Hall than a thousand police, mounted and on foot, moved in with clubs swinging. *The New York Times* next day headlined: "Reds Battle Police in Union Square; Scores Injured, Leaders Are Seized."[6]

While the police uptown were forcibly dispersing the crowd, other police seized the delegation which had gone to the City Hall. They were Bill Foster, secretary of the TUUL; Robert Minor, editor of the *Daily Worker;* Israel Amter, the New York District Organizer of the Communist Party; and two seamen, Joseph Leston and Harry Raymond. (Harry Raymond later became one of the star reporters for the *Daily Worker.*) They were held without bail and kept in jail for five days while charges were fabricated against them.[7] Initially held for "unlawful assembly," they were rearrested for "felonious assault" and it took habeus corpus and bail of $62,500 before they were released to await trial.

On March 6th jail was the order of the day. A check around the country showed the following partial list of arrests: Los Angeles, 60; Detroit, 45; New York, 30; Milwaukee, 36; Buffalo, 12; Washington, D.C., 13; Houston, 5; Boston, 8; Chattanooga, 7; Atlanta, 2. Another ten cities accounted for fifty more arrests.

Bill Foster, Bob Minor and Israel Amter were found guilty of "unlawful assembly" and each served six months in an assortment of city prisons. The relatively obscure Harry Raymond was given ten months. The totally obscure Joseph Leston got one month.

Foster served his time in the loathsome pens on Welfare Island and Hart's Island. Conditions in these foul institutions have had their ups and downs over the years. Mostly they were down. In 1930 they were deep down.

Foster's 1930 experience in the New York County penitentiary furnished the material for his chapter called "Prison" in *Pages From a Worker's Life.*[8] This chapter is an outstanding contribution to the literature of penology—and to U.S. literature in general. His opening remarks on "Class Lines in Prison" set the tone:

American prisons are, of course, not built to hold rich malefactors but offenders from the oppressed classes. The capitalist system, based on the robbery of the workers and poor farmers, is the greatest stickup game in the world's history, and the capitalists who profit from it are the biggest criminals. But this mass robbery is justified by law, sanctified by religion and enforced by the state power. It is only those capitalists and mass scale crooks who go far beyond the rules of the capitalist robbery system—and then only when their crimes are especially stupid and flagrant—who are occasionally put into jail.

In accordance with the role of our prisons generally, the New York County penitentiary was populated almost entirely by workers, and declassed workers become slum proletarians. Ruthless capitalist exploitation and bad social conditions furnished a steady stream of workers, or the sons and daughters of workers, to fill this institution. And the poorer and more downtrodden the strata of the population the greater their representation among the prisoners. The Negroes, oppressed of the oppressed, stood first in relative numbers, and after them came the poverty-stricken Latin Americans.

While the "big shot" gangsters and other fancy crooks in the jail who had money "... always had ample supplies of eggs, meat, canned goods, ice cream and whatever other foods they might want" the general prison population was served rotten meat, wormy cereals and food that "no real farmer would feed his hogs."

Especially bad was the meat, which in summertime was usually putrid and fly-blown. On Hart's Island is located the Potters Field of New York, and the great numbers of pauper dead are conveyed there three times a week, piled high on a steamer's deck and usually in an advanced stage of decomposition. On the off days when no "stiffs" were being transported, the prisoners' beef was carried by the steamer, exposed to the open air and flies, and stacked at the very same place which the day before had been occupied by ripe, dripping, pauper corpses.

On Welfare Island 1,600 prisoners were crowded into an area built, none too amply, for 1,300. Discipline was based on the theory "that to correct prisoners they had to be cowed at every turn and impressed by all possible means with a sense of utter worthlessness, inferiority and hopelessness." Health services were guided by the theory "that the prisoners were human riff-raff entitled to no serious medical care." Work programs were "stupid and useless ... Amter, Raymond and I ... spent many days weeding the potato and corn fields after the crops had been harvested. Often they had our gang hauling the farm wagons about by hand, while the horses grazed contentedly in nearby fields."

Sections on drug addicts, prison vice, the guards, the Potter's Field burial detail, and the parole system round out Foster's chapter on prison life.

In later years, recalling his months in New York's pestilential prisons, Bill like to quote Richard Lovelace:

Stone walls do not a prison make,
Nor iron bars a cage. . . .

Then he would add: "Maybe not—but they make a damn good facsimile."

The six months' absence of Foster, Minor and Amter—a waste of the valuable time of three able men—did not bring Communist activity to a halt. Far from it! The Party seemed constantly to be rising to the many demands the situation placed on it. In fact the small Party would seem at times to have had the whole world on its shoulders.

The Party was small but between its 1929 and 1930 conventions it gained 6,000 members. Over 90 percent of the new members were industrial workers and 1,000 were Blacks.

The TUUL national office was in the charge of Jack Stachel. Such seasoned veterans as Jack Johnstone and Alfred Wagenknecht worked with him out of the offices at Fifth Avenue and West Fifteenth Street in New York.

Bill, serving his time, missed the Seventh Communist Party Convention in June and a conference against lynching, called by the American Negro Labor Congress, in St. Louis in mid-November.

Foster was the Communist candidate for governor of the State of New York in 1930. But as he sweated out a full six months behind bars, Election Day came and went without much of the candidate's participation.

At the Party convention in June the four-man secretariat was replaced by a three-man body: Will Weinstone was organization secretary; Bill Foster, trade union secretary; and Earl Browder, administrative secretary. Browder had been editor of the *Labor Herald* and *Labor Unity*. During the last, and worst, period of the factional fight he had been in China. After the seventh convention he became the Party's general secretary. Though the record is not clear, it appears that from 1930 on Foster was National Chairman.[9]

The great March 6th demonstration had been preceded in New York by a massive funeral procession for a slain worker, Steve Katovis, a striking bakery worker who was killed by a trigger-happy cop. The tens of thousands who marched behind the casket of Katovis were among the scores of thousands who turned out in Union Square in March.

The March 6th event across the country projected the unemployed as a distinct political force and it turned such questions as unemployment insurance and relief into live political issues.

The next step was to organize the unorganized unemployed. On the initiative of the CP, YCL, and TUUL a National Unemployed Council was organized at a convention which brought 1,320 delegates together in Chicago on the Fourth of July, 1930.

The basic membership of the NUC consisted of unemployed persons who joined local Unemployed Councils. While the councils fought for relief, public work at union wages, against evictions and against anti-Black discrimination, a Committee for Unemployment Insurance and Relief, headed by Louis Weinstock, carried the struggle into the AFL. Weinstock, a Communist, was elected—and ten times re-elected—Secretary Treasurer of District Council No. 9 of the Brotherhood of Painters, Decorators and Plasterers. William Green, president of the AFL, expressing the Federation's position, scorned unemployment insurance as a degrading "dole". But Weinstock and his committee lined up 3,000 local unions, 35 central labor councils, six state federations and five international unions behind this idea whose time had come and was soon to be implemented.

As for the unemployed movement, thousands of smaller local actions backed up large national actions. Hundreds of thousands demonstrated on May Day and on National Unemployment Insurance days. On December 7, 1931, 1,800 marchers, a ragged army, assembled in Washington, D.C., from columns that had fought their way from New York, St. Louis, Chicago, Buffalo, Boston and many other cities. This was the first National Hunger March. In the second such march 3,000 assembled before the Capitol a year later. By that time Hoover was a lame duck president.

Those workers who were still employed were largely unorganized. The employers slashed their wages. And those who belonged to unions suffered the same fate, for the AFL would not fight back. The number of strikes and strikers reached record lows; and the AFL lost another twenty percent of its membership.

With the Unemployed Councils now organizing the unemployed, the TUUL was able to give its major attention to the organization of the unorganized into industrial unions. This Communist-led organization bravely tackled the task which the AFL shied away from. In the four years of depression, 1930 through 1933, the TUUL kept the flag of militancy flying, blocking as well as it could the otherwise unchallenged ruthlessness of the employers. The Trade Union Unity League may not have been an ideal vehicle for its role but, essentially, it was the only one around. And not only did it place itself athwart the road that capitalism was following but it trained a cadre which would strengthen its immediate successors—the CIO—when they came along, and the reluctant AFL as well. The TUUL was a detachment whose job was to hold the line against a superior force until the main reserves could be brought up.

The TUUL did not respect the no-strike policy which the AFL followed in the early depression years. In textile the League led several struggles against wage cuts in New England which brought 75,000 workers out of the mills in a number of strikes. In October 1932 a successful strike was waged against Republic Steel's plant in Warren, Ohio. Republic was part of Little Steel which, five years later, gave battle to the CIO's organizing committee, costing many lives before it was hammered into line.

Youngstown, which in recent years has been a battleground of steel companies and steel workers, was another site where Foster's unsurpassed knowledge of the steel industry was brought into play.

In a number of urban areas the TUUL led strikes in the needle trades and food industries and in others. In 1932 the TUUL's Agricultural Workers Industrial Union (AWIU) led a strike of 18,000 beet workers.

But the AWIU's leadership of a strike of 7,000 agricultural workers in California's Imperial Valley in 1930 was in a special class. The humble, helpless-seeming migratory agricultural workers—the difficult subject of recent struggles led by Cesar Chavez and the United Farm Workers—were the unlikely protagonists in the Imperial Valley struggle. The subservient local and state authorities, reinforced by mercenaries supplied by strike-breaking agencies, waged an unholy war against the impoverished Mexican-Filipino-Japanese-Anglo workers. Hundreds were arrested. In the most serious case eight workers and leaders were tried on the ever-ready charge of "criminal syndicalism." Sentences of up to 42 years were handed down.

The veteran Japanese-American Communist, Karl Yoneda, was in the Imperial Valley strike and there he met young Eugene Dennis, then Southern California head of the TUUL and later to be general secretary of the Communist Party.[10]

The coal fields had been in chronic depression for years before the Great Depression of the thirties added its special measure of misery to the existing situation in coal. After the United Mine Workers of America had been wrecked by the loss of the 1927–28 strike, the mine owners took full advantage of the circumstances. By 1931, in Western Pennsylvania and the adjacent coal areas of Ohio and West Virginia, wages were down to as low as $2.00 a day. Working conditions achieved by decades of struggle were destroyed and arbitrary—take it or leave it—conditions were enforced. Employed and unemployed went hungry.

The National Miners Union, led by a group of Foster's "team", including among others such stalwarts as Frank Borich, Pat Toohey, Tom Myerscough and Tony Minerich, went boldly into this bleak social and geographic landscape. They carried on agitation and won a few local strikes, giving new hope to defeated and demoralized miners. With new wage cuts pending they called for a "Strike Against Starvation."

On May 27, 1931, a thousand men walked out of the Atlasburgh-MacDonald mines and the strike was on. "A strike fever," says Foster, "seized upon the bitterly oppressed miners all around. By June 1st, 16,000 were out and by the latter part of June it reached 42,000, of whom 6,000 were Negroes. The strike involved the mines of many of the greatest trusts in America."[11]

Bill Foster, Bill Dunne, Jack Johnstone, Alfred Wagenknecht and other battle-scarred veterans came into the tri-state area of the strike but still the NMU was desperately short of organizers. A hundred thousand workers were ready to join the strike but organization could not keep up with the spirit and will of the miners.

In some ways the 1931 coal strike showed left-wing unionism at its best. Whole families of the miners were mobilized for big marches and mass picket lines. Blacks and whites fraternized as never before in the mine districts. Rank and file committees controlled the strike at the mines and at the Pittsburgh headquarters. A relief apparatus was provided and tent cities erected for those evicted from company houses.

Theodore Draper, writing of these 1930s mine struggles, in an article otherwise bristling with hostility to the Communists, felt moved to say:

> All unions were fought bitterly in those days. But the most brutal terror was reserved for the Communist unions. Mine companies, courts, police and military, local, state and national officials, combined forces against them. In the face of such a phalanx of powerful and implacable enemies, it was more surprising that the Communists were able to fight so hard for as long as they did than that they were unable to win.[12]

And, referring to the stubborn insistence of the Communists that Black and white should eat together in the miners' soup kitchens in Harlan, Kentucky, Draper says: "It is fair to say that only the Communists in that period, in the heat of battle, would have taken such a firm stand on this issue."[13]

The conduct of the strike recalled some of the great struggles of the IWW—as at Lawrence—and of the CP—as at Passaic, and it foreshadowed some of the coming struggles of the CIO.

But the CIO was not yet even standing in the wings at this time. In fact, its future leader, John L. Lewis, now lent the services of his UMWA to sign a wage-cutting contract with the Pittsburgh Terminal Coal Co. as a bulwark against the radical NMU.

Despite help from the steel workers, despite huge demonstrations by the unemployed, despite mass picketing in which men, women, and children took part, the strike was defeated by a combination of government, owners, and AFL leaders. An army of assorted public and private police, deportation moves against foreign-born militants, legal injunctions; the eviction of a hundred thousand persons from company housing, a flood of strikebreakers; brutal jailings, beatings and shootings, the murder of two strikers—these combined to drive the miners back into the pits. Tom Myerscough and Leo Thompson served two years in jail in the aftermath of the miners' heroic bid for a living wage.

In the years of the Roosevelt New Deal, unionism came back to the mines under the UMWA banner. The hard-fought NMU strike of 1931 then proved to have paved the way for future victories.

"Youngstown, Ohio," "Warren, Ohio." "Aliquippa, Pennsylvania"—these are place names which are current in news of the steel producing areas today and which were the scenes of TUUL activity in the early Thirties.

Foster brought his immense know-how, acquired in the great steel drive a dozen years before, to the newly formed Steel and Metal Workers Industrial Union (a reorganization of the TUEL's Metal Workers Industrial League). Amongst the Ohio and Pennsylvania steel workers he trained a new cadre of fighters who were destined in the decade of the thirties to help bring industrial unionism into the vast open shop fortresses of big and little steel. Among this new cadre was young Gus Hall who came from the Iron Range of Minnesota, where he had worked as a miner and lumber worker, to work in the steel mills of Warren, Ohio. (Hall has been general secretary of the CPUSA since 1959.)

Foster was, besides whatever else may be said in his praise, a teacher. He was to show this most notably in the many pamphlets he wrote during the late 1930's organizing drives. He showed it in 1931 when he wrote "On the Question of Trade Union Democracy." He declared: "The bureaucratic methods which have been so much in evidence in our mass work are the surest road to sectarianism and isolation." He explained: "They sever as if with a knife the contacts of the Party with the broad masses. We cannot maintain our mass contacts with mere talk, however eloquent and revolutionary it may be."[12]

The TUUL had more success ultimately with its Auto Workers Union than with the NMU or SMWIU. Though it lost a strike in the Fisher Body plant in Flint (later the scene of the great sit-down that brought unionism into General Motors) it won strikes at a number of Briggs body shops.

During the five or six years of its existence the TUUL set up thirteen national industrial unions besides a number of local organizations. It is impressive to read how the TUUL, led by a relatively small group of Communists in the main, with energetic, dedicated fervor reached out to achieve organization of workers in so many fields— restaurants and food shops, shoe and leather workers, tobacco workers in Tampa and New York, lumber workers in the Pacific Northwest, furniture and upholstery workers, packinghouse, building maintenance, fishermen and cannery employees, barbers, jewelry workers, office workers, printers, taxi drivers, doll and toy makers, photo finishers, laundry workers. The TUUL, spreading itself thin perhaps, did reach out.

It filled a gap in U.S. labor history which would otherwise have existed between the somnolence of the AFL after The Crash and the upsurge of the New Deal period which produced both the mass industrial unions of the CIO and a regenerated AFL.

14

A Crack in the Pitcher

William Z. Foster spent five months in the areas of the 1931 coal strike, giving minute-by-minute guidance. The minutes added up to 18-hour days and Foster recalled it as "one of the severest strike tests I ever went through." For Foster, now in his 51st year, it was not only a physical grind—of which he was hardly aware—but an emotional one. "It was heartbreaking to see the starving miners being cut to pieces by the ruthless operators." By the end of the strike, he says, "I was almost finished myself."[1]

How close he was to being finished would be made evident before the last quarter of the year 1932 had started.

Foster's long, hard stretch on the coal strike front was not followed by a rest, however well-earned that might have been. Rather he went on following his regular routine—beside which he wrote a book of 350 pages in his "spare" time.

The book was commissioned by a commercial publishing house— Coward and McCann. The ordering of this book reflected the prominent position the Communist Party had attained as a result of its work in the early years of the depression. In 1932, as the economy continued to sink toward the bottom, people were looking for answers and the Communists had them. The purpose of the book, said Foster, "is to explain to the oppressed and exploited masses of workers and poor farmers how, under the leadership of the Communist Party, they can best protect themselves now, and in due season cut their way out of the capitalist jungle to Socialism." The book was called *Toward Soviet America.* Foster finished it on May 1, 1932.[2]

The title of the book caused little stir at the time but later was used by the CP's enemies to cause the Party some embarrassment and to waste some time on explanations. If for the alien word "Soviet" the word "Socialist" had been used the aim of the book would have been more precisely defined.

But in 1932 the socialist world was identical with the Soviet world. The word *soviet* (council) was more related to form than to content. This form had been derived from experience gained during the Russian Revolution of 1905. That the form would not necessarily suit the national style of other revolutions was a lesson that would soon be learned. If the book had been written in, let's say, 1935, it would certainly have had a different title.

"For a revolutionary way out of the crisis" was a slogan of the early 30s. The slogan was raised in the context of militant struggles around immediate issues but as a slogan it remained bogged down in abstraction.

The book also reflected the prevailing Communist slogan of "class against class," a narrow slogan which would be modified as the development and threat of fascism made the struggle for peace and democracy the first order of the day. Later there would be more emphasis on the *allies* of the working class—the farmers, professionals, small business. In 1932 every people's struggle for the most elementary right to food and shelter seemed to be answered with violence, and strikes against starvation became local civil wars.

Bill Foster, although he had served six months for his role in the March 6, 1930, demonstration, was still on parole under a three-year sentence when March 7, 1932, came around. If March 6th is memorable in labor history for the first great demonstration of the unemployed, March 7 will be recalled as the day of the Ford Massacre.

Henry Ford, the founder, and in 1932 the head, of Ford Motors, had a cultivated public relations image of a philanthropist whose primary interest was the welfare of his employees. His ruthless dismissal of thousands of workers after 1929 tarnished his image; and the events of March 7, 1932, in Dearborn, Michigan, smashed it to bits.

On that day the Auto Workers Union (TUUL) and the Unemployment Councils organized a demonstration at the Ford plant in

Dearborn. Half the workers in Detroit were unemployed and many were actually starving. The demonstration was to take the form of a march to the Ford plant gates. There demands for work and relief were to be presented and the marchers were to disperse. But when the marchers crossed the Detroit line into Dearborn the subservient city police and Ford's own army of goons fired on the procession with tear gas, rifles and machine guns. Joe York, Joe Bussell, Coleman Leny, and Joe DeBlasio—four young workers—were killed and fifty wounded.

Foster was on a tour organizing the unemployed and reached Detroit on March 6th where he was the principal speaker at a meeting to mobilize for the next day's demonstration. Several thousands attended this rally and Foster then took the night train to Milwaukee where he was to speak the following day. There he learned of the ghastly attack in Dearborn. He learned also that the press held the demonstrators responsible for the slaughter and that he, having been the main speaker at the mobilization rally, was to be charged with murder.

Foster's parole required that he report semi-monthly in person. He went immediately from Milwaukee to New York arriving on precisely the day he was due to report. The talk of a murder charge was soon dropped as the Ford people were anxious that publicity about the Dearborn affair be as limited as possible. But the parole commission sentenced Foster to serve the rest of his parole confined to New York City. With all due respect to the Big Apple, Bill considered this a heavy sentence, almost as bad as Hart Island itself!

In their first ten years the Communists had been steadily moving away from the old left-wing position that the question of the Black people was merely a facet of the broad workingclass question. The Communists recognized it as a question requiring special attention, but the specific characteristics of the question had not yet been grasped.

In 1930 the Communist Party took up the question of Black liberation with such boldness, vigor and skill as had not been seen on this front since the days of the pre-Civil War Abolitionists. Over the years, since the adoption of its 1930 resolution "The Communist Position on the Negro Question," the Communist Party has often been called the "Party of the Black People," a title of honor won on the field of battle.

The key to the fresh approach taken in 1930 was the Party's recognition of Black liberation as related to the question of an oppressed national minority. This important resolution emphasized the national character of this question, first posed in Communist documents in October 1928. It signalled a stepping up of the active struggle for Black liberation and for Black-white unity.

But the 1930 resolution also insisted on the existence of a "nation within a nation" in the Black Belt of the South—an area of Afro-American majority population in the states which had once constituted themselves the slaveholding Confederacy. From this perception of a "separate nation" was derived a slogan for self-determination for the Black Belt. The later history of this slogan is discussed further in Chapter 18.

Within a short time the Party's strengthened position and activity received recognition in the form of a sharp increase in Black membership. A report on Party membership in March 1929 showed no more than 200 Blacks in the Party. A year later, coincident with the March 6, 1930, nationwide unemployed demonstrations, the CP launched a membership drive which brought in nearly 6200 new members—including some 1,300 Afro-Americans. It was at this time that future leaders such as Henry Winston, then 19 years old, were attracted to the movement. Winston is now National Chairman of the CPUSA.

The Party had made a beginning at rooting itself in the South in 1924 and again in 1928 when William Z. Foster, the Party's presidential candidate, carried the election campaign into Southern territory. In 1932 James W. Ford was nominated as Foster's running mate. Ford was the first Black to run for vice-president of the United States.

In 1930 a quantitative and qualitative change was made in the Party's attention to the South. Foster pinpoints this change as dating from August 30, 1930, when "it established the *Southern Worker* at Chattanooga, Tennessee, with James S. Allen as editor."[3]

The work in the South, and among Black people generally, received a boost through the formation in St. Louis, in October 1930, of the League of Struggle for Negro Rights. The League was a descendant of such earlier left groups as the American Negro Labor Congress, the African Blood Brotherhood, the Equal Rights League, and the League of African Freedom.

The League established its headquarters in New York's Harlem. Langston Hughes, the esteemed Black poet, became its president. Richard B. Moore, an eloquent spokesman for the Black people, was general secretary. Bill Foster and many other leading Communists, together with non-Communists, were on its National Council.

The League's weekly newspaper was called the *Liberator*. In 1936 the League of Struggle for Negro Rights merged with the newly formed National Negro Congress, a much broader organization.

Those who undertook to root the Party in the South and to develop unity of Black and white had to face the unrestrained hostility of the agents of the Southern ruling class. The Communists gave their first attention to the most oppressed and poverty stricken section of Southern Blacks—the sharecroppers. In the spring of 1931 the Alabama Sharecroppers Union was organized, based in Tallapoosa and Lee counties.

The Party's work in the South was by no means limited to the agricultural sector, but reached into the urban areas as well. Hosea Hudson, a Black steel worker, has written an account[4] which tells in vivid detail of how he came into the Party in 1931 while working as a molder in a pipe manufacturing plant in Birmingham, Alabama. (In 1980 the Mayor of Birmingham presented Hosea Hudson with the keys to that city.)

At the same time—in Birmingham, Atlanta and other cities of the South—the unemployed were being organized by the Party-led Unemployed Councils.

On March 25, 1931, began the celebrated case of the Scottsboro Nine, also known historically as the Scottsboro Boys. Of the nine youths arrested on that day, one was 13, two were 14 and the oldest was 21.

The Scottsboro Case was the classic Southern rape frameup, a device which has been used to send untold numbers of Black men to death at the hands of a lynch mob or of the law. It was the fact that the Communist Party had turned its attention to the South less than a year before the Scottsboro events that created the possibility for saving the lives of the young victims.

The legal lynching which the state of Alabama attempted to prepare for the nine youths was based on the accusation that they had all participated in the rape of two white women.

The usual quickie trial reserved for Blacks accused of "violating white womanhood" promptly doomed all except the 13-year old to death in the electric chair. At this point the Party launched an international mass campaign on behalf of the youths and brought the Communist lawyer Joseph Brodsky and the forces of the International Labor Defense into the case. Subsequently the U.S. Supreme Court found the defendants had not been properly represented by their first counsel and ordered a new trial. The legal proceedings which ensued saved the lives of the intended victims, but it was six years before the first four of the Nine were free, and almost twenty years before the last Scottsboro prisoner was free.

Foster says of the Party's leadership in the Scottsboro campaign: "It exposed the terrible situation of the Negroes in the South as had not been done since the days of Reconstruction. Of the most vital importance was the great publicity given to the case internationally. It became especially known all over the colonial world. Thus, much of the anti-Jim Crow spirit, which has since become such a powerful force in restraining the Southern lynchers and modifying to some extent the ferocious Jim Crow system throughout the United States, was built up all over the world."[5]

Another case which further dramatized the oppression of the Black people in the South and set new standards in the struggle for civil rights was that of Angelo Herndon.

Herndon was just 17 years old when a chance leaflet on the sidewalk in Birmingham led him to a meeting of the local Unemployed Council. After listening to the Black and white speakers that afternoon and sitting, to his astonishment, in an unsegregated audience, Herndon joined on the spot. Later he heard Communist Party spokesmen, including William Z. Foster and J. Louis Engdahl. He became active in the Unemployed Council and before long joined the Communist Party.

In the summer of 1932 he was active in Atlanta, Georgia, in the Communist presidential election campaign. The candidates were Foster and James W. Ford. His distribution of a leaflet of the Unemployed Council led to his arrest and, on July 22, to his indictment on a charge of incitement to insurrection. The jury found him guilty and recommended "mercy"—18 to 20 years on the chain gang.

The Communist Party and the International Labor Defense carried on a campaign for Herndon's freedom in the following years, and the slogan "Free Angelo Herndon and the Scottsboro Boys" was heard around the world. It took a five-year struggle and two appeals to the U.S. Supreme Court before Angelo Herndon was finally freed in 1937.

In order properly to gear the Party to its struggle for Black-white unity it was necessary to launch a campaign against white chauvinism, racism, in Communist ranks. The Party chose as a lever to launch this campaign the public trial of August Yokinen. Yokinen, a Communist and a member of a Finnish workers' club in Harlem, participated in the exclusion of three Black workers who sought to attend a social event at the club.

Yokinen was placed on trial on March 1, 1931, before an audience of 1500 persons in Harlem, including 211 elected delegates from 113 organizations. The prosecutor was Clarence A. Hathaway, representing the New York District of the CP; the defense attorney was Richard B. Moore, a leader of the ILD. The 14-member jury found Yokinen guilty of white chauvinism and voted for his expulsion from the Party with permission to apply for readmission after completion of a series of tasks related to the struggle against racism.

In a pamphlet entitled, *Race Hatred on Trial,* James Allen wrote: "By this trial, the Communist Party has done two things. First, it has made clear the anti-workingclass character of race prejudice. Second, it has shown that it will not tolerate any form of race prejudice within its own ranks and will fight tooth and nail to root it out of the working class as a whole."[6]

As the CP in the 1920s developed its program for the Black people and opened up special fronts of struggle against racism it attracted to its ranks Black workers and intellectuals who played an important role in its work. Among them were Cyril Briggs, Cyril Philip, Lovett Fort-Whiteman, Otto Hall, Harry Haywood, Maude White, Richard B. Moore, William Patterson, and James W. Ford, Foster's 1932 running mate.

James W. Ford was the son of a steel worker. He grew up in Alabama and attended Fisk University. He was in the American Expeditionary Force in World War I.

Ford worked as a postal employee in Chicago and became a delegate to the Chicago Federation of Labor. "At one meeting of the federation," writes Philip S. Foner, "he charged the AF of L leadership with discrimination and 'immoral trade union conduct' toward Negro workers. As he had anticipated, several white delegates accused him of defending a class of workers who are mainly strikebreakers. To his utter surprise other white delegates came to his defense, although he was the lone Negro delegate . . . He later learned that these delegates were left-wingers and Communists under the leadership of William Z. Foster and that they were leading a fight in the TUEL for the rights of Negro workers."[7]

James W. Ford joined the CP in 1926 and became an organizer for the TUEL. He helped form the American Negro Labor Congress and its successor, the League of Struggle for Negro Rights. In 1930 he was in Germany as secretary of the International Committee of Negro Workers. He returned to the United States in 1932.

William Z. Foster was liberated from his confinement to New York City through the circumstance of being nominated by his party to run for President of the United States. The nominating convention took place in Chicago, May 28–29, 1932. It was attended by 1,200 delegates, sixty percent of whom were not Party members. Fifteen thousand spectators attended the nominating rally at the Chicago Coliseum.

Foster's nomination put the New York parole authorities in a dilemma. They had kept him on a short tether because they hated the thought of his running around the country "stirring up the workers." But when he became a presidential candidate, keeping him in New York promised to confer on him a martyrdom with which they could not cope. So they lifted the travel ban but warned that the slightest "provocation would result in his return to prison for his unexpired term."

The campaign started in June. It was to be a hard grind and it would have been wise to take a rest before starting out on it. This never even occurred to Foster.

Communist candidates faced a workload beyond that carried by major party candidates. Bill's experience had acquainted him with the rigors of "incessant traveling, perpetual speechmaking, bad food, miserable hotels, boresome newspaper interviews, being talked half to death or kept from needed sleep by comrades who felt it to be the function of a presidential candidate to adjust every local grievance, by after-meeting home gatherings, 'banquets' and untimely talkfests."[8]

Bill's tour was designed to cover 30 thousand miles (all by surface transportation) and include 105 major speeches plus numerous radio talks. Local conferences, demonstrations at railroad stops, and the special ordeal of "banquets" were other items in the plan of work.

On the very first day of this challenging grind Foster experienced heart symptoms which should have signaled the wisdom of calling the whole thing off. The symptoms were harbingers of an ailment of which he was never to be totally free for the rest of his life. But Bill, who had never been seriously ill before, chose to ignore these warning signs, even though there were times when he had to cling to the speaker's stand to keep himself erect.

His running mate also toured the country, covering the principal centers. But James W. Ford, as a veteran of the War, also participated in one of the great struggles of the election year: he was in Washington for the dramatic Bonus March.

This event had originally been proposed by the Communist Party and the Communist-led Workers Ex-Servicemen's League in April. But the mass movement which developed soon outgrew its left-wing sponsorship and by July 28, 1932, 20,000 veterans and members of their families were encamped in Washington to demand the adjusted pay, "the bonus," they had been promised. They stayed ten weeks and then were driven out by federal troops commanded by Gen. Douglas MacArthur. Two men and two babies died; dozens were injured; hundreds were gassed. Many, including vice-presidential candidate James W. Ford, were jailed.

Foster adhered to the schedule he had agreed to until September 8 when he collapsed at Moline, Illinois. "The pitcher," as he put it, "had gone once too often to the well."[9]

He insisted on going on to Chicago where he intended to make an appearance at a scheduled meeting at the Coliseum Annex.

In charge of the Chicago meeting was John Williamson, then the district organizational secretary. He met Foster at the train the morning of the meeting and took him to the Washington Hotel where Bill collapsed on the bed.

Williamson tells us: "Bill insisted he must make an appearance at the meeting. The doctor said this was madness and would mean death. We then brought in a leading heart specialist, who was known as a progressive. He not only confirmed everything that had been said, but insisted on hospitalization. Against this advice, Foster demanded to go home. He was taken to the train on a stretcher and then to his home, still resisting the hospital." Williamson adds:

We got the *Daily Worker* editor, Clarence A. Hathaway, to fly into Chicago from New York to substitute for Foster at our big election rally. As chairman of that packed Coliseum Annex election rally, I had an experience I will never forget.

We had not made public Foster's last-minute illness. After the preliminary speeches and the collection were over, I announced Foster's illness and that we had a substitute speaker. It seemed to me, as I faced over 4,000 people in that barnlike hall, that at least half of them rose from their seats, muttering to themselves, and formed solid lines to every exit. I could already picture the crowd dwindle to a few hundred bitterly disappointed people.

Dropping all further efforts to go on with explanations of Foster's illness and his message to the meeting, I introduced Hathaway. For the first few minutes he could not be heard, finally order was reestablished. We had not lost half of the audience; it was nearer to one-fourth, but that was bad enough. Even a speaker as good as Hathaway was not acceptable to that crowd as a substitute for their own Bill Foster. There was also the fact that many of these workers who came to hear Foster still had certain doubts about the Communists. They thought we had fooled them, using Foster's name to get them there. It was several days and even longer before people generally learned, to their sorrow, that Foster was seriously stricken.[10]

The heart attack that felled Bill resulted in a total breakdown. He was kept in bed for five months and for another 19 months *angina pectoris* required constant medical attention. It was three years before he could make a ten-minute speech.

Bill Foster attributed his eventual substantial recovery to three factors: "the intelligent, tireless and loving care of my devoted wife, the loyal assistance given me by the Party, and my own determination ... to live on and fight in the worker's struggle for emancipation."[11]

Whether the role of his doctors is omitted from this explanation of his recovery by oversight or whether by design cannot now be determined. When he wrote the above words (probably in 1937) he certainly showed no sense of impending doom and, indeed, no doom impended. In 1955 (in a talk with the present writer) he recalled his dismay when a doctor cheerily told him, in 1935, "Don't worry, Bill. You can live another five years."

But, never again, after his 1932 illness, was he able to resume the staggering schedule of his earlier years. In any case, there were to be no more whistle-stop campaigns. In the last twenty-five years of his life his activity declined from the phenomenal to the merely extraordinary.

At the end of 1934 Foster began a slow and gradual return to work. For two years he had had no involvement in the rapidly unfolding history of the thirties.

The political framework for developments during the period of his absence was principally provided by Franklin D. Roosevelt's accession to the presidency.

In the November election Roosevelt defeated Hoover with 472 electoral votes to Hoover's 59. FDR's vaguely defined promise of a New Deal and his gestures toward "the forgotten man" stirred the people, and the dynamic quality of his administration, after the torpor of Hoover, created hope among the hopeless.

The vote for Foster and Ford was 102,991. It was the Party's biggest vote yet, but did not correspond to the big struggles the Party led and it did not truly measure the Party's increasing influence. Even those who followed the Party into battle were still kept captive by the two-party system and the fear of the "wasted vote." The Party also showed a left-sectarian tendency by stressing slogans too advanced for the immediate situation—such as "For the revolutionary way out of the crisis" and "For a Workers and Farmers Government."

Hoover remained in office after his defeat in November until Roosevelt was inaugurated on March 4, 1933. Meanwhile the economy stagnated and declined while the nation waited impatiently for FDR to bring salvation.

Roosevelt brought with him to Washington a "brain trust" of innovative assistants who helped him frame a legislative program that swept through a bemused and dazzled Congress. New "Acts" and "Administrations" proliferated, bringing a shower of new initials into the language: AAA, NRA, CWA, CCC, PWA, NLB.[12]

In the mode of capitalist rule, which alternates the carrot with the club, the carrot now became prominent though the club was brought into play all too often. The essence of New Deal policy was class collaboration, and the National Recovery Administration, with the Blue Eagle as its symbol, furnished the principal vehicle for advancing this policy.

Neither the social-democrats, who saw a socialist content in Roosevelt's programs and applauded, nor the monopolists, who saw socialist content and booed, were seeing things correctly. Actually Roosevelt advanced the integration of monopoly and government and promoted the development of that state-monopoly capitalism which has characterized our economic system for the past several decades.

The Communist Party took a dim view of the early Roosevelt program and was especially critical of the National Industrial Recovery Act (NIRA) which created the National Recovery Administration and provided for setting up price and labor codes in various industries. Big Business dominated the entire code-making machinery. The Communists found that the NIRA was patterned after Mussolini's "corporative state." General Hugh Johnson, the man Roosevelt put in charge of the NRA, was an open admirer of Benito Mussolini.

For the labor movement the most important part of the NIRA was Section 7(a) which stated that workers had "the right to organize and bargain collectively through representatives of their own choosing." This ambiguous "right" was not backed by any enforcement machinery and did not distinguish between company unions and the genuine ones. The Communists urged "Write your own codes on the picket line."[13] This corresponded to the mood of the workers.

In July 1933 the Party assembled an Extraordinary Conference of 350 delegates which drafted an Open Letter to the membership. The effect of the Conference and Open Letter was to turn the Party to the shops and industries, to give it a firmer proletarian base, and to enable it to play an important role in the great events of 1934 to 1938 which built the Congress of Industrial Organizations and revitalized the American Federation of Labor.[14]

A new strike wave swept the country, the greatest since 1919, involving 1,300,000 workers by the end of 1933. This took place with a minimum of input by the TUUL which, in 1931-32 had almost single-handedly guided the strike movements. In 1934, after the message of the Open Letter took hold, the Communists became involved in a way which stimulated the union organization drive and advanced the formation of the CIO. By 1935 the Communist Party had 500 shop branches which helped promote in the labor movement the principles, strategy, and tactics which had for years been advocated by the Party and the TUUL.

The year 1934 was marked by one of the greatest class struggles in U.S. labor history. This was the general strike which took place in the San Francisco Bay area on July 16-19.

The general strike grew out of a West Coast strike of 35,000 maritime workers. From 1932 on a Communist-progressive coalition organized the maritime workers of the Pacific Coast. A strike of 12,000 members of the AFL longshoremen's union led by Harry Bridges, starting May 7, 1934, was joined by the Marine Workers Industrial Union (TUUL) and, by May 23, by eight AFL maritime unions. West Coast shipping came to a standstill. As the maritime strike wore on other unions began to call for a general strike.

Then, on July 8th, two workers—one of them Nick Bordois, a Communist—were shot to death by the San Francisco police. On July 10th the Alameda Labor Council called for a general strike. On July 16th 160 AFL unions pulled out 127,000 workers, tying up the entire Bay area.

President Roosevelt denounced the strike and sent Hugh Johnson to break it. Vigilantes wrecked the Communist Party headquarters and its paper the *Western Worker*. The police, militia and deputies attacked the strike from without and the AFL maneuvered to end it from within.

When the general strike was called off the maritime workers remained out and won a partial victory. The coast strike also laid the basis for establishing the International Longshoremen's and Warehousemen's Union which, under the leadership of Harry Bridges, became one of the most outstanding labor organizations in the United States.

Quite inadvertently William Z. Foster found himself involved in the highly flammable West Coast situation in a way he had not intended. He was on a visit to San Francisco, as a change of scene for the purpose of rest and recuperation, when he ran smack into the San Francisco General Strike.

It is only necessary to understand the importance of this event— and to understand Bill Foster—to appreciate why the excitement of the occasion made his "shattered nerves . . . about ready to explode." After the strike had been on for a couple of days, he says, he "was virtually in a state of collapse from excitement and my inability to give any real help. . . . And to make the hazard more acute, William Green [president of the AFL], like a faithful capitalist henchman, had condemned the general walkout and declared that 'Foster is the man behind the strike.' So, in the midst of the struggle, I had to be withdrawn to a less exposed position in the nearby country."[15]

During the years of Bill Foster's illness Jack Stachel presided over the Trade Union Unity League. He was therefore at the helm when the TUUL began to phase itself out. The first two years of the New Deal brought a million workers into the AFL. They were mainly from among the unskilled and foreign-born—categories formerly unwelcome in the AFL. Their presence undercut the conservatism of the old-line officials and stirred some of the top leaders to get out and organize.

The conditions that had brought the TUUL into existence were now fading out and the left forces now looked toward getting back into the AFL. The dual policy of forming new unions where necessary and working within the AFL where possible had generally favored the first part over the second. By 1934 the TUUL forces began to find their way into the AFL—not without hesitations and not without resistance from the AFL. As a matter of fact, as early as 1933 they began to join and help rebuild the United Mine Workers.

Early in 1935 the TUUL unions in steel, auto and the needle trades voted to join the AFL, as a body where possible and as individuals where not.

Now the contacts made in the basic industries, and the shop units created after the Emergency Conference and Open Letter of the CP, would help in the creation of the powerful CIO. The TUUL—a ragged, gallant, and never very large band—justified its existence. It had held the fort and kept the flag flying when there was no other force to do it. With the main troops now in sight the Trade Union Unity League, on March 17, 1935, voted to dissolve.

The Committee for Industrial Organization was exactly that at first—a committee composed of representatives of eight AFL unions for the purpose of winning the federation's support for bringing unionism to the millions of unorganized workers in the basic trust-ified industries. And this would have to mean industrial unions. The craft unions had shown they could not do the job, even assuming that they wanted to.

But the entrenched craft union bureaucrats looked with fear on a shift of power from their own hands, where it had traditionally and comfortably been held. They were by no means ready to lose their prerogatives, or even to share them with what they saw as an unskilled, radical rabble.

The conspicuous leaders of the industrial union movement, such as John L. Lewis, Philip Murray and Sidney Hillman, were nobody's wild-eyed radicals. Their essential conservatism remained. But their recognition that the old ways of narrow craft unionism would no longer do, compelled them—under the additional pressure of a mass upsurge—to adopt progressive measures and play a progressive role.

The industrial unionism which John L. Lewis and his allies proposed came to a vote at the October 1935 convention of the AFL, held in Atlantic City. It went down by a vote of 18,025 to 10,924. The top brass were voting to keep their cozy set-up intact.

But before the year was out, the CIO launched campaigns in the largely untouched areas of auto, coke-processing, rubber, steel and textile.

The response of the AFL was registered in October 1936 when, at its convention in Tampa, it suspended the eight unions of the Committee for Industrial Organization.

The Communist Party favored preserving unity, if possible, within the AFL. But John L. Lewis was not inclined to fight it out in that unpromising arena. The CIO delegates did not even go to Tampa. The split was on. It would last twenty years.

And the Communist Party, Foster wrote, "gave everything it had . . . to the building of the CIO at all stages, and in the organization of the basic industries for which it had fought so long and militantly."[16]

Browder announced to a Central Committee meeting in September 1934 that Foster would be back to work "in two or three weeks." During the next year or so he gradually regained his strength and, as the CIO drive was taking hold, he was providentially able to make his contribution to its success.

From July 25 to August 20, 1935, William Z. Foster attended the Seventh World Congress of the Communist International in Moscow and was a member of its presidium. He turned his position on this honorary body to real account by insisting on making the question of the role of youth a major point on the agenda. His point was accepted and, as a result, the discussion of the role of the youth greatly enhanced.[17]

In October and November 1935 articles by Foster appeared in *The Communist,* his first in that organ since 1932. This proved that, at long last, Bill Foster indeed was back.

15

Fighting for Peace and Democracy

William Z. Foster's long illness took him out of activity during a period of big changes in the United States and in the world.

It was a period in which Roosevelt replaced Hoover in the White House. This was not the familiar Tweedledum–Tweedledee exchange which the two-party trap normally affords the voters.

Though Roosevelt's liberal demagogy created many unfortunate illusions among working people it would be wrong not to see the positive elements in his administration as he responded to overwhelming mass pressure. While the four terms of his tenure were marked by serious shortcomings, and his years in office included times when he made unpardonable concessions to the monopoly system which he principally served, he is judged historically as superior to his predecessors—Harding, Coolidge, Hoover—and his successors one and all.

On January 30, a few weeks before Roosevelt took office, Adolph Hitler became the German chancellor. With the establishment of the nazi dictatorship most peoples of the world had to choose, where they still had a choice, between bowing to fascism or fighting to create, preserve, and extend democracy.

The Communists through most of Roosevelt's presidency, after a couple of years of justified skepticism and testing, gave him critical support (barring the early years of World War II). If sometimes the support was not critical enough, a tendency of Earl Browder in 1937-38, the CP position was nevertheless basically correct and no other political entity of this period surpassed the accuracy of its judgments.

As we have noted in the previous chapter, the Communists were hostile and suspicious toward the first years of the New Deal. The strong support FDR initially received from Wall Street, the parallels of the NIRA to the "corporate state," the Mussolini-style bluster and bombast of Hugh Johnson, head of the NRA—all promised no rescue to people who were loaded down with the whole weight of the depression.

While the people expected much from Roosevelt they did not passively wait for him to perform miracles. The struggles of the unemployed and of the newly organized unionists pushed Roosevelt forward faster and further than he intended to go. The Committee for Industrial Organization became, in 1935, the principal vehicle of the people's advance both inside and outside of the labor movement.

The most reactionary section of the U.S. monopolists recovered their poise as the economy began to recover. They had no patience with Roosevelt's course which was saddling them with the accursed unions. They spurned the neo-imperialism of the Good Neighbor policy—they had much more confidence in the good old Gunboat Imperialism. They broke with Roosevelt, formed their neanderthal American Liberty League to oppose the "radical" in the White House, and encouraged an assortment of fascist-type organizations.

Bill Foster slowly eased himself back into his post as chairman of the Communist Party, with the organized labor movement, as before, his principal focus of attention. Earl Browder, as general secretary, had meanwhile become the Party's accepted spokesman and recognized leader. Foster, by the time he had acquired sufficient health to "make a ten-minute speech," resumed a highly productive level of activity.

The invasion of Manchuria by Japan in 1931, the unconcealed aggressiveness of Germany after 1933, the Italian invasion of Ethiopia in 1935—these events cumulatively showed that there was an identifiable fascist camp of war makers. At the same time it was possible to discern a camp of non-aggressors consisting—besides the Soviet Union—of those imperialist countries which had emerged from World War I with their empires either intact or enlarged. The Soviet Union joined the League of Nations; the fascist states withdrew from it.

There also emerged evidence that fascism was not necessarily invincible. When it made its bid in France in 1934 it was rebuffed by the united front of Communists and Socialists on February 12, 1934, and by the People's Front on July 14, 1935, which brought together Communists, Socialists, Radical Socialists and other anti-fascists. In Spain a people's front was formed in 1935 and won the parliamentary elections on February 16, 1936.

The Seventh World Congress of the Communist International, which Foster attended in 1935, studied the nature of fascism and of the struggle against it. It determined that unity of the working class and united action with its allies were indispensable to a successful fight against fascism. The Congress declared further that "the central slogan of the Communist Parties must be: struggle for peace."

Foster and the rest of the CPUSA delegation returned to the United States and proceeded with all their energy and skills to carry the policies of the world Communist movement into life under the conditions of American reality and in forms suitable to the American political and social conditions.

It was the opinion of the U.S. Communists, concurred in by the Seventh World Congress, that the electoral form of the People's Front in the United States would be a Farmer–Labor Party. This was the form which independent political action had tended to take in the past, though not always under just that name.

In 1936 the CPUSA was part of a national conference held in Chicago by the Farmer–Labor Party of Minnesota. But there it was decided that the time was not ripe for a national Farmer–Labor Party. The CP, though it had grave reservations about Roosevelt, felt that the main task was to defeat reaction. The economic royalists were out to defeat Roosevelt and return the country to Hooverism or worse. The Liberty League and the Republican Party had to be blocked. The Communists, at their Ninth Convention, decided to run their own candidates and preserve an independent stance. They did not support Roosevelt but directed their main fire against Alfred Landon, the Republican candidate, and the forces behind him which included the most reactionary sections of U.S. finance capital. The Communist candidates were Earl Browder and James W. Ford, for president and vice-president respectively.

The successful launching of the CIO in 1935, which tilted the U.S. labor movement toward the dominance of industrial unionism, which brought organization to millions of the unorganized, and which brought the basic mass production industries into the scope of unionism, was probably the outstanding event on the domestic scene during the hectic period of the thirties. It represented also a major validation of the entire course Bill Foster's life had taken to this point.

If the triumph of the CIO is publicly, and justifiably, associated with the name of John L. Lewis, it must also be said that no one worked harder and longer than William Z. Foster to bring this triumph about. As Len De Caux says: "Foster, a lifelong radical, was for years a voice crying for industrial organization."

The left wing—which is to say the TUUL and the CP—had helped to keep Lewis's United Mine Workers alive when it was being stifled in the prosperity of the 1920s—and it had helped rejuvenate it when it began to revive in the 1930s. Lewis's anti-Communism had scarred the bodies and wrecked the livelihoods of many Communist miners. But he nevertheless had a respect for their intelligence, knowledge, courage, militancy and honesty. When he undertook to organize the unorganized he made good use of the Communists and their rare combination of good qualities. The CIO's Steel Workers Organizing Committee (SWOC), for instance, hired 60 Communists. It would never admit it, but it did.

Saul Alinsky, John L. Lewis's biographer, wrote in 1949: "Then, as is now commonly known, the Communists worked indefatigably, with no job being too menial or unimportant. They literally poured themselves completely into their assignments. The Communist Party gave its complete support to the C.I.O. . . . The fact is that the Communist Party made a major contribution in the organization of the unorganized for the C.I.O."[2]

Two later biographers of Lewis confirm Alinsky's statement:

> Determined by late 1936 to build a new national labor center, one that would surpass the AFL, he needed all the help he could find. And he found no more dedicated and selfless union organizers than the young Communists who rallied to the CIO cause. Here were men and women who risked bodily injury and even death; who worked anywhere, anytime; and who asked little material recompense to organize the unorganized. For a labor movement such as the CIO, lacking its own sound financial base, unpaid or poorly paid organizers were a boon.[3]

Certainly Lewis could not expect this kind of help from such AFL "leaders" as Daniel J. Tobin, president of the Teamsters Union. "Tobin," according to labor historian Foster Rhea Dulles, "scornfully characterized the unskilled workers in mass production industry as 'rubbish.'" Lewis had to turn to those whose heart was in the job. Dulles, in his *Labor in America,* says of the Communists: "Lewis did not hesitate to draw upon their experience and skill in building up the C.I.O."[4]

Len De Caux, who was editor of the *CIO News,* has observed that "In America's new-unionism sweep, it was . . . natural that communists should be to the fore. Rather than Lewis, a man like Eugene Debs, William Z. Foster, Big Bill Haywood, might have been expected to lead . . . Foster's big 1917–19 packing and steel drives were the most immediate precursors of the CIO campaign." De Caux also reminds us that "At the 1926 AFL convention in Detroit, he [John L. Lewis] pointed dramatically from the platform to William Z. Foster in the visitor's balcony, denouncing him as 'the Archprince of communism in the United States.'"[5]

In the new situation of the second half of the 1930s, Lewis's "Archprince" appeared in a more work-a-day guise. His health was no longer equal to the demands of long speaking tours. But Art Shields, the veteran labor journalist, remembers him as "a splendid teacher. . . . He trained an entire generation of trade union activists in the Communist Party. . . . I cannot think of the CIO and its millions of members without thinking of William Z. Foster and his pupils. . . . I used to listen to him as he met with the CIO's Communist organizers when I was covering the steel drive in the Pittsburgh area in 1936. . . . They listened intently to his advice on strategy and tactics. They studied his pamphlets on organizing methods and put them into practice. And Foster must be regarded as one of the fathers of the CIO steel union."[6]

One of those who was among the gallant band who faced the hardships and dangers of organizing steel in the 1930's was Gus Hall, the present general secretary of the CPUSA. He joined the Communist Party in 1928 at the age of 18. Hall became a steelworker in Ohio after having worked in the Mesabi iron range of his native Minnesota. He became sub-regional director of the Steel Workers Organizing Committee in Warren, Ohio, where he led the strike against Little Steel.

Gus Hall has noted in his article "Thirty Years of Struggle in Steel" that:

> It is a matter of record that the only working-class organizations which had continued to provide genuine leadership to the steelworkers since 1920 were the Communist Party, the Communist-led Unemployed Councils, rank-and-file committees, and the S.M.W.I.U. The work of these organizations had also been supplemented in the early 'thirties by the Communist- and Left-progressive-led organizations of the nationality groups and the National Negro Congress. Our Party was already engaged in mobilizing capable forces for the campaign long before the S.W.O.C. had established its offices or staff. It was inevitable, therefore, that the various district directors of the S.W.O.C. established close working relations with the local leaders of the Communist Party. Many leading Communists went on the staff of the S.W.O.C. Almost without exception, the first union contact in the steel mills, the organizing core, proved

to be a club of the Communist Party or individual Party members, an ex-member of the S.M.W.I.U., a reader of the *Daily Worker,* a member of the National Negro Congress or a member or supporter of one of the Left-progressive-led nationality organizations. Many of these activities had also been the spark for the union in 1919 and 1930.

But the Communist contribution to the campaign did not end here. Before the drive started, Comrade Foster wrote two pamphlets addressed to the steelworkers: *Unionizing Steel* and *Organizing Methods in the Steel Industry.* These pamphlets reflected the rich, accumulated experiences of the working class in general and of the steel workers in particular. They immediately became the guide for the work of all Communists in the steel industry, and especially for those of us who were on the organizing staff. Through us, the ideas and policies put forward by Comrade Foster were passed on to the whole staff.

Comrade Foster also gave personal leradership to the drive. He spent many days and nights in meetings with those directly involved in the campaign. He met with Communists and non-Communists in the staff and leadership of the S.W.O.C. . . .

The campaign very closely followed the proposals made by Foster in his pamphlets. The very heart of these proposals is guaranteeing full rank-and-file participation.[7]

The two pamphlets mentioned by Hall (above) were preceded by one (April 1936) titled, *Industrial Unionism.* This launched a series of writings by Foster which became manuals of instruction to those building the new unions. It was 48 pages long and like *Unionizing Steel* (August 1936, 48 pp), *Organizing Methods in the Steel Industry* (October 1936, 24 pp), and *What Means a Strike in Steel* (February 1937, 64 pp) it sold for five cents, a price within the reach of its entire readership.

The curious syntax of the title of the last-named pamphlet aroused much debate among friends of Bill Foster but Foster always defended the propriety of this odd locution. In any case, none of his friends took issue with the contents, which put the capstone on the previous three pamphlets just as the strike in Little Steel put the capstone on the work of the SWOC.

Let us cite a page or so from *What Means a Strike in Steel* as a sample of Foster's pamphleteering style. (Readers will recall that Bill Foster had been a roustabout in a traveling tent show some 25 years before he wrote this):

The perspective of a huge national strike confronts the workers' leaders with the necessity of bearing closely in mind another basic principle of strategy, that of mobilizing a full sufficiency of forces to achieve their objective. A good strategist never sends a boy to do a man's job. This strategic principle may be illustrated by an old-time circus story: A boss canvasman was explaining to a visitor how vitally important it was that the cook-wagon should arrive early on the circus lot in order that the men could breakfast, or else they would not put up the big top.

Said he: "No cook-wagon; no breakfast, and no breakfast, no work," and he explained therefore, that they always used the precaution of having eight of the strongest horses to pull the cook-wagon over the muddy roads.

"But," inquired the visitor, "suppose the roads are so poor that your eight horses can't pull the cook-wagon, what then?"

"Oh, then," said the circus boss, "we put on more horses, and if they can't do the job we get out old Babe the elephant, to push it from behind."

"Still," persisted the visitor, "suppose the roads are so terribly bad that even all these horses and old Babe together can't haul the cook-wagon through the mire, how about that?"

"Oh, hell," declared the boss with finality, "we just put on more horses and more horses. The damned cook-wagon simply has to go through."

It is in this spirit of unconquerableness that the workers' leaders must face the eventuality of a national steel strike. They must be prepared to throw more and more forces into the struggle until finally they budge the "immovable" steel trust. The steel campaign must come through and that is all there is to it. Nothing will be handed to the workers gratuitously, either by the bosses directly or by the government. All they will get is what they are willing and able to fight for. The key to the winning of the movement of the steel workers is the greatest mobilization of labor's forces ever made in the United States.[8]

In addition to the four pamphlets we have named, Foster wrote an introduction to *Get Wise—Organize* (sub-titled, "What Every Young Steel Worker Should Know"). The pamphlet was by Dave Doran, who worked in the Western Pennsylvania steel and coal regions helping to build the new unions and the Young Communist League. He became the YCL's trade union director. His pamphlet was published in 1937. In 1938 Dave Doran was killed fighting fascism in Spain.

In the general organizing scheme of the CIO it was planned that steel would be organized first. After this formidable giant had been vanquished the other giants would be more vulnerable. But that's not the way it happened.

Workers everywhere were clamoring for organization, and for union contracts. Hosiery and hotel workers, shoemakers and ship-builders, restaurant employees and rug weavers, transport and tobacco workers, seamen and saleswomen, printers and pressmen, garbagemen and gravediggers, farmhands and foodpackers—all wanted in.

It was the great sitdown strike in General Motors, which started in Fisher Body plant No. 1 on December 30, 1936, that proved to be the key in the CIO's sweeping campaign. With the strikers still hanging in at Fisher 1 (the sitdown had spread to Chevrolet 4) negotiations began on February 3, 1937. On February 11 the mighty GM signed an agreement with the United Auto Workers. The first contract was for a six-months term, but GM and the UAW have now had contractual relations for over 40 years. William S. Knudsen, the GM president, led the list of signers for the company; for the union the list was headed by Wyndham Mortimer, UAW vice-president, a great Communist labor leader raised in the "Foster School."

The defeat of General Motors, the biggest corporation in the world, by a new and relatively small union, opened the gates for an organizational sweep. The victory was accomplished by a united front of the Communist Party and Socialist Party. It had the support of Frank X. Martel, head of the Detroit AFL, the CIO leadership, the Catholic trade unionists, and the language groups of the left-wing International Workers Order (IWO). It was helped by the fact that Michigan governor Frank Murphy feared that to use force to end the sitdown would doom the Democratic Party in that state.

Outstanding in the victory, besides Wyndham Mortimer, was Robert Travis, organizer of the GM strike, another Communist.

Right-wing Socialist lawyer, Larry Davidow, admitted in 1960 that an important element in the srike was militant workers who had been in Foster's TUEL and learned from him militant tactics of the class struggle.[9]

The UAW victory spurred the entire CIO. The Communists were not now "borers-from-within"—they built the UAW. Non-Communists in the GM strike have acknowledged that William Weinstone, as Communist organizer in Michigan, played "a very considerable role" in assisting the victory.[10]

The Chrysler Corporation was soon forced to follow GM into the unionized camp, but Ford, with its notorious "service department," its hired thugs, in-plant terrorism, and old Henry Ford's personal cussedness, was not brought into line until April 11, 1941.

Between that date, when a strike truce was declared, and May 21, when Ford workers voted overwhelmingly for the UAW in an NLRB election, Ford still tried to stem the tide, desperately using racism in an attempt to foil the union's final victory. Neither this nor any of Ford's last minute dirty tricks availed. On May 19 a huge rally was held in Cadillac Square in downtown Detroit. CIO president Philip Murray spoke and so did Paul Robeson. Two days later the UAW was in.

"The Ford organizing drive of 1940–41 followed the basic lines recommended by Bill Foster in a series of articles in the *Daily Worker* in November 1937," says Lou Saperstein, who was there when it all happened. "Foster presented a basic plan for a really mass organizing campaign with the full mobilization of the entire UAW. Auto workers responded enthusiastically to the drive. . . . Every local union headquarters became a recruiting office for the Ford drive. Local unions throughout Detroit set up committees to aid the campaign. A joint committee of three Left-led locals, 51, 155 and 208, was the pacesetter. . . ." In short, the plan applied Foster's thesis that the "cook-wagon has to go through." And it did.[11]

But—back to 1937.

The UAW victory at GM brought an unforeseen response in Big Steel. Without the push and shove of a strike, the US Steel corporation gave recognition to the SWOC on February 28 and signed an agreement on March 2, 1937. Members had been flocking into the union at the rate of two thousand a day. The House of Morgan, owners of US Steel, "capitulated" to the union in the hope of "taming" it.

Not so Little Steel. Republic Steel, Jones and Laughlin, Youngstown Sheet and Tube, and Inland Steel gave battle. A strike was called on May 26, 1937.

On Memorial Day ten strikers and sympathizers were killed and ninety wounded at Republic Steel in Chicago. Six more were killed before a month was over. After four months the union was forced to retreat. It retreated in good order, without demoralization. But it took four more years before Little Steel was brought under union contract.

The SWOC was forced to fight the pitched battles of class war almost in spite of itself. The hardbitten, old line bureaucrats who headed the organizing committee (and later entrenched themselves in the United Steel Workers) kept the reins of power tightly in their own select hands. Len De Caux, who had an inside view of the situation states:

> SWOC leaders particularly wanted to liquidate the memory of the last drive's leader, William Z. Foster. He was now at the head of the Communist Party, which some of his ablest steel organizers had also joined. Communists had kept alive some union activity. They had influence among foreign-born steelworkers, some following among the Black. They had promoted a shortlived Steel and Metal Workers Industrial Union and been active in 1933-35 efforts to organize through the AFL.

> The SWOC leaders, coming mostly from coal, had little background and few contacts in steel. They found the ready help of the communists invaluable. Foster, who should know, wrote later that 60 of the first organizers hired by SWOC were members of the Communist Party. Bill Gebert, a party leader, was liaison man and in charge of mobilizing foreign-born groups.

Rallying all their supporters and contacts, the communists threw themselves into the campaign more unconditionally and self-effacingly than is usual in politics. SWOC used their help and, rather underhandedly, tried to rub out their faces completely. It put communist steelworkers on the payroll, if needed, but each one was a marked man, closely watched at all times and dispensed with as soon as possible. Any move he might seem to make to win personal following would be countered quickly by undercover redbaiting or slander, by transfer to other territory, or by firing.[12]

Bill Foster was always a railroad man at heart. (He favored his old Hamilton pocket timepiece over any new-fangled wristwatch!) So he turned easily from the CIO and steel to the question of the railroads, a section of basic industry where the CIO had little impact and where entrenched, moss-backed leadership prevailed.

Bill's 64-page pamphlet, *Railroad Workers, Forward!* (October 1937) was addressed to the rank-and-file. In his usual simple style, using the special jargon of railroading, fortifying his assertions and conclusions with facts and statistics, Foster combined a restrained critique of the railroad union bureaucrats with a program of demands, and recommendations on how to win them.[13]

The railroad union officials were not at all pleased with the airing of their shortcomings and the unsolicited advice which Foster offered to the railroad workers. One of the most hard-bitten of the railroad labor executives, President T.C. Cashen of the Switchmen's Union of North America, "answered" Foster in the March 1938 Switchmen's *Journal*—answered with a blast of red-baiting and a barrage of slanders and lies. Cashen's blast was reprinted widely in the journals of the various railroad unions. Foster replied in April with a second pamphlet, *Stop Wage Cuts and Layoffs on the Railroads*. In this he makes no special effort to be "nice" to Mr. Cashen. One issue, at least, that Foster dealt with in *Railroad Workers, Forward!* Cashen did not and could not answer. This was Bill's denunciation of the shameful treatment of Black workers in the railroad industry and their exclusion from the union. A constitutional provision of Cashen's union made membership available to "male, white persons" only.[14]

When the railroad corporations in 1938 called for a general reduction of 15 percent in the wages of all railroad workers, Bill Foster addressed the workers again in a pamphlet, *Halt the Railroad Wage Cut* (October 1938). The threat of a strike, followed by government mediation, resulted in the wage cut being cancelled.

The great and positive changes in the labor sector, largely brought about by the successes of the CIO, paradoxically helped the AFL as well. Organization was the order of the day. The long dammed-up energy, initiative, and inventiveness of the U.S. working class, which Foster had labored for so many years to unleash, now found an outlet. Despite the expulsion of the original CIO unions from the AFL, by 1944 the AFL had a membership of approximately 6,800,000 (compared to 2,608,011 in 1934) and the CIO had approximately 6,000,000.[15]

The great advance of the U.S. labor movement was made during a period when the people of this country, along with the rest of the world, lived under the shadow of a lowering war cloud which in 1939 burst into a storm of war.

In William Z. Foster's 1937 book, *From Bryan to Stalin*, he says: "Humanity now stands upon the very brink of a gigantic war, far more cruel, bitter and destructive than the war of 1914–18. Mass executions of prisoners by Spanish fascists and air bombardment of Madrid and other cities show how terrible the coming war will be." The reality, as we now know, turned out to be even more terrible than this anticipation.

"And," Foster predicts accurately, "there is every reason to believe that the next general war, which is now so rapidly in the making, will provoke such a mass revolt as to cause the overthrow of capitalism in many European countries and bring about a huge expansion of Socialism."

Does this mean that the socialist-minded people should passively contemplate the inevitability of war, and even welcome it as the bearer of the society they seek? Foster does not ask this question, but he answers it when he says:

"The toilers want peace. They want to accomplish the inevitable transition from capitalism to Socialism through the ordinary processes of democracy. . . . They know it is they and their families who must always bear the brunt of war. . . . But in the present relation of forces the decisive word may rest with the fascist capitalists who hold power in many countries. . . . In spite of mass resistance they are striving to plunge the world into a holocaust of murder and destruction, that will threaten civilization with a return to barbarism. On their heads, therefore, be the heavy responsibility. By war they cannot save capitalism, and history will inexorably visit upon them condign punishment for their monstrous crime."[16]

The very fact of a growth in the size and quality of the organized labor movement was no doubt the largest single factor enhancing the democratic struggle in the United States during the Roosevelt era. But there were other components of the democratic front.

The most significant of these was the spirit of struggle among the Black people and the organized forms it took. One such was the National Negro Congress (NNC), founded in Chicago in February 1936 by 817 delegates representing a "combined and unduplicated" membership of 1,200,000. Ralph Bunche and W.E.B. Du Bois attended, as did such different notables as A. Philip Randolph, John P. Davis and James W. Ford. Ford had suggested such a Congress two years before its founding.

The NNC adopted a progressive program; it helped in building the CIO and promoted trade union membership among Black workers.

A year later Black youth, under mainly Communist leadership, came together in the Southern Negro Youth Congress (SNYC) at Richmond, Virginia. SNYC brought to prominence a new cadre of Black leaders including Edward Strong, James Jackson, Louis Burnham and Esther Cooper. It played a vital role over the next ten years. Foster calls the SNYC the most important movement ever conducted by Black youth.[17]

Another youth organization, the American Youth Congress (AYC) was one of the largest and most vital of the democratic organizations which were born in the New Deal period. It came into being at a convention in New York in 1934. The Roosevelt administration—with Eleanor Roosevelt, a half dozen governors, and New York's liberal mayor, Fiorello LaGuardia, as its front runners—hoped to control the AYC. Its nominal founder, Viola Ilma, who had studied youth organization in nazi Germany, now faced the representatives of 1,500,000 organized youth with her blueprint for a new organization. There were delegates present from the YMCA, YWCA, YM and YWHA and many other traditional organizations. Also present were the Young People's Socialist League and the Young Communist League (YCL). To the consternation of Mrs. Roosevelt, the leadership slipped out of Miss Ilma's hands when she was balked by the democratic spirit of the youth. Until the outbreak of World War II, the AYC remained the most influential voice of the youth of the land. Gil Green, leader of the YCL, became a prominent leader of the AYC. And Mrs. Roosevelt, swallowing her disappointment, remained as a sort of den mother to this dynamic organization.

The women's movement did not succeed in forming any such large or representative organization. But a Women's Charter was drafted by a group of liberal and labor women and attracted the support of a large and varied group of organizations, including the Communists.

Communist women leaders, such as Ella Reeve Bloor, Ann Rivington and Margaret Cowl Krumbein, were not content merely to endorse the Charter with its limited assertion of the right of women to full equality in all spheres of social activity. The Communists paid special attention to women's trade union activities, to the people's health movement and the mass movement for federal health insurance, including maternity coverage. They advocated child care programs and devoted special attention to the needs of Black women.

The prosperity period of the 1920's generated illusions among the majority of the working class. This was not a case solely of spontaneous generation. Overwhelmingly the mass media of that day promoted capitalist ideals. There seemed to be a conscious effort to confirm the observation of Marx and Engels (in the *Communist Manifesto*) that "The ruling ideas of each age have ever been the ideas of its ruling class."[18] The motion pictures, the fiction magazines and the best selling books—with some exceptions—dealt with capitalist success stories, happy-ending romances, and other forms of wish fulfillment.

A radical, mostly Communist, Left was a voice of sanity in the pervading babble of distortions and cynicism. First *The Liberator*, then the monthly *New Masses,* furnished a rallying point for a real people's culture. Talented, humanistic and socialist-minded artists and writers—such as Fred Ellis, William Gropper, Lydia Gibson, Robert Minor, Art Young, Moissaye Olgin, Meridel LeSueur, Countee Cullen, Michael Gold, Joseph North, Josephine Herbst, Langston Hughes, Oakley Johnson, Ruth McKenney, and others—built *New Masses* (which in 1934 became a weekly) and helped found the John Reed Clubs for the encouragement of progressive writing. The Pierre DeGeyter Society gave similar inspiration to musical artists and composers.

Hardly had the Great Depression begun when the more honest and searching intellectuals, shaken by the fierceness of the economic crisis, began to heed the voice of the Communist Party, the sanest and soberest voice around. For the next ten years the best intellectual and artistic products of the country bore the stamp, to greater and lesser degree, of Marxist influence.

Many who approached the Party in this period were fellow travelers or sympathizers who proved to be transients in the working class and national liberation ranks. Others signed up for the duration.

As the years of the thirties recede the tide of reminiscence advances, and many volumes have been written in retrospect of those times, especially by writers trying to come to terms with their embarrassment at having been "mixed up" in a movement from which they have since sought to move as far away as possible.

Former faith now leads to present slander. Reviewing a book by Malcolm Cowley, one of the best of the fellow-traveling group, Alfred Kazin, himself a veteran of the grim decade, smugly remarks: "Mr. Cowley, like virtually every talented and honest writer caught up in the movement, eventually learned that the Communists who seemed to be leading it were in fact distrustful of talent and dishonest on principle."[19]

The talented and the honest, then, were all betrayed according to Mr. Kazin. The rich, successful, Harvard-educated, worldly Malcolm Cowley, Kazin seems to say, allowed the Communist "Pied Pipers" to lead him blindly out West to report the drought and the dust storms; to Washington to witness the dispersal of the Bonus Army; to "Bloody Harlan" in Kentucky to observe the plight of the coal miners! What nonsense! These were the grim realities of the time and Cowley reported them as he saw them. If the Communists helped bring these realities to his attention, it was because no one else did so.

In 1932, when William Z. Foster ran for President, and James W. Ford was his running mate, a League of Professional Groups for Foster and Ford was constituted. In October 1932 this ad hoc league published a 32-page pamphlet called *Culture and the Crisis.* It concluded:

> In the interests of a truly human society . . . ; in behalf of a new cultural renaissance which will create integrated, creative personalities, we call upon all men and women—especially workers in the professions and arts—to join in the revolutionary struggle against capitalism under the leadership of the Communist Party.[20]

This statement was signed by 53 prominent figures in the arts and professions, mostly non-Communists. From Sherwood Anderson to Ella Winter, Erskine Caldwell to Edmund Wilson, Malcolm Cowley to Lincoln Steffens, Theodore Dreiser to Sidney Howard, Countee Cullen to Langston Hughes, it was a list of names for which Bill Foster's own reputation had been the principal attractive force.

The idea for a professionals' committee for Foster and Ford took shape after a meeting at the home of Edmund Wilson. "W.Z. Foster made a very fine impression by his talk at E.W.'s home last week," wrote Matthew Josephson to a friend of his late in May 1932. A "fairly large group of intellectuals" had been there. Foster dressed in "unfashionable though well-brushed clothes, stood in marked contrast to the Ivy League radicals in that living room. He was a tall, bony Irish-American of about fifty, with thinning red hair, lined face, and blue eyes. . . ."

Josephson asked Foster about his differences with the Socialists and got the reply: "The socialists see more in capitalism than the capitalists; they see socialism in it."

In the summer, a dozen or so writers met at a dinner party, and an *ad hoc* committee of intellectuals to support the Communists' 1932 election campaign began to take shape—if "shape" is not too firm a word for such an amorphous group.

Thirty-five years later, after the Cold War and McCarthyism had done their worst, the honest liberal, Matthew Josephson would say:

> In the light of later recantations and "revelations" by some of the persons involved in the left-wing activities here described, and their later claims that it was part of a vast underground "conspiracy" to use writers as "dupes" who would deliver the people into the hands of the Bolshevists, I should like to deny all such allegations with all my heart. I cannot for the life of me recall anything partaking of the nature of a conspiracy . . . The

climate of opinion in the United States of those days was far more favorable to freedom of thought than it is nowadays.[21]

Foster, as he grew older, continued to develop as a writer. In literary quality he reached a high point with *Pages from a Worker's Life* (1939). He was one of the self-educated intellectuals who are found in large numbers in American life, particularly among those who are active in the labor movement. This great pool of talent makes one wonder why our Congress must be overwhelmingly composed of lawyers and business people to the utter exclusion of ordinary working people. Self-education may not be the best road to becoming a nuclear physicist, but it works wonderfully in the fields of culture and social science!

Bill Foster had a respect for literature which extended to those who produced it, and this respect was reciprocated.

Joseph Freeman, one of the prominent talents on the literary Left wrote his memoirs in 1936 in a mammoth volume (when he was still at a rather tender age for such a grand enterprise). In his *American Testament* (Farrar and Rinehart) he has given us a valid sketch of the mid-1930s Foster:

> His thin, wiry body was surmounted by a large head which rose from a round, strong chin to a broad forehead and temples enlarged by baldness. His clear blue eyes were by turns austere and mild, his voice soft.
>
> . . . Foster was a man of wide cultural interest; his library was as full of literary as of socialist classics, and he had an unusual knowledge and appreciation of the best in music.[22]

This statement is accurate except insofar as it exaggerates Foster's appreciation of music. A friend who visited Bill in his last years, when he was house-ridden after a stroke, recalls him saying that he never paid much attention to music. "I guess I missed a lot because of that," Bill mused. Then after a short silence he said, "Hell! I suppose I've had plenty to make up for it!"

Mike Gold, the poet, editor, and all around literary voice of the Left, whose work scolded, encouraged and set a model for emulation for two generations of writers, recalled (in 1951) a day in 1924 when Bill Foster stopped Mike on the street and congratulated him on a poem he had recently had published. "I cannot tell the young writers of today," said Mike Gold, "how much his words of praise warmed my spirit and helped me continue writing in that milieu of hostile Philistines—both bourgeois and 'Communist'."[23]

Another author who was encouraged by Foster's interest in his work is Lloyd L. Brown, the highly regarded Black novelist and biographer. When his novel, *Iron City*, came out in 1951, Brown sent a copy to Foster as well as to a number of other busy people whose comments he was eager to have. Only Foster replied. He told the author he had "enjoyed the book immensely" that it was a "splendid piece of writing" and called it "one of our best expressions of Negro rebellion." Foster asked to be excused for not making a more analytical criticism, pleading that he lacked time because he was "up to my neck working on the *History of the CPUSA.*" Lloyd Brown was greatly impressed that Foster, despite poor health and the tensions of a difficult time, had taken the trouble to write a warm personal letter to encourage a young writer.[24]

Theodore Dreiser, who is probably best known for his powerful novel *An American Tragedy*, sent a message to Foster's 60th birthday celebration (1941) in which he said of him:

> To me he is a saint—my first and only contact with one. It was ten years ago in San Francisco that I got to know him well. That was at the time when the "end of the rainbow" . . . had come to its drab finale in "Hoovervilles" and hunger. . . . The forgotten man has never been forgotten by William Foster . . . a man among men, a leader among leaders, who has always kept faith with the common man.[25]

Joseph North recalled a personal experience with Dreiser, whom he met in the Pennsylvania coalfields during the 1931 strike which Foster led. At that time Dreiser spoke to North of what he called Foster's "Christ-like devotion to the poor and dispossessed."[26]

(Lloyd Brown also thinks Bill was a saint but, he adds, "a saint who could cuss like the Devil!" Bill Foster dismissed the attempt to canonize him with a chuckle and a blush.)[27]

H.L. Mencken, America's most urbane, witty and scholarly cynic (and author of *The American Language*) made an honorable distinction between Foster and some of his labor-movement contemporaries when he wrote in 1923:

> Try to think of an American labor leader writing good English, or even ordinary intelligible bad English. The effort takes one into mysticism. Is William Z. Foster an exception? Then don't forget that Doctor Foster has been repudiated by the Sacred College of American Labor, and that in most American states the circulation of his compositions is forbidden by law, always with the consent of the local Federation. Old Gompers is a far

better specimen of the normal American labor leader. He can neither think nor write.

Some may feel this comes down a bit hard on Gompers and his cronies, but who will dispute that it does simple justice to Bill Foster?[28]

16

Fascism Leads to War

" . . . In defending the interests of the working class and other toilers, the Marxist party is thereby defending the interests of the overwhelming majority of the people. It is functioning in the interests of the nation against a reactionary bourgeois nationalism, against an exploiting capitalist class which always advances its own class interests at the expense of the people in general." (Foster.)[1]

As fascism at home and abroad cleared the road to war, the Communists paid increased attention to their responsibility to defend and champion the nation against a treacherous bourgeoisie. This was a central point of the policy adopted at the Seventh World Congress of the CI.

After August 1934 the American Liberty League loomed as the personification of the internal fascist enemy. It was sponsored by the principal monopolist families of the country—duPont, Morgan, Rockefeller, Mellon—and by the giant industrial corporations, US Steel, General Motors, AT and T, International Harvester, and most of the rest of really big business.

The Hearst press opened its pages to League publicity. The demagogic Huey Long and Father Coughlin switched from the Roosevelt camp to the Liberty League's. There was a division of labor here: the Liberty League's naked reactionism had no appeal for the vast majority of Americans. The pseudo-populist demagogy of Senator Huey Long, with his slogans of "Share the Wealth" and

"Every Man a King" allured many people who were desperate in their misery. Similarly the unctuous rabble-rousing of Father Charles Coughlin—the "Radio Priest"—reached many who tuned out the message of Morgan and Mellon.

Roosevelt was now under pressure from the most reactionary section of monopoly capital on the one hand and, on the other, the great, new mass movements intent upon achieving economic and political advance. He tried to follow a middle course which he himself described as "a little left of center." In firming up his popular base he signed into law in 1935 a number of reform measures of which the Wagner Labor Relations Act was the most important in the short run. In the long run the most important was the Social Security Act. The Communist Party supported such reform measures while combating illusions created by them among the working people.

The Communists initially took a dim view of the Wagner Act for it seemed to invite the government—the bosses' government—to participate as a third party at the collective bargaining table. They soon changed their position to one of approval, recognizing that the balance of forces then prevailing ensured advantages to the labor movement under the Act. The Wagner Act gave the force of law to gains already won in struggle through the great organization drives.

The 1936 elections took place at a time when an international situation was developing which would explode into war in 1939. The Spanish Civil War had been added to the problems troubling the peace. The reactionary forces, with fascism and war in their hearts and minds, rallied to defeat Roosevelt.

Eighty-five percent of the press supported Alfred Landon, the Republican candidate. But the mass support for Roosevelt was overwhelming. Workers and farmers chose FDR; and so did the Blacks in the North who, for the first time since the passage of the Fifteenth Amendment (1869), abandoned the party of Lincoln to support the Democratic candidate.

While local and statewide independent parties—of the labor and farmer-labor type—grew during the '36 elections and after, the goal of a national farmer-labor party remained out of reach. Labor expressed itself politically mainly through the instrumentality of Labor's Non-Partisan League. The Communist Party called for "the defeat of Landon at all costs." Its campaign brought the issues before the people but was not geared to win votes for its candidates, Earl

Browder and James W. Ford. Roosevelt won a spectacular victory carrying every state except Maine and Vermont. The Communists' correct policy in 1936, Foster says, "was eventually . . . distorted by Browder into an impermissible subordination of the Communist Party to the bourgeois Roosevelt program in general."[2]

The Soviet Union, which joined the League of Nations late in 1934 after the axis powers had left it, advocated what it called a policy of "collective security." Its gist was that the peace-loving countries were to form an international peace front to restrain the aggressive fascist powers. But there were no takers among the capitalist states. Roosevelt proposed to "quarantine the aggressors" in 1937 but this proved to be mere rhetoric. The reality was the phony "neutrality," which embargoed aid to the legal government of Spain in its fight against the fascists; the weak support of oil sanctions against Italy, which involved Ethiopia; and the continuing sale of scrap iron and other war materials to Japan.

Against all these policies the U.S. Communists fought with a consistency unmatched by any other political formation in the country. In the case of Spain the Party organized the sending of some 3,000 volunteers to fight against Franco, Hitler and Mussolini on Spanish soil. Half of them died in that democratic struggle.

By the time Madrid fell in 1939 other events had taken place which paved the way to world war. In February 1938 Hitler occupied Austria. In May the governments of Germany, Italy, Great Britain and France, with the approval of the Roosevelt administration, consented to German seizure of Czechoslovakia's Sudetenland, which soon led to the occupation of the entire country.

The western European countries, in all their actions, showed that they were ready to "appease" Hitler by posing no impediments to his territorial ambitions so long as they were directed eastward—and ultimately against the Soviet Union.

In an address to the 18th Congress of the CPSU on March 10, 1939, Joseph Stalin made the low-key statement: "Far be it from me to moralize on the policy of non-intervention, to talk of treason, treachery and so on. . . . It must be remarked, however, that the big and dangerous political game started by the supporters of the policy of non-intervention may end in a serious fiasco for them."[3]

These words, which provoked no diplomatic stir when they were uttered in March, were a warning, the meaning of which became clear when the Soviet Union, on August 24, 1939, bought time for itself by signing a non-aggression pact with Germany.

The Soviet Union had made many attempts to establish collective security with Britain and France, and to sign a mutual-assistance agreement with them. These attempts were rebuffed. The combined strength of these countries could have halted Hitler's drive to conquer Europe.

If the USSR, in the face of opposition to collective security had rejected Hitler's offer of a non-aggression pact, it would have been isolated. It would have become the victim of the British and French appeasers who wanted Hitler to move against the Soviet Union. The Soviet-German pact, which gave no material aid to Hitler, gained for the Soviets time to prepare for Hitler's unprovoked June 1941 assault.

When Hitler attacked Poland the British and French offered only expressions of sympathy, notwithstanding their existing agreements to come to the aid of that country. The United States stood neutral. The Soviet Union's offer of aid had been rejected in advance of the attack.

With Hitler's invasion of Poland on September 1, 1939, the long-feared Second World War started.[4]

Despite differences in the ranks of U.S. capitalists, despite judgments which leaned variously to the carrot or the club, and despite partisan conflicts which did not affect basic policy, the aim of the imperialists was to ensure that the war, when it came, would be a war against the Soviet Union. This had been the common goal in the years before the war actually broke out, and it explains the "neutrality" policy of the United States, the government willingness to appease Hitler, and the U.S. approval of the infamous Munich betrayal.

With the actual outbreak of hostilities, the long-standing split in the American bourgeoisie took a sharper form and the lines became distinct as between the Roosevelt camp—which favored Britain—and the Liberty League crowd, which now came up with its America First Committee and, as discreetly as possible, favored Germany.

The section of the class which supported Roosevelt was swayed by the large mass of capital they had invested in Britain—42 percent of all U.S. foreign investments—and the danger to U.S. imperialism stemming from Hitler's covetous intentions toward Europe, the Far East and Latin America. The anti-Roosevelt capitalists, including many of the biggest, were partial to fascism and would have welcomed a stalemate in the existing war. Some would gladly have seen it turned into a mutually destructive war between Germany and the Soviet Union. In fact, when the war took on a changed character in June 1941, Senator Harry S. Truman of Missouri proposed that the United States follow a policy designed to produce such an outcome.

In an address delivered to the closing session of the Nominating Convention of the CPUSA at Madison Square Garden on June 2, 1940, William Z. Foster spoke on "The Three Basic Tasks of the Communist Peace Policy." These can be summarized as follows: "The first of these tasks is to keep America out of the war. . . . The second great task presented to us by the present war is to achieve a just and lasting world peace . . . The third task presented to us sharply by this war . . . is for us to work towards putting an end forever to the monstrous social system, capitalism, which, in addition to its endless other mass miseries, has given birth to this dreadful war."[5]

Leaving aside the third task—a task always on the agenda of a Communist Party with varying degrees of urgency—the other two tasks were dictated by the character of the war as of June 2nd, 1940, when Foster made his speech. Up to a few weeks before, Neville Chamberlain, whose umbrella was the very symbol of the anti-Soviet, fascist-appeasing Munich policy, had still been Prime Minister of Britain. In the higher echelons of the Western allies there appeared to be no will to fight an anti-fascist war and it was evident no preparation had been made for such a fight. Preoccupation with "strangling the Communist baby" (to use a phrase of Winston Churchill's) had left the countries disarmed, ideologically and otherwise, for an anti-fascist war. No wonder that 96 percent of the people of the United States favored staying out of it.[6] They were no more interested in "knittin' for Britain" than in "purlin' for Berlin"—to use the words of an anti-war song of the period.

Lenin had said that "For a Marxist, clarifying the nature of the war is a necessary preliminary for deciding the question of his attitude toward it. . . . It is necessary to consider the war in the historical environment in which it is taking place."[7]

So viewed, the war arose as a collision between two groups of imperialist powers. However, a parallel with World War I will not serve. The main difference arises from the existence of the Soviet socialist state. The imperialist powers had sacrificed the interests of smaller states in order to achieve their objective of turning Germany against the USSR. Then they were themselves attacked. Within the countries invaded by nazi forces, resistance grew among the peoples, giving an increasing national liberation content to the ongoing war.

With the United States outside the arena of armed struggle, it was difficult for the people of this country to support the allies who still bore the stamp of Chamberlain and Daladier appeasement.

The sudden, treacherous invasion of the Soviet Union by Germany on June 22, 1941, and the subsequent alignment of the Western powers with the Soviet Union, changed the character of the war beyond dispute: it was a war for the freedom and national independence of peoples, for the crushing and defanging of the fascist serpent, and for the preservation of socialism.[8]

The CPUSA, in a statement signed by William Z. Foster and Robert Minor, then called for "full and unlimited collaboration of the United States, Great Britain, and the Soviet Union to bring about the military defeat of Hitler."[9]

But before this stage had been reached, before the new character of World War II had become unambiguously clear, almost twenty-two months passed during which the Communists in the United States had to face the heightened hostility of the government and the press as penalty for their principled position. This was true despite the fact that the 1939 conventions of both the AFL and CIO went on record against intervention in the European conflict. In November 1939 the three major farm organizations did likewise. The vast majority of Americans favored neutrality.

The Communist position was more complex than this. Foster stated it as follows: "The Communist policy was not one of isolationism or neutrality but of dynamic struggle to defend the rights of the conquered peoples, to prevent the spread of the war, and to bring the war to the quickest possible democratic conclusion."[10]

Following the signing of the Soviet–German non-aggression treaty, the start of World War II, and the Roosevelt administration's tilt toward Britain, the Communist Party came under a pall of harassment. In the fall of 1939, Earl Browder, William Wiener, leader of the International Workers Order, and Harry Gannes, foreign editor of the *Daily Worker,* were charged with technical passport violations. Browder was convicted and sentenced to prison; Wiener and Gannes were both terminally ill and could not be brought to trial.[11]

The Dies Committee (House Committee on Un-American Activities) cited a number of Communists for contempt for refusing to supply the Committee with Party membership lists; eighteen Party election workers were held under $100,00 bail each in Oklahoma for violation of that state's criminal syndicalism law.

In Detroit sixteen persons were arrested by the FBI in February 1940, charged with recruiting soldiers for the Spanish Loyalists in 1937 and 1938. At the same time, in Milwaukee and New York, the FBI raided the offices of the Veterans of the Abraham Lincoln Brigade. Private homes were raided by the "Red Squad" in Chicago. Dies Committee agents ransacked the Washington, D.C., offices of the American League Against War and Fascism. Communist Party offices in Washington, Pittsburgh, and elsewhere were raided. People who had signed Communist nominating petitions were intimidated by the FBI. Vigilantes participated in incidents too numerous to mention.[12]

In October 1940, the CP was obliged to dis-affiliate from the Communist International under the terms of the Voorhis Act. In June of the same year the Smith Act was passed. Under the guise of an Alien Registration Law, the Smith Act contained provisions which, after the war, resulted in the prosecution of almost 200 CP leaders for conspiracy to teach and advocate "the overthrow of the United States government by force and violence."

On the night of March 17, 1941, 18,000 persons assembled in Madison Square Garden in New York to attend a celebration of William Z. Foster's sixtieth birthday and 46 years of activity in the labor movement. Among those on the platform was Paul Robeson who sang a vocal tribute to Bill Foster.

The occasion was also used to protest the imprisonment of Earl Browder who was on the eve of entering the Federal Penitentiary to begin serving a four-year term for a technical violation of passport regulations. During Browder's enforced absence his post was filled by Robert Minor who had the title of Acting General Secretary. Foster continued as Chairman.

When Hitler had driven the British forces into the sea at Dunkirk, he subjected most of Europe to his dictatorship and was able to draw upon the productive capacity of the subject countries and on the physical effort of a host of slave laborers. He had two strategic choices.

One was to launch war against the Soviet Union; the other was to attack the practically defenseless British Isles.

"Nevertheless," says Foster regarding the latter choice, "Hitler did not venture to seize the great prize lying so temptingly before him. This was primarily because of his fear of a two-front war, his dread of the Red Army in his rear in the East. . . . Hitler kept three-fourths of his army in Eastern Europe, on guard against the Russians. . . . Then, considering that Great Britain could be no danger in his rear for the next period, he delivered his major blow—against the U.S.S.R. . . . " That was June 22, 1941.[13]

Much of the U.S. military and naval establishment expected the Soviet Union to be vanquished in short order. *Time* Magazine remarked complacently that Germany and the Soviet Union were now "at each others throats." And Harry S. Truman expressed his hope that "the Nazis will kill lots of Russians and vice versa."[14]

This vicious cynicism, fortunately for the United States, did not prevail in Washington and did not guide President Roosevelt's thinking. By October 1 a billion-dollar lend-lease agreement was in effect between the USA and the USSR.

After June 22, 1941, it became easier to distinguish, for those formerly had been confused in the matter, between the anti-fascist, pro-peace position with which the Communists identified themselves, and the isolationism which continued to be advocated by the America First forces. The latter, though sponsored by the most reactionary stratum of the monopolists, attracted a number of presumably well-intentioned liberals (even the Socialist Party leader, Norman Thomas, spoke from its platform) and gave all possible aid to the Axis camp under a demagogic "peace" cover. Not for long.

The entire country was swept into the fervor of an anti-fascist war when the Japanese made their infamous sneak attack on Pearl Harbor on December 7, 1941. After that, "peace" talk was relegated for the duration mainly to certain religious sects and to the clandestine circles of Axis supporters.

By December 11, Germany and Italy declared war on the United States after the United States had formally declared war on Japan. Now the sides were drawn up *for* war on the lines the Communists had urged they should be to *prevent* war. For the next three-and-one-half years, until first the Germans and then the Japanese had surrendered to the overwhelming force of the Soviet Union and its war-time allies, the politics of the United States were the politics of a country engaged in a defensive, anti-fascist war. Within this context the capitalist powers and members of their ruling classes maneuvered as always for their own advantage but such maneuvering was subject to the need for military success. Meanwhile the working people of the Allied side made the necessary sacrifices for victory. The Communist Party, USA, conformed its immediate domestic program to the implications of its slogan: "Everything for victory over world-wide fascist slavery!"[15]

With Earl Browder absent in prison, William Z. Foster took the lead in voicing the Communist Party's position. Even before the bombing of Pearl Harbor exploded all remaining illusions of the possibility of US neutrality, Foster had stated the CP position in a major speech delivered at the Stadium in Chicago, August 20, 1941. He declared in his opening words.

> The American people, on pain of disaster, must fully realize that a Hitler victory over the Soviet Union and Great Britain would place in acute jeopardy the most fundamental national interests—the very national existence of the United States. They, therefore, should take all necessary steps, jointly with Great Britain, the U.S.S.R., China and other anti-fascist peoples, to repel the developing fascist world offensive and militarily to destroy Hitlerism, root and branch. This is the only means by which the United States can be effectively defended against the growing Hitler threat.[16]

In the course of his speech Foster articulated—probably for the first time—an issue which was to be the Communists' major foreign policy demand for the next three years: the opening of a "second front." Foster said: "Great Britain and the United States should cooperate in opening up a great Western front, so as to force Hitler into a fatal two-front war."[17] This strategic necessity did not become a reality until June 6, 1944.

Winston Churchill was the main opponent of a 1942 second front. He pretended to favor one for 1943. When it finally came in 1944 it was because of fear that the Soviet Union might defeat Hitler herself and play a predominant role at the peace table. The United States and the Soviet Union had issued a communique in May 1942 which contained the statement: "In the course of the conversations complete agreement was reached with regard to the urgent tasks of the creation of a second front in Europe in 1942." The agreement was reached, but it was not carried out.[18]

On the home front the Communists threw themselves into the campaign for an all-out national war effort. They exerted themselves with the same whole-heartedness that had always characterized their major campaigns. They led in the Battle for Production; they participated in all aspects of civilian defense. Communist women replaced those men in Party leadership who left to enter the armed services or to work in war industries. (Gus Hall later observed that "the worst symptom of male superiority tendencies in our ranks" in the immediate postwar period was "the speed with which we released the bulk of our leading women comrades after World War II and our slowness to correct this error.")[19]

In the Battle for Production labor's no-strike pledge played a vital role. This pledge had been adopted by conventions of both CIO and AFL and, except at the local level, it was almost universally observed. John L. Lewis and the coal miners conducted several big mine strikes; and a number of walkouts took place in auto plants, where the UAW was under the leadership of Walter Reuther. Nowhere was the pledge more scrupulously observed than by those unions under Communist and left leadership. Foster later observed that the left-led unions may have been overscrupulous, enforcing the pledge "too rigidly where shop grievance stoppages were concerned."[20]

One honorable exception to the Communists' "too rigid" adherence to the no-strike pledge took place in the Winston–Salem, North Carolina, plants of the R.J. Reynolds Tobacco Company. On June 17, 1943, a Black worker died on the job after a foreman refused him permission to leave his post to see a doctor. A strike started almost spontaneously among the super-exploited workers. Eventually 11,000 joined the strike. Soon more than 9,000 of them, mostly Blacks, joined Local 22 of the Food, Tobacco, Agricultural and Allied Workers. Moranda Smith, a highly regarded Black woman Communist, played a leading role in the strike and in winning recognition for Local 22.[21]

The patience and control exercised by the working class in the Battle for Production were a product of their anti-fascist spirit and discipline—maintained in the face of endless provocations by the employers. Ingenuity and perseverance were applied to keep wages abreast of rising prices as the capitalists went about "business as usual," the business of capitalism being to make as high a profit as possible. In the early periods of the war the monopolists conducted a "sitdown strike of capital" to force the government to approve the levels of profit they demanded. The workers as a class were aided in their struggle with the high cost of living by the availability of overtime at premium pay and the phenomenon of full employment—a strictly wartime phenomenon not encountered since.

The historic inequality of wages and employment opportunity as between white and non-white workers had not been affected by any law ever, up to June 25, 1941.

On that day, however, with the country gearing up for war. President Roosevelt issued his Executive Order 8802, declaring it to be the "policy of the United States that there shall be no discrimination in the employment of workers in defense industries or government because of race, creed, color, or national origin."[22] A few weeks later Roosevelt appointed a Fair Employment Practices Committee (FEPC) to enforce his order.

This was a very limited step, albeit in the right direction. The spirit of Order 8802, for one thing, had no impact on the armed services where almost a million Black men and women served under customary segregated conditions. This was an area where the Commander-in-Chief could have simply ordered an end to this indignity. "If the FEPC was set up," says Foster, "it was due primarily to the need for workers in the war emergency, to the pressure of the mass of Negro trade unionists, to the fighting spirit of the Negro people, and to the growing unity in struggle between Negro and white progressives."[23]

The timing of Roosevelt's order was not by any means spontaneous. In January 1941, A. Philip Randolph, president of the Brotherhood of Sleeping Car Porters, demanding a fair employment policy, called for a March on Washington to take place on July 1, 1941. The aim was for 10,000 Afro-Americans to assemble at the Lincoln Memorial. Black workers responded enthusiastically to the call and soon it appeared that 50,000 would participate. The Roosevelt administration made strong efforts to have the March called off. As the target date approached it appeared that 100,000 were ready to go on to Washington. After Roosevelt signed his June 25th order the threatened March was called off.

A broad and vigorous campaign by the CP for the release of Earl Browder was concluded when he was freed from Atlanta Penitentiary on May 16, 1942. President Roosevelt commuted Browder's prison sentence saying it was "in the interest of national unity" to do so.

Browder resumed his post as General Secretary of the Party and it gradually became evident that his conception of national unity, while it may have coincided closely with that of Roosevelt, did not serve the working class. In Foster's opinion it "was essentially of a Social-Democratic character" and "subordinated the political role of the working class to bourgeois dictation."[24] While some in the Communist leadership felt national unity required a coalition government in which labor would hold cabinet posts, Browder vetoed this concept and tailed along with John L. Lewis, William Green, and Philip Murray. This tailing negated the leadership role of the Communist Party. It muted the Party's expose of the imperialist goals of Wall Street in the midst of a just war.

Browder's euphoric, self-serving, self-centered view of "national unity" under wartime conditions led to successive steps to the right. Within the span of two years this journey would lead him to propose the liquidation of the Communist Party itself.

During the war years the left-center unity which had helped make the CIO possible continued. The CIO leadership was clearer than John L. Lewis and the AFL bureaucracy on the aims and tasks of the war. The availability of Communist support was useful to the Philip Murray forces in beating off the CIO's rivals, which were infected with rabid anti-Soviet bias.

Browder, however, smugly accommodated himself to the difficult navigational problems of the wartime seas while confidently spinning dreams of a utopian "organized capitalism" as a wartime necessity, taking his cue from certain conclusions of the House Committee on Wartime Migration headed by Congressman John H. Tolan.[25]

Browder tended to take at face value the pretensions of Roosevelt's "good neighbor" policy toward Latin America. In 1942 he was expressing the pious hope that the peoples of Latin America could be induced to feel "that the 'good neighbor' policy was something deeper than the expediency of the historical moment."[26]

Browder's half-hearted criticism of bourgeois theory and practice in the period after his release from Atlanta stirred opposition within the Communist Party's ranks. "But," says Foster, "this opposition was neither clear nor strong enough . . . to defeat the revisionist system that Browder was rapidly building up."[27]

The city of Teheran was the site, from November 28 to December 1, 1943, of a meeting of the Big Three—Roosevelt, Churchill and Stalin. The conference produced a declaration that agreement had been reached on the opening of the second front. It also declared the determination of the allies "that our nations shall work together in war and in the peace that follows" to "banish the scourge and terror of war for many generations."[28]

Two of the "many generations" have already had time to discover that these fine words have proved to be no more than fine words. But for Browder these words were as good as the deed. He seized upon them and, from the moment he heard them, all his planning for the immediate moment and for the distant future was based on the diplomatic declaration at Teheran.

By December 12, 1943, when the ink had barely dried on the Teheran declaration, Browder told a meeting in Bridgeport, Connecticut, that the "Teheran conference has not only strengthened the fighting alliance of the anti-Hitler Coalition, but has established a relationship for peaceful post-war collaboration between the Soviet Union, Britain and the United States."[29]

In his book, *Teheran: Our Path in War and Peace,* he asserted that "Upon our judgment of Teheran, therefore, depends our answer to all national and world problems." And, a few pages further on: "Teheran represents a firm and growing common interest between the leaders who gathered there, their governments, the ruling classes they represent, and the peoples of the world."[30] By May 1944 class struggle had disappeared and Browder was explaining that "We want to guarantee that the achievement of well-being and democracy for all within our country . . . will be the product of intelligent collaboration of all intelligent men in America."[31] (Presumably, while the intelligent men were talking it over, the women would be readying the coffee and sandwiches!)

William Z. Foster has fingered the doctrine of "American exceptionalism" as the classic form of revisionism in the U.S. Marxist movement. In each of the three principal crises which have threatened the viability of the Communist Party—the Lovestone revisionism of 1929, the Browder revisionism of 1944, and the so-called Gates movement of 1958—the root source of the problem has been the view that U.S. capitalism has fundamental (and superior) features which distinguish it from capitalism elsewhere in the world. In short *our* capitalism is better than *their* capitalism—more immune to crisis and more intrinsically democratic.[32]

The Leninist view, of course, is that, despite the superficial impact of purely national influences, the fundamental laws of capitalist development apply in all capitalist countries. Incidentally, while

Browder salted his Teheran writings and speeches liberally with the words "Marx" and "Marxism," he used no references to "Lenin" and "Leninism." Leninism, of course, is uniquely the Marxism of the imperialist epoch. The word "imperialism" also became scarce in Browder.

On other pages of his *Teheran,* Browder embraces the goal of making "free enterprise" work, abandons the task of heightening the class consciousness of the workers, suspends the Marxist critique of capitalism and asserts that the Afro-American people are convinced they can achieve complete equality in the present period and under the present system.[33]

Apparently Browder had not discussed his brand new Teheran thesis with his closest co-workers, for in the December 14, 1943, issue of *New Masses* appears an article by Chairman Bill Foster which takes a stand just the opposite to Browder's new line of the day before. Foster's article was titled "War and Postwar—planning for the era after victory." Here is a brief extract:

> The great democratic mass of American people are now fighting to make this a better country than it was before the present holocaust began.... As for the great business interests, however, their postwar plans are something else again and do not contribute either to world peace or security.... This means that the power of monopoly capital, the poison source of fascism all over the world, will have to be drastically curbed and eventually broken. To do this the nationalization of the banks, and of such industries as the railroads, coal, and steel is imperative. Nor can the danger of war, fascism, and mass pauperization be finally liquidated in our country until the American people establish socialism....[34]

Assuming Browder was right in his Teheran thesis, there was no role left for a Marxist-Leninist Communist Party. And that is the conclusion Browder came to. The Teheran Conference ended on December 1. On January 7 to 9 the CP National Committee met, heard Browder's report on his new line, and agreed to form a non-party organization. This was done. The new organization was called the Communist Political Association.

By means of the CPA, said Browder, "We will participate in political life as independents, through the established Party organizations of our progressive associates, without committing ourselves to any party label."[35]

The proceedings of the January National Committee were detailed extensively in the February 1944 issue of *The Communist.* William Z. Foster's name does not appear among the contributors to this issue.

17

War Ends—Cold War Begins

If William Z. Foster's name was absent from the sheaf of reports to the January 1944 National Committee meeting it was not because he was not among those present. Actually, as Party chairman, he presided at the meeting. When Browder finished his report to the plenum (about 500 persons were present) Foster put his name on the speakers' list. At the same time he notified the Political Committee that he intended to speak against Browder's report. Then, as Foster tells us: "Several members of the Committee strongly urged him not to do this, on the ground that it would throw the Party into grave confusion in the midst of the war. They also assured him that Browder had spoken without previous review of his speech and that the whole matter would be taken up shortly for reconsideration by the Political Committee." Foster then withdrew his name from the speakers' list.[1]

The promised reconsideration did not take place. Therefore, on January 20th, Foster addressed a letter to the National Committee taking issue with Browder's position and proposals. Foster rejected the illusionary forecast of a "progressive," non-imperialist American capitalism and warned of a postwar U.S. drive for world domination. While endorsing the aims of the Allied agreement at the Teheran conference, he rejected Browder's conclusion that the agreement mandated class collaboration as a postwar perspective.[2]

No meeting of the National Committee was called to discuss Foster's letter. Instead, an "enlarged meeting" of the Political Committee was held, on February 8, with about 40 Party leaders present. When Foster's letter was presented to this body it was rejected with only one person joining Foster in voting for it.

Between the first public proposal for dissolving the Communist Party on January 9 and the actual deed on May 20, Communists had time to adjust themselves to Browder's bold proposal. When the plan was announced in a lengthy statement to the press on January 9, the dissolution of the Party was mentioned only in the final sentence, where it was alluded to gently, merely as a change of name.

When the national convention took place, however, on May 20, the act of dissolution was the sole business of the convention, which lasted only a few minutes and adopted Browder's motion. He presented it in what some must have felt were chilling words: "I hereby move that the Communist Party of America be and hereby is dissolved. . . ."[3]

That being done, the body was reconvened as a convention to found the Communist Political Association.

It would appear that Foster had three options when he found himself in a dissenting position on the Teheran thesis. He could resign from the Party; he could carry on a struggle inside the Party, which would lead inevitably to his expulsion; or he could accept the discipline of the organization, avoid direct conflict and await a favorable opportunity to press for a correct policy. In the "everything-for-victory" atmosphere then prevailing he saw the wisdom of taking the third option. He felt sure the Party would see its error and correct it.

Hence he was in the incongruous position of presiding at the opening session of the Convention to found the CPA. He also presided at the penultimate session on May 22.

During the course of the Convention Foster played what may be described as a muted role and this could also characterize his conduct in the fourteen months during which the CPA continued to exist.

Foster made an interesting contribution in the course of discussion at the final session during an observance of the "Twenty-Fifth Anniversary of the Communist Movement [sic] in the U.S.A." The report on the subject was made by Robert Minor. Then Alexander Trachtenberg made brief remarks in introducing twenty-five invited guests who were being honored for their long years of service in "the American Communist and labor movement." Four of the old-timers, including Pat Cush and Ella Reeve Bloor, spoke briefly. Then, say the minutes, "Chairman William Z. Foster delivered an impassioned reply to the greetings of the honored guests."[4]

The moment must have been a poignant one for Bill Foster. The brief speech he made sounds today as if he were trying to reduce the change in the Party to just a change of name, though this was implicit rather than explicit when he said of the old Party veterans: "we will do our very best to live up to the splendid traditions that they have set for us in their life's work."[5] Of course, Bill himself had made a major contribution in the creation of those traditions.

The convention elected Earl Browder to be president of the Communist Political Association. It also elected eleven vice-presidents, somewhat after the fashion of banks or advertising agencies. William Z. Foster was one of the eleven. He saw as his immediate task "to help to keep the C.P.A., in fact, if not in name, the Communist Party."[6]

The leaders of the Communist Party, who became the leadership of the Communist Political Association, were a body of men and women who had the gravest sense of responsibility toward the necessity of carrying on a successful struggle for victory in the war. They were single-minded on this question. Browder, who may be credited with the same aim, had acquired enormous prestige within Party ranks and as a public figure during his fifteen years as an international Communist leader. He was able to carry his comrades along his impossible Teheran line, says Foster, because under Browder's leadership there had been "drastic curtailment of real political discussion, the virtual abolition of self-criticism, the cultivation of bureaucratic methods of work, the general development of a super-centralization, and the almost complete abandonment of the fight against right tendencies in the Party."[7]

Browder's Teheran policy did not long survive. The trust and faith in his leadership which had manifested itself in the near-unanimity of the Party's leading bodies were soon undermined by a hard-headed sense of reality.

In the year that followed the founding of the CPA, the evidence accumulated that the "intelligence" of the capitalists—on which Browder relied so much—was not going to preserve the wartime friendship of the Allies, not even to the end of the war.

An American historian has summed up the period in this way:

> Domestic Communism was meantime being revived as a menace. We have seen how Dewey tried to exploit latent anti-Communism in the 1944 election. *Newsweek* was warning the next spring of the "imminent possibility that the American Communists might revert to their 1939–41 position of sabotaging national defense." The editors of *Life* embraced Truman for forcefully pointing out the direction of postwar U.S. foreign policy—"U.S. leadership in world affairs." But the Russians, they complained, were being uncooperative about it. If they opposed American predominance in a reasonable way, it might be tolerable. But the United States was unfairly handicapped. "The fellow-traveler is everywhere: in Hollywood, on college faculties, in government bureaus, in publishing

companies, in radio offices, even on the editorial staffs of eminently capitalist journals."

... So now, wherever one looked—among conservatives, among liberals, among those in between and those at the fringes—there was a growing consensus on one point, at least: Russia was the mortal foe of the United States. As early as 1943 one journal had reported that among military men there was already talk of "the next war"—against the Soviet Union. When Kenneth Crawford returned home in the spring of 1945 after a year overseas, he was shocked by what had happened since he left. "War with Russia is unthinkable, yet it is being thought about constantly. It is, in fact, America's great pre-occupying fear."[8]

P.M.S. Blackett said: " . . . we conclude that the dropping of the atomic bombs was not so much the last military act of the Second World War, as the first act of the cold diplomatic war with Russia now in progress."[9]

Browder sought approval of his Teheran thesis from other Communist parties. He found support in the Western Hemisphere, from parties in Colombia, Peru and Puerto Rico. The Canadian Communist Party was to some extent influenced by Browderism but it refused to dissolve itself. In general it recognized that "Browderism was an attempt to relegate the Communist movement to a role that a section of the bourgeoisie wanted it to play. . . . The [Canadian party] did not advocate or support any of those anti-Marxist ideas."[10]

The South African Communists rejected Browderism and so did the Australians—as the present writer had occasion to learn first hand in the fall of 1944. At that time the writer (then a GI on furlough in Sydney, Australia) had an unexpected interview with A. Sharkey, general secretary of the Australian C.P. Sharkey's opinion of Browder's view was expressed in a curt statement: "Well, it just wouldn't do for us."

Doubt about the line was also beginning to gnaw at the vitals of the Political Committee of the Communist Party. Eugene Dennis, Gil Green, Benjamin J. Davis, Jr., Jack Stachel, Bob Thompson and John Williamson manifested doubts about one or more aspects of the Party's line. "Foster cultivated all these doubts about the correctness of the Party line and lost no occasion of criticizing the Browder policy and exposing its fallacies. Browder, therefore, had all plans laid for Foster's expulsion in the near future."[11]

The catalyst in this increasingly tense situation was the publication in *Cahiers du Communisme,* the theoretical journal of the French

Communist Party, of an article by Jacques Duclos, the party secretary, "On the Dissolution of the Communist Party of the U.S.A."[12]

There must have been many who were unfavorably impressed by the changes wrought in the Communist Party. Many thousands of Party members failed to register as members of the Association. Interestingly, the weekly *New Masses* carried, in its issue of June 12, 1945, a critical letter which had been received several weeks before—prior to the publication of Duclos' article. The letter-writer remarks: "The disastrous effects of the new Communist line on *New Masses* are apparent both politically and culturally. . . . The magazine dropped whatever pretensions it had to being Marxist. . . . Your political articles have degenerated to the level of showing that black is black and examining capitalists through a magnifying glass to separate the 'patriotic' capitalists from those who are not patriotic (whatever that means). . . . We still believe in Bolshevik self-criticism, a practice we respectfully recommend to the editors."[13]

Self-criticism was forthcoming in abundance as soon as the contents of Duclos' article became available. The English text was received on May 20, 1945, and was immediately discussed in the Political Committee. Duclos' critique of Browder's policies was based largely on Foster's February letter to the National Committee. Duclos had been moved to write his article because a French Communist paper, *France Nouvelle,* had published an article in praise of Browderism and because Browder's liquidation of the CPUSA was encouraging liquidationist tendencies in the French party.

Events moved rapidly following receipt of the Duclos article, which was published in the *Daily Worker* on May 27. The entire policy of the CPA came under discussion and when a vote was taken it was found that two-thirds of the Committee was against the policy. Soon after, the vote became unanimous—except for Browder.

Browder would make no acknowledgment of error and stuck to his discredited position. He was suspended from his post as general secretary and replaced by an interim secretariat consisting of Foster, Eugene Dennis and John Williamson.

The National Committee met June 18-20 and made Browder's suspension permanent. There was unanimous agreement on condemning Browder's line, accepting the Duclos article, endorsing Foster's earlier letter to the National Committee, and adopting a new draft policy resolution. A special convention was called for July 26–28 in New York City. The convention declared: "The source of our past revisionist errors must be traced to the ever active pressure of bourgeois ideology and influence upon the working class."[15]

The Convention reconstituted the Communist Party, returning it to a Marxist-Leninist basis. A secretariat was chosen consisting of Foster, Dennis, and Robert Thompson. The main resolution repudiated Browder's absurd thesis of a progressive American imperialism. It stated: "If the reactionary policies and forces of monopoly capital are not checked and defeated, America and the world will be confronted with new aggressions and war and the growth of reaction and fascism in the United States." On the domestic front the resolution rejected class collaboration and embraced a program of class struggle saying, "It is of central importance to build systematically the political strength of labor, the Negro people, and all true democratic forces. . . ."[15]

The expulsion of Earl Browder from the Communist Party became inevitable. Although he promised to abide by convention decisions he refused a minor Party post, and engaged in factional correspondence within the Party. He started a newsletter, *Distributors Guide*, which made sly attacks on the Party, and tried to build a factional grouping. He was expelled by the National Committee at its meeting of February 12–15, 1946.[16]

At the June 1945 plenary meeting of the CPA National Committee, at which the process of departure from Browderism officially started, the incomparable Elizabeth Gurley Flynn spoke in eloquent terms of the process by which she came under the influence of Browder's thinking. In concluding her speech she turned to Browder and said: "Break down your reserves, which have been a barrier between you and your fellow-workers and find your answer among people, not in research and study alone. You are a hard man to talk to, nobody feels he knows you, nobody feels free to approach you. . . . If you had mixed with the people, gone into their homes, checked your thoughts with them, as Lenin did—you would not be so isolated today. If you had even mixed with your own comrades—you could have understood them better. Take a trip around the country, alone, unknown, unhonored, and unsung, but *meet the people*, Earl, and learn to be one of them once again."

Needless to say, Flynn's eloquence was wasted on Earl Browder, "a hard man to talk to."[17]

When the war came to an end both victors and vanquished, in

Europe and Asia, were sorely hurt by the physical and human damage the war had brought. The colonial possessions of Great Britain, France, and the Netherlands resumed, with mounting success, their struggles for independent statehood. Among the capitalist countries, the United States, its productive plant intact, even enhanced, stood dominant.

In Eastern Europe new People's Democracies began to build socialism on the cooling ruins. The Soviet Union, began to heal its scorched earth. Its wartime loss of twenty million of its citizens did not curb for long the rebuilding of its socialist means of production.

The new U.S. president, Harry S. Truman, was in the White House. On April 23, 1945, Molotov, the Soviet Foreign Minister, who was on his way to San Francisco for the founding of the United Nations, paid a courtesy call on the President, but was received with anything but courtesy. The coldness and rudeness with which Truman treated Molotov were a sign of what was to come. The spirit of Teheran was not hovering over the White House.[18]

In 1946 the domestic front was enlivened by labor's postwar fightback. Five thousand strikes brought out 4,600,000 workers. Steel, coal, automobile, electrical equipment and packinghouse workers struggled to break out of the war-imposed wage freeze which kept their wages out of reach of soaring prices. The cost of living jumped by 70 percent.

The minimal protections of the National Labor Relations Act were an impediment to unrestrained profit-making. The monopolies set out to subvert labor union militancy, from within, by anti-Communist penetration and, from without, by the restrictions of the infamous Taft-Hartley law.

It was class warfare with a vengeance. The spirit of Teheran did not float over this arena either. Foster, and the Communist Party, which now united around his leadership, did not expect it would.

With almost the formality of a minuet, the Cold War, which had already started, was proclaimed on March 5, 1946, in a speech by Sir Winston Churchill at Fulton, Missouri. He was introduced by President Truman who stood by approvingly while Churchill launched into his notorious, anti-Soviet, "Iron Curtain" speech. In 1961 the historian D.F. Fleming called the speech a " . . . world crusade to smash world communism in the name of Anglo-Saxon democracy. In print Churchill's battlecry became the bible of every warmonger in the world."[19]

Just two days after the Fulton spectacle the Communist Party rallied 15,000 persons to an open air meeting in New York City at which William Z. Foster made the principal address. "We are gathered together in historic Union Square," he said, "at a grave moment in world history. The imperialists in the United States and Great Britain are trying to stampede the peoples into another war. . . . It used to be that they would let a generation elapse between world wars, but now, like chain cigarette smokers, they light one war from the other. . . . Winston Churchill's speech. . . . was a call for a general capitalist war against the Soviet Union. . . . His speech was built around the Red bogey and the whole business stank of fascism."[20]

The labor fightback of 1946 spurred counter-measures by the employers. Their principal weapon was the Taft-Hartley Law of 1947. This measure canceled a number of protections which labor had won in the 1930s and which were codified by the Wagner Act of 1935. This was bad enough, but Taft-Hartley also required union officials to sign affidavits which certified that they were not members of the Communist Party. This counter-democratic measure was disruptive and divisive. It was freely used by the right-wing leaders in the unions to drive the Left out of leading posts and, in 1949, it was the pretext which enabled the CIO top brass to expel ten unions and their one million members, alleging "Communist domination."[21]

Of course, Taft-Hartley's provisions were not limited to its anti-Communist clauses. Its provisions were designed to weaken the trade union movement generally: it abolished the closed shop, established a 60-day "cooling-off" period in strike situations, outlawed mass picketing, barred secondary boycotts, legalized injunctions, made unions vulnerable to suits for "unfair labor practices," prohibited use of union funds for political purposes, and gave decisive powers to the National Labor Relations Board. To this day the labor movement is hobbled by Taft-Hartley.

Later there would be critics who blamed the Left itself for the punishment it took, especially in the CIO. Criticism focused on three or four issues on which, according to the critics, the Left was doomed to defeat: The Cold War, the Korean War, the McCarthyite repression, the Marshall Plan and the Henry Wallace Progressive Party campaign. The Left, they say, should have just played it cool, steered clear of these issues, and quietly rode out the storm.

Gil Green in his thoughtful book, *What's Happening to Labor*, deals with this question of Left culpability in its own defeat. He marshals convincing argument that the Left did, in the main, what it had to do—and not all of it was in vain, notably in opposing the Korean War. He points out that the splitting tactic which worked so well for capital in the CIO was part of a global capitalist strategy. It split the World Federation of Trade Unions. It split the powerful labor federations of France and Italy.

In short, says Green, "The argument that the Left should not have fought for its views really says that the Left could have saved itself by ceasing to be Left."[22]

In the winter of 1947 Bill Foster sailed for Europe for a three months' trip which kept him abroad into the spring. His itinerary took him to England, France, Switzerland, Italy, Trieste (which was then a bone of contention between Italy and Yugoslavia), Bulgaria, Czechoslovakia, and Poland, in that order. His intention to visit Germany was defeated by the U.S. State Department's failure to provide the necessary permit.

Foster was shocked by the extent of the damage to cities and industries that he saw wherever he went. Wreckage could be seen in London and Calais, in Prague and Warsaw.

"About 80 per cent of the city of Warsaw had been destroyed, most of it obviously cold-bloodedly and to no military purpose. The destruction was especially complete in Warsaw's big ghetto. . . . One could vividly feel the anti-Semitic hatred of Hitlerism expressed in the devastation the fascists had wrought upon the ghetto." The casualty figures were equally shocking—6,000,000 killed in Poland (including 3,000,000 Jews); 1,700,000 in the small country of Yugoslavia.

As a railroad man he was appalled at the devastation of the railroads. Italy lost 85 percent of its locomotives and 81 percent of its rolling stock; Poland, Bulgaria and Czechoslovakia suffered comparable losses.

Bill wrote a book about what he had seen and what he thought about it.[23] It was not a travelog nor a tourist's diary. In Europe he found confirmation of what he had believed for most of his political lifetime: imperialism was the enemy of the people everywhere; imperialism's long drawn out terminal illness was responsible for the wreckage he had seen and the slaughter of which he knew. But its dominance was not unchallenged. In Poland and Bulgaria he saw democracy being born; in Czechoslovakia it was reborn. In Italy the classic fascism was replaced by democratic forms and Communists played a role in government. Soon the U.S. Mediterranean Fleet would cruise off Italy's coast to make sure that democracy did not "go too far." Bill Foster, however, would always remember with a pleased smile the day he accompanied Palmiro Togliatti, a founder and leader of the Italian Communist Party, to an important government building in Rome. Togliatti had been a member of the cabinet in 1944 and 1945. As he and Foster approached the door, two ceremonially dressed guards snapped to a smart salute. Bill liked to think of that as a portent of things to come.

New democratic systems, mass Communist parties, dynamic trade union movements, these were the hopeful signs in "the new Europe."

"Europe, by and large, is on the march toward a new and higher type of democracy. As a result of the ravages of fascism and war its democratic millions have moved to adopt a whole series of progressive economic and political measures, which constitute the new Europe. . . .

"Now Wall Street big business, with a subservient Administration and Congress at its command and in alliance with every category of European reaction, is out to undo all this. . . . Nevertheless, the democratic peoples of Europe will be able to withstand the reactionary threat now coming from the capitalists of the United States."[24] So Foster wrote in 1947. In 1949 he would generalize on this theme, globally, in a larger work, *The Twilight of World Capitalism.*

At its 1946 convention the CIO resisted the penetration of the Cold War into the organization. After that it surrendered. In 1947 it wavered and waffled. Philip Murray, unable to bring the Marshall Plan into the convention by the front door, brought Gen. Marshall in person to the platform and declared afterward that the convention had endorsed both him and his plan.

In 1948 the CIO adopted a pro-war line, engaged in uninhibited redbaiting, and thereafter acted like "a labor branch of the State Department."[25]

Doing for the capitalists what they could not do for themselves, the CIO Murray-Reuther leadership set out to isolate the Communists, the left-wingers, and the progressives from the millions of trade union members, as part of a global attack taking place against the advanced forces in the worldwide labor movement. During the year-and-a-half following its 1947 convention, the CIO expelled, drove out, or "converted" to its jingoist view, the progressive-led unions which had contributed so much of its backbone in the ten previous years.

The years from 1947 on were marked by a government drive to render the Communist Party impotent and to intimidate and silence all persons and organizations that were pro-peace and refused to accept the Cold War and anti-Sovietism as necessary and proper.

In furtherance of this drive in 1947 the leaders of the Joint Anti-Fascist Refugee Committee were convicted of contempt of Congress; the "Hollywood Ten" were imprisoned on a similar charge. Perjury or contempt charges sent dozens more to prison for up to three years as case after case violated First and Fifth Amendment rights. Hundreds of foreign-born persons faced deportation for political nonconformity.

Eugene Dennis, a former seaman and teamster from the Pacific Coast, who had succeeded Browder as general secretary in 1946, was summoned before the House Committee on Un-American Activities (HUAC) in 1947. He refused to answer questions which violated his First Amendment rights and he refused to testify because, in his view, the committee was illegal. It was illegal, he maintained, because one of its members, John E. Rankin of Mississippi, was sent to Congress in an election which barred Blacks from voting. Dennis was convicted in June 1947 and, after appeals, served a one-year sentence in prison starting in May 1950. (Some of those who served time in federal prison for political "crimes" had the dubious pleasure of having as a fellow prisoner, J. Parnell Thomas, chairman of HUAC in the 80th Congress, who had been convicted of charges growing out of his padding of the federal payroll.)

In an escalation of repression, President Truman issued an Executive Order in March 1947 prescribing procedures to test the "loyalty" of federal employees and to purge those found "disloyal." In December the U.S. Attorney General published a list of organizations membership in which, past or present, was presumptive evidence of disloyalty. Subsequent additions to the list brought the number of "proscribed" organizations into the hundreds.[26]

William Z. Foster and eleven of his comrades on the National Committee of the Communist Party were indicted by a Federal Grand Jury on July 20, 1948 and charged with a conspiracy to "teach and advocate the overthrow and destruction of the Government of the United States by force and violence." The Jury had been investigating the Communist Party for 18 months but had found no overt subversive acts. The publishing of books, newspapers and magazines, the establishing of schools and classes, the re-establishing of a political party—these were the acts charged in the conspiracy indictment under the provisions of the Alien Registration Act of 1940 or, briefly, the Smith Act.[27]

(The Grand Jurors probably had not known—and in any case could not have cared—that as long ago as 1853, one of the first Communists in the United States had disposed of the "conspiracy theory" when he noted "that one cannot conjure up revolutions by means of conspiracies, that it is social crises which call forth the revolutions, the cumulative effects of social tensions rather than the petty striving of individuals." This was said by Joseph Weydemeyer who, in the Civil War, became a colonel in the Union Army.)[28]

The timing of the indictment may have been related to the administration's wish to embarrass the presidential candidacy of Henry Wallace.[29] The founding convention of the Progressive Party which nominated him took place at the end of the week in which the charges against the Communists were announced. The Communist Party was a strong supporter of the Wallace movement.

The eleven Communists indicted with Foster were:

Eugene Dennis, General Secretary
Benjamin J. Davis, Jr., only Black member of the New York City Council
Henry Winston, National Organization Secretary
John Williamson, Labor Secretary
Jack Stachel, National Educational Director
Robert Thompson, New York CP Chairman
John Gates, Editor of the *Daily Worker*
Irving Potash, Manager Joint Council of the Fur Workers Union
Gil Green, Illinois CP Chairman
Carl Winter, Michigan CP Chairman
Gus Hall, Ohio CP Chairman

The trial began on January 17, 1949. Foster's case was severed from the others on January 18, after four court-appointed doctors affirmed that his serious heart ailment would endanger his life over the course of a long trial. The trial lasted nine months.

On May 22, 1949, William Z. Foster issued a statement giving the Communist Party position on the issues presented in the Government case against the Eleven. (The prosecution had rested on May 18.) His statement, which was published in July as a 96-page pamphlet, was written as if he was one of the defendants, acting as attorney *pro se,* making an opening statement to the jury.[30]

Before World War II Communist parties had only the Soviet

example before them as the road to socialism. After the war, in Eastern Europe, more than half-a-dozen countries began to find their own roads. In capitalist countries the road to socialism, was studied nation by nation—in Italy, France, Great Britain. No blueprints were devised. It was apparent that in each country the road would correspond to the conditions prevailing and be affected by national culture and traditions.

In the government case the question of force and violence was behind the "conspiracy" charge—a charge which was supported not by proof of violent overt acts but by the interpretation given by hired informers and perjurious witnesses to selected passages in books and pamphlets.

Foster in his statement was willing to accept the formulation of the United States Supreme Court in the case of William Schneiderman, a California Communist leader. The court said in 1942:

> A tenable conclusion from the foregoing is that the Party in 1927 desired to achieve its purpose by peaceful and democratic means, and as a theoretical matter, justified the use of force and violence only as a method of preventing an attempted counter-overthrow once the Party had obtained control in a peaceful manner, as a matter of last resort to enforce the majority will if in some indefinite future time because of peculiar circumstances, constitutional or peaceful channels were no longer open.[31]

"American Communists," added Foster, "consider this expression by the Supreme Court to be a fair and objective statement of the fundamentally peaceful and democratic character of Communist policy. . . . "

Bill Foster later returned, in a self-critical vein, to some of the points he made in his trial-statement pamphlet. He felt he had dealt too cursorily with some matters and had oversimplified some questions.

In *Political Affairs* of June 1950 he sought to clarify some theoretical points, especially insofar as they concerned People's Fronts and People's Democracy. But as for the main line followed in the Dennis Case, Foster concluded "it was politically sound and correct."[32]

But the nine-month trial did not give the Communists their day in court. The day belonged to the vain and irascible Judge Medina who, in the course of the trial, badgered the defense witnesses, sent five of the defendants to jail for "contempt," and admonished City Councilman Ben Davis to "be a good boy." At the end of the trial, during which he had relentlessly bullied the defense attorneys, he sentenced all six lawyers to jail for contempt, setting terms varying from one month to six.

On October 14th, after brief consideration of the nine months of trial proceedings, the subservient jury found all eleven guilty. Ten of them received sentences of five years in prison plus $10,000 fines. Robert Thompson, who had won the Distinguished Service Cross for bravery in World War II, got a $10,000 fine plus three years.

The bail of the Eleven was revoked by Medina and it took weeks to regain it as the case made its way through the appeals process. On May 12, 1950, Eugene Dennis began serving his one-year sentence for contempt of Congress. Gus Hall replaced him during his absence, with the title of National Secretary.

In March 1948, prior to his indictment under the Smith Act and before a bad turn in his health curbed his mobility, Bill Foster made a trip to Puerto Rico by ship where he had a chance to see at first hand the conditions of the people in San Juan, capital of that U.S. colony. While there he spoke at one of the largest meetings of workers and progressives ever held on the island up to that time. Two thousand persons tried to crowd into a 1,200-seat theater to hear him.

Immediately upon his return to New York he released an open letter to President Truman. He focussed attention on *El Fanguito* ("The Mudhole"), the worst of the several huge slums in which almost half of San Juan's population lived. *El Fanguito,* he wrote, "is the very symbol of human misery, exploitation and despair. It is also, no less, the symbol of American colonial domination over Puerto Rico." Today this symbol is gone but the exploitation, misery, and colonial domination remain.[33]

In 1953 the Central Committee of the Communist Party of Puerto Rico sent a Memorandum to the United Nations in the case of Puerto Rico. The Memorandum protested the intention of the United States to discontinue reporting on Puerto Rico under the terms of Article 73 of the UN Charter. The United States claimed that Puerto Rico was now fully self-governing. The Memorandum maintained that the Island was still a colony. The Memorandum was published in the States with a supporting foreword by Foster.[34]

The pressures on the CPUSA increased and the generally restrictive political atmosphere in the country correspondingly intensified. A crass example of this occurred in Peekskill, N.Y., where on August 27, 1949, Paul Robeson was prevented from singing by a mob which shouted anti-Semitic and anti-Afro-American obscenities and attacked the audience.

The program was carried through successfully a week later, before an audience of 15,000, in an open-air setting heavily guarded by volunteers, many of whom were World War II veterans. But, as the crowd dispersed after Robeson's recital, the concert-goers, most of them riding in cars and chartered buses, were attacked by fascist-style hoodlums while state and local police failed to intervene—except to join in the violence. Over 200 persons were injured in this outrage.

One after another, cases arose which signalled the aggressiveness of imperialism, racism, and other forms of reaction, all calculated to intimidate the people in their exercise of civil rights and liberties.

One case after another jeopardized Black people, North and South. In Trenton, New Jersey, six Black men accused of murdering a white man had to fight six years against death sentences based on perjured testimony. In Martinsville, Va., seven Black youths were executed for "rape," a charge for which no white man had ever been executed in Virginia's history. In Laurel, Mississippi, Willie McGee, was executed after six years of struggle, in a lynch atmosphere which doomed him. In 1951, poll taxes still prevented Blacks from voting in six Southern states.[35]

Teachers were subjected to "loyalty" oaths; maritime workers were blacklisted by federal law; the left-wing International Workers Order, a fraternal and insurance movement, was liquidated by New York State authorities because its financial situation was "hazardous" since it was a "subversive" organization.

The McCarran Act was passed in 1950, beginning an unsuccessful attempt, lasting years, to get the Communist Party to register with the government and provide it with a list of all Party members. The broad provisions of the act made even trade unions vulnerable to prosecution.

By 1950 Congressman Richard Nixon had already latched on to the device of making a successful career out of unbridled anti-communism. This attracted the attention of Senator Joseph McCarthy who was in need of a gimmick to save his slipping career, and for the next five years the country was plagued with McCarthy and, even more dangerous, McCarthyism. The "ism" became a menace that cast a chill over the nation's vaunted democracy, driving people into jail, unemployment, and suicide.

On June 25, 1950, the Korean War started, creating a new pretext for heightening "internal security" tensions. In this atmosphere, by August 11, Ethel and Julius Rosenberg had been arrested as "atom spies" and started along the road to death in the electric chair. Afterward, Justice Hugo Black would reveal that the Supreme Court "had never reviewed this trial record and therefore never affirmed the fairness of this trial."[36]

The 1949 conviction of the Communist leaders was argued on appeal before the Supreme Court on December 4, 1950. On June 4, 1951, the conviction was upheld. On June 20, seventeen more leaders of the Communist Party were arrested in New York City on Smith Act charges. Arrests soon took place in other cities as well—Baltimore, Los Angeles, Honolulu, Pittsburgh, Detroit, Chicago, Seattle, St. Louis, and elsewhere.

By the end of January, 1953, there had been 98 arrests. Forty-four had already been convicted of conspiracy "to teach and advocate" in violation of the Smith Act.

The Fifteenth National Convention of the Communist Party was held in New York City, December 28-31, 1950. The conditions were maturing which would prevent the holding of another convention for over six years.

The Korean War and rampant McCarthyism provided the social ambience in which the 1950 convention took place. But there was no concession made at the Convention to the difficulties the Party and the American people were facing.

Eugene Dennis was absent from the Convention, a prisoner in Atlanta. William Z. Foster was present for only one hour due to his illness, but he sent a message which was read to the Convention. Gus Hall, National Secretary, made the main political report, titled *Peace Can be Won!* The Main Resolution was on "Working Class and People's Unity for Peace." Benjamin J. Davis's report was published as *The Negro People in the Struggle for Peace and Freedom.*[37]

Six months later, of the eighteen or so Party leaders who made reports at the Convention, all were either in prison, under indictment, political refugees, or (in the case of Robert Minor) disabled by illness.

When the Convention adjourned it was less than two months to Bill Foster's seventieth birthday. Gus Hall referred to this coming event in the course of his summary remarks to the Convention saying that the activities being organized for that occasion would be "a big political event for our Party. . . . In these plans the new book of Comrade Foster . . . must be an important factor."

The "new book" was the subject of a report made by Robert Thompson. The title was *Outline Political History of the Americas.* The publication of this 667-page volume was a fitting capstone on Foster's three score years and ten.

18

Three Score and Ten Plus

William Z. Foster's 70th Birthday was observed with warmth, joy and sober appreciation. Around the date of February 25, public celebrations were held in a number of cities across the country. In New York City thousands attended observances in The Bronx, Queens, Harlem, and Manhattan. Gus Hall made the principal address at the Manhattan celebration.

Political Affairs called its 96-page March 1951 number the "William Z. Foster 70th Birthday Issue." The entire contents—with one exception—were devoted to tributes, greetings, evaluations, and reminiscences pertaining to Foster. (The exception was a piece by Foster himself on "Truman's State of National Emergency," a bit of business as usual.)[1]

Greetings came in from dozens of countries around the globe— from the socialist world, from the countries of imperialism, from the colonial and neo-colonial countries.

Coinciding with the birthday observance was the publication of Foster's *Outline Political History of the Americas.* For Bill that was the best present and greeting of all.[2]

At age 70, Bill lived with Esther Foster in the one-bedroom apartment which had been their home since the 1930s. It was located on Nelson Avenue a few blocks north of Yankee Stadium, close enough for the roar of the crowd to be heard when a big game was on.

The bedroom was also Bill's workshop. A table and desk were

squeezed into the room. After the heart attack which caused his severance from the *Dennis* Smith Act case, Foster spent a great deal of his time in this room and the adjoining livingroom, writing his five last books as well as several pamphlets, dozens of magazine articles and scores of *Daily Worker* pieces. Before most people had eaten their breakfast, Bill had usually gone down to the newsstand for the daily papers and written a thousand words of a book or article.

This writing was done in ink with a fountain pen on a pad of Woolworth's "Fifth Avenue Brand" correspondence stationery, size 7¼ × 10½ inches, a size which he had adopted as his standard long before.

Foster's illness was not evident in his physical appearance, which was that of a lively, vigorous person. He had learned how to manage his health problem. ("I know more about my body than any doctor," he would say.) It was largely a matter of diet, discipline, and avoidance of tension. (Bill would walk away from the TV set when the ball game he was watching became too exciting.)

Physical exertion had to be measured. Normally he walked at a brisk stride; when taking a recreational walk it became a stroll. He could climb stairs when necessary but he had to take it easy. A bit of gardening in the summer (which he spent in a rented cottage in northern Westchester County) fulfilled part of his need for exercise.

High speeds, especially in an automobile, were to be avoided. ("We are never in a hurry," he told his driver.) Fifty miles an hour was the top limit. (This was one of some twelve or so commandments he had written down for the driver's guidance.)

In the spring of 1951 he was accumulating material for his *History of the Communist Party, USA*. In connection with this he made an overnight trip by train to Chicago where he wanted to interview some old-timers—including Sam Hammersmark and Alfred Wagenknecht. An aide made the ticket reservation for him at Grand Central Terminal and requested a certain train. The ticket agent pointed out that that was a local and that through passengers could save six hours by taking one of the expresses. But Bill liked to go slow.

(Henry Winston, then the CP National Organizational Secretary insisted that Bill be accompanied on the Chicago trip by someone who could assist him. But Bill adamantly refused. Nevertheless, a discreet young comrade from the Party's national office "just happened" to be on the same train, in the same sleeper—and only Winston knew how he came to be there.)

Foster's trip to Chicago was the last long journey he was to make until almost ten years later, when he went to the Soviet Union for health care.

A recreational ride, often combined with a recreational walk, was a frequent mode of relaxation for Bill Foster. In the spring and fall he liked to go to City Island where a pleasant esplanade faced Long Island Sound and seagulls busily opened mussel shells on a stone jetty. At other times he might walk along Manhattan's Twelfth Avenue taking in the busy maritime scene and stopping for coffee at a diner. He got a kick out of listening to the jiving of the waterfront workers who ate there. (Once, seeing a big bonfire in an open lot, where a pile of dunnage was being disposed of, he remarked: "If a French peasant saw that wood going up in smoke he'd lose a month's sleep.")

Summers were spent at the rented cottage. The move began at the end of May when he would be driven up, the car loaded with a carefully stacked cargo of household goods. On this trip, always made on a Saturday, his pre-school great-grandson, Joseph, might accompany him. A stop would be made to pick up tomato plants, seed and fertilizer, and a beginning would be made at starting a garden.

Other trips followed on successive Saturdays, a load of cargo each time pre-empting the rear seat. Then, before the Fourth of July, a final trip, this time with Esther Foster sharing the back seat with the last of the necessary cargo. (Because of her arthritis, Esther could not be made comfortable in a front seat.)

Bill's summer in the country was a working vacation. He escaped the discomforts of his hot and stuffy apartment and enjoyed the domestic congeniality of his daughter, Sylvia, and her husband and young Joseph. (Joseph, until he was old enough to assert his distaste in the matter, was called "Butch" within the family.)

In his Westchester retreat Bill continued his writing and consulted with visitors. About once a week his typist, Jean Smith, would come up from the city to transfer the current accumulation of handwritten manuscript to neat and accurately typed sheets. (No one could transcribe Bill's scrawl as well as Jean—not even Bill.)

Occasionally he would go into the city when it seemed his on-the-spot intervention might help resolve some current problem. Or a visitor would come up from the city for a confab.

Paul F. Douglass, a former president of American University, visited Foster for an interview in connection with a book Douglass was then writing. He says: "As Foster settles back in an easy chair in his book-lined Bronx apartment, he gives the appearance of a retired university professor of philosophy, or a church deacon who has been especially interested in youth work."[3] Douglass may have expected to find the stereotype of a "wild-eyed radical." Foster was much less stuffy than the stereotypes his visitor used in describing him. (Bill's benign appearance may have derived in part from the clothes he wore. On the rare occasions when he purchased a new suit he shopped at one of New York's most conservative men's stores—so conservative that it had a special department "for the clergy.")

Paul Douglass also noted that Foster "meticulously extracts his notes and checks his material for accuracy of fact and citation. Although he may give an interpretation to facts which is completely different from capitalistic orientation, he is objective in insisting on being in possession of the facts. . . . At every available opportunity Foster reads. In moments of complete relaxation he reads the classics and science—especially volumes dealing with new scientific developments."[4] Bill did wish that over the years he might have been able to indulge more than he had "in the reading of the science and history that I love so much."[5]

Outline *Political History of the Americas,* published on the occasion of its author's seventieth birthday, is Foster's largest book. It is a pioneering work in that, for the first time, it brings together in a single connected narrative, an account of the discovery, settlement, and development of the Western hemisphere.

Beginning with a discussion of the Aztecs and the Incas and their social organization, it then relates the conquest of the hemisphere by its Spanish, Portuguese, English, French, and Dutch conquerors. The importation of African slaves, the exploitation of the indigenous Indian peoples, and the varied development of colonial empires are presented in an integrated outline. This unified treatment was necessary, in Foster's view, "because of the geographical, economic, political, and cultural ties which throughout four centuries have bound all these countries together in a closely related history."[6]

In the book the colonial history of the hemisphere is followed by a study of the years from 1776 to the start of World War I. It traces the course of the bourgeois-democratic revolutions which, one after another—inspired by the example of the thirteen English colonies—expelled the rule of the European overlords from most of the area. The growth of capitalism and the fight to end chattel slavery are depicted. In a final section Foster deals with the era of imperialism and especially the growing domination of the United States over the two Western continents.

A unique feature of the book is the many pages devoted to matters affecting the Indians—the Native American population. Included is a section dealing with the special oppression of present-day descendants of this population in the United States. In his writings on the American Indians Foster thus began the process of correcting the traditional neglect of this question by the North American left. Recent conventions of the Communist Party have not failed to single out the problems affecting the Native Indian population for deserved attention.

Without attempting an over-detailed account of the general hemispheric history, Foster analyzes "the broad course of economic, political, and cultural growth and decay." He "especially bears in mind the relationship of the peoples and nations of our hemisphere to the most fundamental social process of our times; namely, the developing general crisis and decay of world capitalism, and the birth and growth of world socialism."[7]

At the time that *Outline Political History of the Americas* appeared in February 1951, Bill Foster was well-advanced on his next project— *History of the Communist Party of the United States.* This appeared a year and a half after the previous volume and—at 600 pages—was another giant feat, especially considering the other writing its author carried on simultaneously with work on this book.

The publication of the Party *History* was timed for the thirty-third anniversary of the founding of the CPUSA. It appeared in September 1952.

By the time this volume was published some drastic changes had taken place in the Communist Party as a result of the impact of extraordinary events.

Ever since their Smith Act conviction at Foley Square on October 14, 1949, the eleven national leaders of the Communist Party had seen their case going through the appeals process and working its way up to the Supreme Court. On June 4, 1951, the high court upheld the lower court's rulings.

The decision was six to two. Justice Robert H. Jackson, one of the majority, was perceptive enough to note in his concurring opinion "I have little faith in the long-range effectiveness in this conviction to stop the Communist movement. Communism will not go to jail with these Communists."

Justice Hugo Black was in the minority. He declared: "These petitioners are not charged with an attempt to overthrow the government. . . . The charge was that they agreed to assemble and to talk and publish certain ideas at a later date. . . . No matter how it is worded, this [the indictment] is a virulent form of prior censorship of speech and press, which I believe the First Amendment forbids." Black was joined in dissent by Justice Douglas who stated, "Not a single seditious act is charged in the indictment. To make a lawful speech unlawful because two men conceive it, is to raise the law of conspiracy to appalling proportions. That course is to make a radical break with the past and to violate one of the cardinal principles of our constitutional scheme. . . ."[8]

On July 2, 1951, seven of "The Eleven" started serving five-year terms. Four others did not surrender but became political refugees. Two of these, Gus Hall and Robert Thompson, were subsequently apprehended and were given additional sentences for their presumed contempt of court. Two remained at large for several years to continue their political work. They were Gil Green and Henry Winston. They eventually surrendered, in 1956, and began to serve their sentences plus an additional term for failure to appear in 1951.

The FBI was furious at having "lost" some of its victims. Thirteen others of the Party's leaders in the New York headquarters had already been convicted and were out on bail. The FBI said it would "wake them up in the morning and put them to bed at night." Close surveillance was maintained at the Party office. Hard-eyed men sat in pairs in cars parked near the office with engines running; and FBI men, dressed in what they hoped looked like "workers' clothes," ambled nearby, conspicuously trying to look inconspicuous.

When Foster would give a lift in his car to one of his indicted comrades out on bail, a car would peel away from the curb and provide "escort." If there were two extra passengers in Bill's car, two cars would follow. On one occasion his car headed a motorcade of five vehicles.

Late in October 1952 Foster was summoned to a Foley Square courtroom to show cause why he should not submit to a medical examination to determine his physical fitness to face trial under his 1948 Smith Act indictment. In May 1953 Judge Sylvester Ryan ruled, on the basis of the opinion of government-appointed doctors, that Bill could not be tried.[9]

At one period early in 1954, Bill Foster was subjected to closer than usual surveillance. For two weeks there was always a car in front of his apartment house in the Bronx. When he left to go for a ride the car would follow. The purpose of this close following did not become clear until some weeks after it ended.

The government used the results of their surveillance to argue his fitness to stand trial. On such and such a date he went to the party offices, they said, and remained for so and so many minutes; on another day he visited at such and such an address and did not emerge for so and so many minutes; another day he went for a ride to City Island and spent two hours away from home.

In April 1954, Foster, then in his 74th year, was ordered to submit once again to examination by the government's doctors. Actually, not long before, Bill had experienced two "cerebral vascular accidents" which had confined him to bed or armchair for several weeks. It appeared to be the Federal attorney's intention to try him on the "membership"—as distinct from the "conspiracy"—indictment. A conviction on that charge could have led to the actual illegalization of the Communist Party.

But the findings of the doctors were not different from what they had found on previous occasions: William Z. Foster had coronary artery heart disease, coronary insufficiency with angina pectoris, and cerebral arteriosclerosis. These conditions enforced on him an essentially sedentary life and "required him to avoid any emotional strain or excitement."[10]

It was the last attempt to bring Bill to trial under the Smith Act. His cardio-vascular illness was judged as making it impossible for him to survive the ordeal of a long, long trial.

But petty harassment continued. On December 15, 1955, the Social Security Administration ruled that a number of Communist Party employees and their spouses who were receiving Old Age Benefits were ineligible because "service for the Communist Party is service in the employ of a foreign government." Bill Foster (or William E. Foster as the SSA correctly called him) was one of those affected by this bizarre ruling. The government moved to recover the eleven monthly checks of $91.50 each he had thus far been paid. But on June 22, 1956, a legal referee reversed the Social Security action because he could find no evidence "either oral or documentary" to support the premise "that persons allegedly working for the Communist Party in the United States are employees of the Soviet Union."[11]

Foster's history of the Communist Party has become an invaluable record of the pre-history of the Party and of its first thirty-two years. All future historians of United States politics have had their tasks simplified by its availability. Foster's own personal knowledge and involvement in much of what he wrote about was supplemented by the sources he consulted and by his consultations with survivors of several generations of participants in the labor and socialist movements.

The first 170 pages of *History of the Communist Party of the United States* deal with its roots in the early years of the Republic and sketch all the relevant contributory circumstances to the founding of the Party in 1919. He succeeded brilliantly in showing the specific connections of the Party's development to the American past while, at the same time, emphasizing the common heritage of all workingclass revolutionary movements internationally and their theoretical basis in the thought of Marx, Engels and Lenin.

Appearing at the time it did, the book constituted a thorough refutation of the premises behind the manifold prosecutions and harassments of the Party which were then underway. "The Communist Party," Foster wrote, "is not an intruder among the toiling masses, as the Department of Justice alleges, seeking to thrust an alien program upon them. Instead, the Party is flesh and bone of the working class."[12] (Both the author and the publisher—Alexander Trachtenberg—were under Smith Act indictment at the time *History of the CPUS* was published. Trachtenberg was sent to prison not long after.)

The writing of the book was complicated by the severe repressive measures that were being taken by the government at the time. But Foster consulted as freely as possible with all persons he could reach. Mimeographed copies of the manuscript were sent to some who were absent, inviting their criticism and comment.

Many names which might otherwise have been included in the text were omitted to avoid playing into the hands of would-be persecutors.

Like Communists generally in 1950, Foster based his estimate of Joseph Stalin on what appeared to be the Soviet leader's remarkable achievements in guiding the Soviet Union for twenty-five years in the face of hostile capitalist encirclement. Later revelations of Stalin's tragic weaknesses prompted modifications in Foster's view of the man but, until some years after the book was published, there was no knowledge of this painful matter.

Mao Tse-tung, who was judged only by the achievements credited to him by the Chinese party, was also admired by Foster. In the years just before the book was written China had driven its mandarins, warlords and compradores into the sea and had cut off imperialism's roots and branches. The distortions of the Chinese Revolution only began to be evident in the last years of Foster's life, and those years were saddened by the situation then developing. What appears in Foster's book is merited approval of the early years of the "New China." In those days not only Mao, but such stalwart Marxists as Liu Shao-chi and others of his stature played a leading part. After long years of helpful guidance and aid from the Comintern and from Communist parties around the world, China seemed then to be moving along the lines of Marxism-Leninism—along the lines of anti-imperialism—taking a direction which, it is hoped, she will someday take again.

William Z. Foster's *History of the CPUS* is notable, among all other things which may be said in its praise, for its handling of the many theoretical questions which the Party confronted in its activity. Foster had frequently given leadership in aspects of ideological struggle in the course of his Party work. In 1951 a tribute to him by the National Committee of the Party on his seventieth birthday summarized his ideological leadership as follows:

> Thus, he has trained the guns of Marxist-Leninist theory against such harmful bourgeois ideologies as American "exceptionalism," pragmatism, technocracy, Keynesian economics, national chauvinism, white chauvinism and all expressions of racism, male "superiority," cultural obscurantism, and various other general bourgeois and specifically American bourgeois reactionary ideologies.[13]

By February 1954 William Z. Foster had published the third volume in the great series of historical works which poured from his pen in the first half of the 1950s. This was his 608-page *The Negro People in American History,* a book which is still in print.

While intent on completing this book—so that he could get on with his next one—Foster by no means dropped everything else. He continued to write frequently for the *Daily Worker* and, in the year 1953, he published no less than nine articles in *Political Affairs.*

It was in 1953 that the National Association for the Advancement of Colored People raised the slogan: Free by Sixty Three! Behind the slogan was the intent that by 1963, one hundred years after the Emancipation Proclamation, the Black people should have freedom and equality at last. It may have seemed in 1954 that the goal was soon to be in reach: on May 17, 1954 the U.S. Supreme Court, in a unanimous decision, outlawed racial segregation in public schools thereby reversing the "separate but equal" doctrine of *Plessy* vs *Ferguson,* established in 1896. "In the field of public education, . . . separate educational facilities are inherently unequal," said the Court.[14]

In the decades which followed, millions of Afro-Americans and their supporters fought to implement and extend the 1954 decree. Martin Luther King, Jr., Malcolm X, Fred Hampton, Viola Gregg Liuzzo and many, many others have since fallen in the fight. Despite all the gains which struggle has won, the goal remains unreached. Angela Davis, the Black woman who was Communist candidate for Vice-President in 1980, told an interviewer: "It's dangerous to harbor the illusion that because we have one Black at the UN, because we have a few Blacks on TV, because there are a smattering of Blacks here and there, we've made qualitative progress on the road to liberation."[15]

Bill Foster interrupted work on his book in 1953 to do an article, which proved to be of particular interest, for the July 1953 issue of *Political Affairs.* It was titled: "Left Sectarianism in the Fight for Negro Rights and Against White Chauvinism." In this article Foster does more than deal with leftist errors and distortions in the struggle for Black rights and against racism. He criticizes Party left-sectarian weakness on a number of points, surveying the period 1948-1953. He sharply defines and characterizes the evil of white chauvinism (or racism) and the absolute need for resolute struggle against it, both outside the Communist Party and within Communist ranks. Having done this he proceeds to tackle boldly some manifestations then current of left-sectarianism in the fight against racism.

But first he makes clear that "The fight against white chauvinism is of basic importance to both Negro and white workers. It is not simply a matter, important though it is, of relieving the Negro people of this bitter hardship. Even more significant is the fact that the fight against white chauvinism is indispensable for developing the Negro-white solidarity, without which the labor-progressive movement can make little real headway. . . .

"White chauvinism, of course, must especially be combated and eradicated from the ranks of the Communist Party. There can be no place in our Party for such bourgeois poison."[16]

Gus Hall, as General Secretary of the Communist Party, had occasion to refer back to Foster's 1953 article when, in 1971, Hall made a report on the question of racism to the Party's National Committee. He observed that "while Foster's article helped to correct a momentary one-sidedness, it became a factor in creating another one-sidedness. This is not so much a criticism of Foster's article. It is more a criticism of the Party for not guarding against or being vigilant enough against wrong side-effects."[17]

Foster was not unaware that his July 1953 article on left-sectarianism might be misapplied. In the May 1955 issue of *PA* he has a lengthy and wide-ranging article: "Notes on the Struggle for Negro Rights" in which, while discussing a number of other aspects of the general question as well, he returns specifically to the particular question of white chauvinism—that is, racism.

"The greatest menace we have to be on guard against in this respect is the Right danger," he says. "This is the failure or refusal in general to fight against white chauvinism under one pretext or another." Further on, referring to the "Leftist" danger, he observes: "In correcting this glaringly wrong policy, however, some have hopped to the other harmful extreme, to the Right, of slackening the fight against white chauvinism."[18]

The Negro People in American History proved to be yet another of those volumes which bear Foster's distinctive stamp. That is to say, the documentation is reliable, the language accessible to any functionally literate person, and the viewpoint consistently Marxist-Leninist. It is the viewpoint which is particularly important in Foster's work even when the material is basically familiar. His thesis, stated in his own words is: "the worst of all the crimes of expanding capitalism in this country has been the centuries-long outrage it has perpetrated, and continues to perpetrate, against the Negro people.... The most shameful pages of American history are those dealing with the exploitation and oppression of the Negro masses." But there is also the fact that "The long and heroic struggle of the Negro people against the outrages to which they have been subjected is the greatest epic in our nation's history."[19] The outrages and the struggle against them are the essence of Foster's book.

A few months after the publication of the book, the Supreme Court handed down its unanimous landmark decision that "separate educational facilities are inherently unequal," thus setting the stage for a whole new level of struggle for Afro-American liberation.

Foster's 1954 book argued for the validity of the position adopted by the Communist Party in 1930 (see Chapter 14) which called for "self-determination of the Black Belt."[20] This derived from the perception of an area of Black majority in 286 contiguous counties of the states in what had once been the Southern slavocracy.[21]

Foster acknowledges in his book that the self-determination slogan had not won wide acceptance among the Black people. Nevertheless he was not yet ready to give up the idea. In December 1946 a major plenary session of the National Committee of the Communist Party gave its principal attention to the question of Afro-American rights and self-determination, reaffirming the slogan. Foster, Benjamin J. Davis, Jr., Eugene Dennis, James E. Jackson, Edward Strong, William L. Patterson and others participated in the discussion.[22]

But by 1957, James E. Jackson had taken the lead in demonstrating that the self-determination slogan was not valid. Even those who maintained that it once had validity had to acknowledge that great movements of Black population to urban centers North and South, together with entry into workingclass ranks of large numbers of Black people, had voided the premise for the slogan of self-determination. The Seventeenth National Convention of the CP, December 10, 1959, adopted a resolution incorporating this position.[23]

This did not negate the special national character of the question of Afro-American liberation.

A resolution adopted at the Communist Party's 22nd National Convention, August 23–26, 1979 put the matter this way:

"The Afro-American question is a national question of a special kind, of a specific type.

"Afro-Americans are a component people of the U.S. nation. They are an oppressed national minority. . . . The national aspect of the oppression of Afro-American people manifests itself in the fact that racism subjects all social strata of Black people to racist humiliation and violation of their dignity as human beings."[24]

In 1955, in his "Notes on the Struggle for Negro Rights," Foster was not yet ready to drop the self-determination slogan but he clearly recognized the population shifts, urbanization and changes in class structure. It is no wonder that we find him in 1959 supporting James Jackson's thesis.[25]

During his year-and-a-half of intensive work on *The Negro People in American History,* William Z. Foster followed his usual method of consulting with as many people as possible and reading all available material on his subject. His own highly functional library yielded much of what was needed. His secretary would bring him materials from private collections. Borrowed books were scrupulously returned within a few days.

Foster had a quick way of getting what he needed from a book. "I tear the guts out of it," he said. Sometimes he would be finished with a borrowed book in a few minutes. "Hold it for a couple of days," he'd tell his secretary. "I don't want the lender to think I didn't use it."

When other sources failed, trips would be made to the New York Public Library on Fifth Avenue, a rather tiring excursion for Bill and not to be undertaken lightly. For his *Negro People in American History* a number of visits were made to the Schomburg Collection in Harlem. There was no elevator and the collection was on the top floor of the inadequate quarters in which it was then housed. The stairs had to be carefully scaled.

An aspect of Bill's mode of work may be illustrated by the following anecdote:

On a fine fall day in 1953—a perfect day—Bill took Betty Gannett for a drive one Saturday morning for the purpose of discussing some theoretical points of his work-in-progress—his history of the Black people in America.

Bill had great respect for Gannett's abilities in the theoretical field. She was then the Communist Party's national educational director and in 1966 became editor of *Political Affairs.* (She was imprisoned under the Smith Act in 1955 and 1956.)

The drive this day took them north from the Bronx up Westchester's Saw Mill River Parkway. On this bright, crystal clear day, the fall leaves along the parkway were at their peak of color. As the car moved between Ardsley and Hawthorne, Bill expounded his views on a point in his book that was giving him some trouble. Betty, excited by the autumnal spectacle through which they were moving, kept interrupting Bill with exclamations about one red, yellow or golden tree after another. Bill, deeply into his subject, talked on unhearing. Finally he concluded, asking Betty if she did not agree. Betty agreed, and for a while there was silence as the car rolled on. Then, Bill turned to Betty and said: "Here we are driving through all this beautiful foliage and you're not even noticing!"

Bill Foster was in his usual summer retreat and therefore did not immediately receive a letter which was sent to his home on July 7, 1954, by a Catholic clergyman of Bill's Bronx neighborhood. But by July 27 the letter had caught up with him and he sent the Monsignor a reply on that date, apologizing for the delay, and for not being home when the priest called at his home during his absence.[26]

It seems the clergyman had become aware that a leading Communist—and one-time Catholic—resided in the vicinity of his church. The clergyman evidently felt it his obligation to bring the lost sheep back into the fold. He was apparently aware, through the press, of Foster's poor state of health and his fullness of years. He wanted to offer Bill an opportunity to return to a state of grace and be prepared to pass on to his reward.

Bill made a courteous and thoughtful reply expressing his appreciation of the priest's sincere concern regarding his spiritual welfare. He told him he intended to publish his own reply and asked for permission to publish the priest's letter. The priest was irritated by Bill's intention to publish the reply and was quite firm against Bill making public use of the original letter. Bill accordingly conformed to the priest's wishes.

If the good Monsignor had read the section on religion in Foster's *The Twilight of World Capitalism* he might have saved himself the trouble of stirring up the question. Bill's "Reply" is an expanded version of the section in *Twilight*.[27]

He told the priest that "It is now about sixty years since I parted company with religion." He says: "as a Marxist, I find that the dialectical materialist viewpoint fully satisfies me in meeting the everyday problems of life, as well as in confronting the perspective of eventual natural dissolution by death. In my outlook on life there is no place for religion."

Bill assures the priest that: "We Communists fully recognize that there are great numbers of honest and intelligent people who still retain, in greater or lesser degree, their religious beliefs, and we would be the last to offend them in these convictions. At the same time, we likewise recognize that these masses of religious workers, peasants and other toilers also have the same economic, political, and social interests as ourselves."

Foster's four-page reply to the priest ends with the statement: "I am one of those countless millions who are being carried along in the great ideological progress of our age, which heads away from metaphysical-religious concepts and toward a rational-materialist outlook on life. The possiblity of reversing this trend, so far as I personally am concerned, is utterly unthinkable to me."

William Z. Foster's graceful prose style, his unlabored and clear language, together with his political and social tact, are perfectly displayed in his "Reply to a Priest's Letter." This short piece could profitably be studied by any writer on the Left who is young enough to learn from it.

With the publication of *History of the Three Internationals* in February 1955, William Z. Foster seemed on his way to establish a definitive Marxist historical library. He had never announced that as his goal, but that's the way it was turning out.

When he had finished his *Outline Political History of the Americas* he would have liked to write a one-volume history of the United States, and he would also have been pleased to work on a one-volume history of the labor movement. But younger writers had staked out that territory for future efforts and Bill had no wish to trespass. With the publication of his fifth volume, *Outline History of the World Trade Union Movement*, in 1956, the series came to an end. This did not mean he had stopped writing—not at all: he had lengthy pieces in every 1956 issue of *PA* except one.

History of the Three Internationals, like all the other Foster histories, started with pre-history. Though it was intended as a history of Marxist international organizations from the founding of the International Workingmen's Association (1864) to the end of the Communist International (1943), the author starts with the Industrial Revolution and the emergence of industrial capitalism and carries his narration to the Communist Information Bureau (1947) and beyond, ending with his true theme: "The Historical Advance of Socialism (1848–1954)."

It has been stressed in these pages that the Communist Party, and all progressive forces in the country, had been under severe attack since the end of World War II. Space will not permit the cataloging of the manifold modes of attack, of the hundreds of cases it generated, of the thousands of victims it produced and of the silent, unmeasurable terror that prevailed.

But the Communist Party continued to function. The *Daily Worker* appeared regularly as did *Political Affairs*. Pamphlets and books were published in a continuing flow.

Much of the Party's energies and finances were inevitably diverted to defense, to the struggle to stay alive and keep its adherents out of jail. But the government unrelentingly kept up its effort to destabilize, if not destroy, the Communist Party.

In August 1954 the CP held a National Election Conference. Before the month was over, President Eisenhower signed into law the "Communist Control Act of 1954," originally sponsored by Senator Hubert H. Humphrey, the notorious "liberal." The Control Act essentially outlawed the Communist Party. The passage of this Act led William Z. Foster to write an article for *Political Affairs* asking "Is the United States in the Early Stages of Fascism?"[28] The answer was that the passage of the Act had further increased the ongoing fascist danger but there were democratic forces at work in the United States and abroad which made possible a successful anti-fascist, pro-democratic struggle. For the Party the struggle was a long and costly one. Not until 1967 was the repressive legislation directed against it essentially nullified.

But, until 1967 arrived, cases proliferated. The New York Eleven were followed by the New York Thirteen, the Baltimore Six, the Pittsburgh Five, the Los Angeles Fifteen, the Hawaii Seven, the Seattle Five, the Detroit Six, the St. Louis Five, the Ohio Ten, the Philadelphia Nine, the Connecticut Seven, the Colorado Seven. And there were others.

Beside these federal cases there were the state cases—mostly sedition, or anarchy, or syndicalism. There were such cases in Pennsylvania, Massachusetts, Kentucky and elsewhere. A touring company of discredited informers was on the road appearing in case after case, for suitable witness fees and travel expenses.

Early in 1955, the Thirteen lost the last of their appeals and in January and February, entered an assortment of penal institutions. Among those who went into prison that winter were a number of Communist leaders who had been resident in New York City and operative with Foster and others in national leadership of the Communist Party. These included Alexander Bittelman, Elizabeth Gurley Flynn, Pettis Perry, Betty Gannett, Claudia Jones and William Weinstone.

But, as the Thirteen were going "inside," most of the Eleven were coming out, and would soon return to their accustomed places.

In March 1955 John Williamson (soon to be deported to Great Britain), Jack Stachel, Eugene Dennis, Carl Winter, and John Gates were released from prison. In April, Benjamin J. Davis was released. Parole conditions forbade the released Communists to return immediately to the "scene of their crime" but by early 1956 conditional release was terminated and all were back at their posts.

19

One Final Conflict

The year 1956 started well enough for Bill Foster. Some of his closest comrades were now once again within arm's reach. In February there was his 75th Birthday, an important milestone in anyone's life, and again it was enthusiastically marked by *Political Afairs* with a Foster anniversary issue.[1] A birthday dinner on March 9 featured an address by Benjamin J. Davis, in his first major public appearance since his release from prison.

Perhaps best of all, *Outline History of the World Trade Union Movement* appeared, the last of Foster's "history series," another big (592-page), blue-covered, clothbound volume—the fifth to be issued between 1951 and 1956.[2]

Sidney Lens has described Foster as "an immensely resourceful organizer, a description" he adds "confirmed by virtually everyone, including Sam Gompers." This organizational ability was a trait which Foster succeeded in applying to his own life and work and accounts for the prodigies of productivity he was able to achieve despite the limitation of his health and circumstances.

Lens has also described other qualities of Foster which enhanced his efficiency: ". . . he was of strict personal habits, disciplined, stable . . . and one always felt in his presence that his mind was always in motion, filled with plans for the next foray."[3] Those who have spent more time with Bill Foster than Lens did, can confirm the restless quality of his mind, always tossing around ideas, bouncing them off the wall of other people's judgment, testing and refining.

But the year 1956 was to prove a troublesome one for Bill Foster. Before it was over he would be in yet another battle—to help defend the Communist Party from enemies within and without. It was a battle he certainly did not need, considering his age and state of health.

On January 20, 1956, an enthusiastic, overflow crowd at Carnegie Hall gave an emotional welcome-home to Communist leaders who had been absent for almost five years.

Eugene Dennis, the Party's general secretary, and John Gates, editor of the *Daily Worker,* made the principal addresses.

Gene Dennis, in the course of his remarks at Carnegie Hall, said: "Our Communist Party, guided by its socialist principles and scientific outlook, is going to take a new look at all problems confronting our nation and our people."[4] The audience warmly applauded this promise.

From April 28 to May 1, 1956, the Communist Party's National Committee held an enlarged meeting in New York City. In the form of a report delivered on behalf of the National Board by Eugene Dennis the Communists "took a new look."

Dennis's report sought especially to single out left-sectarian errors of the Communist Party during the preceding five-year period, and even going back ten years—to 1946. The Party, as he saw it, had suffered serious losses in membership and influence as a result of these errors.[5] Foster acknowledged that some errors had been committed, but he attributed the losses the Party had suffered, and even the errors themselves, mainly to the intense persecution it experienced during the Cold War. This persecution had derived both from government sources and from the top bodies of the AFL and CIO. Bill Foster was proud of the way the Party—its members and its leaders— had stood firm during the whole period of McCarthyite repression.

McCarthyism was not quite over, by the way. The government at this point took yet another occasion to show that its commitment to democracy was no more to form than to essence.

To the embarassment of some who are inclined to favor form over content, the U.S. Treasury Department, on March 27, 1956, seized the offices of the *Daily Worker* on the preposterous charge that the paper had failed to pay taxes on its "profits." The charge was preposterous if only because the *Daily* was notoriously a deficit operation—to the tune of $200,000 a year—which survived through the generosity of its supporters. The Communist Party offices were also seized.

The T-men, emulating various inquisitional committees, demanded the names of every donor, of every person who had lent money to the paper and of its volunteer distributors. It got none of these.

The occupation of the offices lasted into April. But the *Daily Worker* continued to appear. Its staff functioned from improvised offices and the paper was printed on its usual facilities which were owned by a printing company not involved in the phony tax suit.

A right wing was forming in the Communist Party at the time of the April National Committee meeting. It was amorphous, but more and more it tended to group itself around the person of John Gates.

General Secretary Dennis proposed for discussion in April the eventual formation of "a new mass party of socialism." This proposal, although intended as a long-range perspective, provided a small opening for the right wing, an opening which, in the ensuing months was widened and reshaped to fit a short-range intention to liquidate the Communist Party, drop Leninism from its advocacy and form again a "political association" of the Browder mold. As may be supposed, Foster was among those vehemently opposed to any "opening" through which such a political juggernaut could pass.

It so happened that as the April Plenum was drawing to a close the news arrived that, at its Twentieth Congress, the Communist Party of the Soviet Union had heard a report on the serious excesses of Joseph Stalin, his gross violations of the norms of socialist democracy.

The news had a shocking impact on the leadership stratum assembled at the NC meeting. When the news became generally known it caused grief and even disorientation in Party ranks. The right wing now splashed around in the waters which had been muddied.

In his 76th year, and with an illness that was not improving with age, William Z. Foster found himself plunged into a political battle which he did not feel he could avoid. The essential health, sanity and loyalty of many of his fellow members on the National Board, and of the majority of Communist Party members, braced him in this struggle—the Party's third struggle against "American Exceptionalism." The pro-party group opposed a numerous right wing (and also a small group of ultra-leftists) and they had also to win over a well-intended "center" group.

The Sixteenth National Convention of the Communist Party took place, February 9 to 12, 1957, on New York City's Lower East Side in a hall which was soon to be levelled by the wrecker's ball.

Foster pointed out that the bourgeoisie and its press had their eyes on the Convention and that nothing could please them more "than for a split to take place in the ranks of the Communist Party." Then he added to applause: "there is not going to be any split at this convention."[6]

He was right about that. There was no split at the Convention. Unity was maintained—but precariously, for it was based on compromise among the contending views. But, in the compromise, there was an earnest of success in the fact that the Party was still the Party, and that it remained committed publicly to Marxism-Leninism.

In the year following the Convention the Right discovered it was isolated from the Party membership, despite its ability to "score points" in internal debate and through its control of the *Daily Worker's* editorial policies. The "Gates group" became more and more hostile. Members of the group left the Party.

"Throughout his years in the leadership of the Communist Party Foster was always associated with the forces who fought the influences of opportunism," says Gus Hall. " ... It is possible to say that at times this led to some one-sidedness. But this is very much secondary to his correct fight against opportunism."[7]

In December 1957 and January 1958 *Political Affairs* carried a two-part article by Foster on "The Party Crisis and the Way Out."[8] The warm logic of this well-thought out piece foretold the failure of the Gates tendency. It also refuted the roseate fancies of an old Communist, Alexander Bittelman, who was beguiled by the possibilities of a "Welfare State."

Foster's two-part article appeared in *PA*, then edited by Herbert Aptheker, rather than the *DW* because the *Daily* was by this time down to four-page editions and there was no room for Bill's article.

The inner-Party struggle, in which the Right used events in Eastern Europe (e.g., Poland and Hungary) to negative effect, cost the Party dearly. One of its costliest losses was the *Daily Worker,* which published its last issue on January 13, 1958, exactly 34 years after its first issue came out in Chicago. Gates, with some of his editorial cronies, left the paper and the Party. He was hailed by the Republican Party mouthpiece, the *New York Herald-Tribune,* with an editorial headed: "Welcome Home."

The *Worker* continued publication as a weekly. In September 1961, with James E. Jackson as editor, it began twice-weekly publication. In July 1968 it again became a daily newspaper under the name *Daily World.*

The tensions of the struggle to preserve the Communist Party from the depredations of its rampant right wing were precisely what the doctor had not ordered for Bill Foster. But though Bill could walk away from the tension of a TV ball game he could not walk away from a fight to save the Party which had been his life for forty years. He attended all the critical meetings where the differences within the leadership were thrashed out. He generally reclined on a couch during these proceedings, his felt hat shading his eyes, accumulating vigor for the moments when he would take the floor to make a slashing statement of his views.

In October 1957, Bill suffered a cerebral hemorrhage which, among other effects, drastically impaired his ability to hold a pen. He was handicapped and mostly bedridden for the rest of his days. His mind and his will continued to function and his optimism cheered visitors who came to see him during these last years.

His writings continued to appear in *Political Affairs* and betrayed none of the physical difficulties which limited his movements.

He would make notes in a shaky handwriting and dictate his articles to a typist. In this way he wrote eight articles for *Political Affairs* in 1959.

Beginning on September 10 of that year, the Communist Party began a discussion period leading toward its Seventeenth Convention to be held in New York on December 10 to 13. Foster got into this discussion with an article on the pre-Convention Draft Resolution. His article, which made more than a dozen main points, sought to strengthen the resolution by moving it further away from the elements of compromise which had served the purpose of saving the Party at the critical Sixteenth Convention. Many of Bill's ideas were incorporated in the final Resolution.

But, by December 1959, Bill had not achieved any stable improvement in his general condition and he sought to take advantage of offers he had received from some socialist countries to visit them for treatment and recuperation.

To be able to do this he had first to be released from the bail restrictions under two Smith Act indictments which had been pending since 1948. The government opposed his application and refused to remove legal obstacles to his overseas travel. Permission came via the Supreme Court a year later—by which time there had been further deterioration in his condition. Arrangements were then made for his early departure.

In the meantime he had continued to express himself on a variety of subjects. He wrote six articles for *PA* during 1960, with titles ranging from "The Japanese Mass Movement" to "The Latin-American Revolution of 1810–1826."

The Soviet Union offered to make available the finest resources at its disposal for Bill's treatment and to place him in an environment which might promote his recovery from the paralytic strokes which had afflicted him. Early in 1961 he made arrangements to go abroad.

Bill arrived in Moscow on January 12, 1961, and was taken to a hospital on a stretcher. He had pressed hard for the trip, the only obstacles to be overcome being the legal ones. Forty years before, he had embarked on the political road which he was to follow for the rest of his life. He had found it in this city. The road had proved to be longer and more roughly paved than he had at first imagined. But he never doubted that the road led to where humankind must go.

So it was that when he boarded a plane called "The Flying Dutchman" at New York's international airport he waved triumphantly to Elizabeth Gurley Flynn and the other of his comrades there to see him off, and he gave them that broad smile which he always had ready for friends.[9]

He had worked hard for the U.S. passport he now carried, and as he was helped aboard the plane he felt gratified at this victory over bureaucratic vindictiveness.

Bill was soon established in a sanatorium some twenty miles from Moscow's center. Everything was done to make him comfortable. No head of state could have been treated more royally. The kid from Taunton, Mass.; the slum-youth from Philly; the sailor and homesteader; the laborer and railroad man; the organizer of Packinghouse and Steel; the single-minded Communist against whose iron will all attempts to destroy his Party were shattered—now was made to feel the appreciation and gratitude of an international movement expressed by its most powerful component.

On February 25, Bill was given a surprise birthday party and had some surprise visitors. A photo exists of the occasion of Bill sitting up in a chair, dressed in a well-fitted dark suit, smilingly receiving the hearty congratulations of Premier Khrushchev, Frol Koslov and other Soviet leaders. The Russian Civil War hero, Semyon Budyonny, and the writer Boris Polevoi were also among the visitors.

Perhaps most pleasing of all to Bill was the presence of his dear friend Paul Robeson. Twenty years before, at Madison Square

Garden, on Bill's sixtieth birthday, Robeson had honored him by singing Marc Blitzstein's song "The Purest Kind of a Guy," a song which might have been written with Bill Foster in mind (and quite possibly was!).

Over the years circumstances granted Robeson and Foster fewer occasions than they wished for face to face meetings, but a warm relationship had grown up between them based on the highest degree of mutual respect for each other's character and achievements.

On another occasion Bill was visited by Yuri Gagarin, the first cosmonaut to make the venturesome trip to outer space. But, in that same April in which Gagarin had been rocketed into space, Bill Foster's condition worsened. In June, Esther Foster came to stay with him and she was with him when the end came on September 1, 1961.

On September 7, the funeral ceremonies were held in Red Square where thousands had gathered. They were delegates representing the working people from various districts and enterprises of the capital.

A funeral procession with military escort carried the urn with William Z. Foster's ashes to Red Square from the House of the Unions.

On the tribune of Lenin's Mausoleum were L.I. Brezhnev, O.V. Kuusinen, M.A. Suslov, N.M. Shvernik, K.Y. Voroshilov and other Soviet dignitaries. Elizabeth Gurley Flynn, Chairperson of the Communist Party, U.S.A., was there as were Dolores Ibarruri of Spain, Ajoy Ghosh of India, Liu Hsiao of China, and others.[10]

Kuusinen told the assemblage that "William Z. Foster lived a long, difficult and glorious life." Foster would probably have agreed with that characterization. Hadn't he said, some dozen years before, that he would not have lived it any other way?

Kuusinen paid tribute to the "tireless energy, integrity and firmness of William Foster's convictions, the breadth and depth of his knowledge, his personal charm and modesty." He said: "Just because Foster was an American patriot, because he loved his people selflessly, he fought with all his strength for friendship between the United States and the Soviet Union. He well understood that the preservation of world peace depended to a great extent on Soviet-American relations, and he passionately wanted our people to live in peace and friendship always."

Foster's ashes were brought back to the United States where funeral services were held at Carnegie Hall, New York, on September 18. Gus Hall who, since the Seventeenth Party Congress, was general secretary of the Communist Party, made the principal address. Hall paid tribute to Foster as a worker, a trade-union organizer, a crusader for Black-white unity, a fighter for peace.

"Above all else William Z. Foster was a Communist—a student, a teacher, a theoretician of the science of Marxism-Leninism. . . . He brought to the Communist Party a great heritage of American struggle. For as you know, like the roots of a great oak, the roots of William Z. Foster, while respected and honored in all parts of the world, are deep in the soil of the aspirations, hopes and struggles of our people."[11]

Ten years later, paying tribute on the 90th anniversary of the birth of William Z. Foster, Gus Hall summed it up by saying: " . . . he was the very best that the U.S. working class has produced."[12]

On October 5, 1961, a memorial meeting was held in Chicago, Foster's favorite arena of workingclass struggle. The next day his ashes were laid in Waldheim Cemetery, close by the monument to the Haymarket Martyrs, back in his native soil.

Notes

1. A Bit of Background

1. Robert W. Dunn, *Labor and Automobiles,* International Publishers, 1929, pp. 185–6.
2. *Labor History Documents, Vol.I.* "Trial of the Journeymen Cordwainers of the City of New York . . . 1809." New York State School of Industrial and Labor Relations, Cornell University, Ithaca, 1974.
3. See Philip S. Foner, *History of the Labor Movement in the United States,* Vol. I, International Publishers, 1947.
4. Bernard Mandel, *Labor Free and Slave,* Associated Authors, 1955.
5. Foner, op. cit.
6. Birth records of Taunton, Mass., give the mother's maiden name as McCoughlin.
7. William Shakespeare, *Hamlet,* Act I, scene vi.
8. William Z. Foster, *The Twilight of World Capitalism,* International Publishers, 1949, p. 162.
9. Gus Hall, "William Z. Foster: A Tribute." *Political Affairs,* February, 1971, pp. 33–7.

2. The Philadelphia Story

1. Foster, *Pages from a Worker's Life,* International Publishers, 1939, p.15 [Hereafter cited as *Pages*].
2. Ibid.
3. *The Book of Taunton,* C.A. Hack & Son, Taunton, Mass., 1907.
4. Elizabeth Gurley Flynn, *Labor's Own—William Z. Foster,* New Century Publishers, 1949.
5. Sam Bass Warner, Jr., *The Private City,* University of Pennsylvania Press, Philadelphia, 1968.
6. Foster, op. cit., p.18.
7. Ibid., p.20.
8. Foster, *From Bryan to Stalin,* International Publishers, 1937, p.13.
9. Ibid., p.14.
10. Foster, *The Twilight of World Capitalism,* International Publishers, 1949, p. 158.
11. Ibid., p. 159.
12. Foster, "How I Became a Rebel," *The Labor Herald,* July 1922, pp. 24–5. ["Soap box orators" were the source of many epiphanies similar to Foster's in 1900 and for generations to come.]

3. Work, on Land and at Sea

1. C. Desmond Greaves, *The Life and Times of James Connolly,* International Publishers, 1961, p. 218.
2. *Pages,* p. 21.
3. Ibid., p. 36.
4. Ibid., p. 52.

2. *Pages*, p. 21.
3. Ibid., p. 36.
4. Ibid., p. 52.
5. Ibid., p. 61.
6. Ibid., p. 69.

4. Homesteading and Railroading

1. Foster, *Pages*, p. 32.
2. Ibid., p. 105.
3. Foster, *From Bryan to Stalin*, p. 26.
4. Ibid., pp. 29–30.
5. Ibid., p. 37.

5. A Syndicalist in the Making

1. Philip S. Foner, *History of the Labor Movement in the United States*, Vol. 4, 1965, p. 178 ff.
2. Elizabeth Gurley Flynn, *The Rebel Girl*, International Publishers, 1973, pp. 109–10.
3. Foster, "Syndicalism in the United States." *The Communist*, Nov. 1935, pp. 1044–57.
4. Foster, *From Bryan to Stalin*, p. 46.
5. Ibid., p. 48.
6. Paul Frederick Brissenden, *The IWW*, Columbia University, 1920, p. 275.
7. See: Foster, *More Pages From a Worker's Life*, American Institute for Marxist Studies, 1979, for his lively account of his Budapest experience. Also, *From Bryan to Stalin*, p. 59.
8. Patrick Renshaw, *The Wobblies*, Doubleday, 1967, p. 166 ff.
9. Brissenden, op. cit.
10. Foner, op. cit., Ch. 18.
11. Foster, *From Bryan to Stalin*, p. 59.
12. Ibid., p. 62. Also: Cf. *I Corinthians, V.6*.
13. It was Foster's belief that the McNamara brothers had been betrayed into pleading guilty in this unhappy affair. See: *History CPUS*, p. 110.
14. *From Bryan to Stalin*, p. 72.

6. Foster's Militant Minority

1. Foster, *Trade Unionism: The Road to Freedom*, Chicago Labor News [1915].
2. Foster, *From Bryan to Stalin*, p. 77.
3. V.I. Lenin, *Collected Works*, Vol. II, Moscow, 1962, p. 213.
4. David J. Saposs, *Left Wing Unionism*, International Publishers, 1926; Jack Hardy, *The Clothing Workers*, International Publishers, 1935.
5. *The Jungle* first appeared serially in the weekly *Appeal to Reason*.
6. Foster, *Pages*, pp. 152–3.
7. Ibid., pp. 155–6.
8. See: *From Bryan to Stalin*, pp. 90–104 for a succinct account of the Packinghouse organization drive; also Paul Douglass, *Six Upon the World*, Little, Brown (Boston) 1954, pp. 74–9.

7. Steel: Organization and Strike

1. Renshaw, op. cit., p. 217.
2. Foster, *Bryan to Stalin*, pp. 88–9.
3. Foner, op. cit., vol. 2, p. 206.
4. Samuel Yellen, *American Labor Struggles*, S.A. Russell, 1956, Chapter III.

5. Ibid., p. 259.
6. Ibid., p. 260.
7. Mary Heaton Vorse, *A Footnote to Folly,* Farrar & Rinehart, 1935, p. 276.
8. Foster, *The Great Steel Strike,* B.W. Huebsch, 1920, p. 21.
9. Foster, *Bryan to Stalin,* p. 106.
10. Ibid., p. 111.
11. *Webster's American Biographies,* G.C. Merriam, Springfield, Mass., 1975, p. 387.
12. *Chicago Tribune,* Sept. 19, 1919.
13. Philip Taft, *The AFL in the Time of Gompers,* Harper, 1957.
14. Cited in: *Recent History of the Labor Movement in the United States, 1918–39,* Progress, Moscow, 1977, p. 37.
15. Cited in Joseph J. Mereto, *The Red Conspiracy,* National Historical Society, 1920.
16. David J. Brody, *Labor in Crisis,* Lippincott, 1965, pp. 136–9.
17. *Public Opinion and the Steel Strike,* Harcourt, Brace, 1921, pp. 279–81.
18. Yellen, op. cit., p. 273.
19. Elizabeth Gurley Flynn, *Memories of the Industrial Workers of the World (IWW),* American Institute for Marxist Studies, 1977, pp. 20–1.
20. The Interchurch World Movement, *Report on the Steel Strike of 1919,* Harcourt, Brace, and Howe, 1920, p. 238.
21. Foster, *The Great Steel Strike,* facing p. 148.
22. The Interchurch World Movement, op. cit., p. 230.
23. Yellen, op. cit., pp. 281–2.
24. Foster, op. cit., p. 209.
25. Cited in: Douglass, *Six Upon The World,* p. 88.
26. Vorse, op. cit., pp. 284–5.
27. Foster, op. cit., p. 233.
28. Vorse, op. cit., pp. 298–9.

8. From Syndicalist to Communist

1. Robert W. Dunn, ed. *The Palmer Raids,* International Publishers, 1948.
2. V.I. Lenin, "Left-Wing Communism: An Infantile Disorder," *Collected Works,* Vol. 31, Progress, Moscow.
3. Foster, *From Bryan to Stalin,* p. 137.
4. Lenin, op. cit. Ch. VI.
5. *Lenin Kak Chitatle* [Lenin as Reader], Political Literary Publishers, Moscow, 1977, pp. 168–9.
6. Foster, "Emma Goldman," *More Pages from a Worker's Life.* pp. 12–13.
7. Foster, *The Russian Revolution,* Trade Union Educational League, Chicago, 1921.
8. Foster, *From Bryan to Stalin,* p. 157.
9. Foster, *The Russian Revolution,* p. 7.
10. Foster, *From Bryan to Stalin,* p. 163.

9. The TUEL: With the Tide

1. Foster, *History of the Communist Party of the United States,* International Publishers, 1952, pp. 177–195.
2. *Labor Herald,* Vol. I, No. 6, Aug. 1922, p.3.
3. Foster, "Draper's 'Roots of American Communism,'" *Political Affairs,* May 1957, p. 36.
4. V.I. Lenin, *Collected Works,* Vol. 24, p. 45.
5. Eugene Victor Debs, *Labor Herald,* April 1923.
6. See: Eugene Staley, *History of the Illinois State Federation of Labor,* University of Chicago Press, 1920, p. 395. (Staley calls Foster a "scintillating agitator.")
7. Foster, *From Bryan to Stalin,* p. 174.

8. Foster, *Pages*, pp. 224-8.
9. Sylvia Kopald, *Rebellion in Labor Unions*, Boni & Liveright, 1924.
10. Louis Levine, *The Women's Garment Workers*, B.W. Huebsch, 1924, pp. 365-7.
11. Foster, *Pages*, pp. 217-8.

10. The TUEL: Bucking the Tide

1. Frederick Lewis Allen, *Only Yesterday*, Harper & Row, 1931, pp. 38-9.
2. Cited in: *The Twenties*, George E. Mowry, ed., Prentice-Hall, Englewood Cliffs, 1963, p. 122.
3. Cited in: Allen F. Davis, *American Heroine*, Oxford University Press, 1973.
4. Foster, *Labor Herald*, May 1923, p. 6.
5. Foster, *Pages*, pp. 232-4.
6. R.M. Whitney, *Reds in America*, Beckwith, 1924, pp. 208-9.
7. *Time*, May 12, 1923.
8. Foster, *Misleaders of Labor*, Trade Union Educational League, 1927.
9. Grace Hutchins, *Labor and Silk*, International Publishers, 1929, pp. 150-1; Robert W. Dunn and Jack Hardy, *Labor and Textiles*, International Publishers, 1931, pp. 222-4.
10. *Program*, Trade Union Educational League. [1927], p. 10. (This pamphlet was written by Foster.)
11. *The Communist*, July, 1928.
12. Foster, *From Bryan to Stalin*, p. 215.

11. Toward a Labor Party

1. Karl Marx and Frederick Engels, *Letters to Americans*, International Publishers, 1953. p. 167. See also: Tom Foley in *Political Affairs*, Sept. 1969 and Arthur Zipser (Simson, pseud.) *ibid.*, Nov. 1974.
2. Of course Engels was not underestimating the importance of a valid program, but he thought the American workers—like the British workers who were predominantly trade unionists—would learn the need for a socialist program through the class struggle.
3. Foster, *Pages*, pp. 277-80.
4. *The American Labor Yearbook*, 1925, Rand School, 1925, p. 156.
5. Foster, *History of the Communist Party of the United States*, p. 220.
6. Foster, in *Workers Monthly*, Nov. 1924.
7. *Labor Herald*, July 1924.

12. The Trade Union Unity League

1. Ben Gold, *The Storm in Riverville*, Ben Gold Book Committee, 1973.
2. Philip S. Foner, *The Fur and Leather Workers Union*, Nordan Press, Newark, 1950.
3. Foster, *History of the CPUS*, p. 255.
4. Robert W. Dunn, *Labor and Automobiles*, International Publishers, 1929, p. 179.
5. Ibid., p. 194.
6. Foster, op. cit., p. 269.
7. *Outline History of the Communist International*, Progress, Moscow, p. 290.
8. Joseph Stalin, *Speeches on the American Communist Party*, Central Committee, Communist Party, U.S.A. [1929] p. 20.

13. Facing the Crisis

1. Bruce Minton and John Stuart, *The Fat Years and the Lean*, International Publishers, 1940; and *Labor Fact Book*, No. 2, International Publishers, 1934.
2. Foster, *History of the CPUS*, p. 276.

3. Cited in: *The Great Depression*, David A. Shannon, ed. Prentice-Hall, Englewood Cliffs, N.J., 1960, p. 12.
4. Foster, *From Bryan to Stalin*, p. 303.
5. Foster, *History of the CPUS*, p. 281.
6. *New York Times*, March 7, 1930, p. 1.
7. *Labor Defender*, March 1930, p. 63 ff.
8. Foster, *Pages*, pp. 243–66.
9. See *The Path of Browder and Foster*, Workers Library, 1941, p. 14, "from the year 1930 . . . Foster was our National Chairman."
10. Sam Kushner, *Long Road to Delano*, International Publishers, 1975, pp. 57–79.
11. Foster, *From Bryan to Stalin*, p. 229 ff.
12. Theodore Draper, "Communists and Miners—1928–33," *Dissent*, Spring 1972, p. 391.
13. Ibid., p. 387.
14. Foster, "On the Question of Trade Union Democracy," *The Communist*, March 1931.

14. A Crack in the Pitcher

1. Foster, *Pages*, p. 180.
2. Foster, *Toward Soviet America*, Coward-McCann, 1932.
3. Foster, *History of the Communist Party of the U.S.*, p. 286.
4. Hosea Hudson, *Black Worker in the Deep South*, International Publishers, 1972.
5. Foster, *The Negro People in American History*, International Publishers, 1954, p. 483.
6. *Race Hatred on Trial*, Communist Party, U.S.A., 1931.
7. Foner, *Organized Labor and the Black Worker*, International Publishers, 1976, p. 165.
8. Foster, *Pages*, p. 282.
9. Ibid., p. 284.
10. John Williamson, *Dangerous Scot*, International Publishers, 1969, pp. 89–90.
11. Foster, op. cit., p. 284.
12. AAA = Agricultural Adjustment Administration;
    NRA = National Recovery Administration;
    CWA = Civil Works Administration;
    CCC = Civilian Conservation Corps;
    PWA = Public Works Administration;
    NLB = National Labor Board.
13. Foster, *History of the Communist Party of the U.S.*, p. 298.
14. William Weinstone, "An Important Chapter in the Party's History of Industrial Concentration," *Political Affairs*, Sept. 1949, pp. 71–81.
15. Foster, *Pages*, p. 195.
16. Foster, *History of the CPUS*, p. 307.
17. Conversation with Gil Green, June 1980. See text of speech by Otto Kuusinen in *VII Congress of the Communist International*, Foreign Languages Publishing House, Moscow, 1939.

15. Fighting for Peace and Democracy

1. *VII Congress of the Communist International*. Foreign Languages Publishing House, Moscow, 1939, p. 591.
2. Saul Alinsky, *John L. Lewis*, Putnam, 1949, p. 153.
3. Melvyn Dubofsky and Warren Van Tine, *John L. Lewis*, Times Books, 1977.
4. Foster Rhea Dulles, *Labor in America*, T.Y. Crowell, 1949, pp. 249, 317.
5. Len De Caux, *Labor Radical*, Beacon, Boston, 1970, pp. 236, 209.

6. Art Shields, "A Great Workingclass Leader," *Political Affairs*, Feb. 1971, p. 38ff.
7. Gus Hall, "Thirty Years of Struggle in Steel," *Political Affairs*, Sept. 1949, pp. 64–5.
8. Foster, *What Means a Strike in Steel?* Workers Library, 1937, pp. 19–21. Foster may have been influenced, subliminally or otherwise, by his recall of a title used in a speech given in New Bedford, Mass., in 1898 by Daniel De Leon: "What Means This Strike?"
9. Roger Keeran, *The Communist Party and the Auto Workers Unions*, Indiana University Press, Bloomington, 1980, p. 183.
10. Ibid., p. 161.
11. Lou Saperstein, "Ford is Organized," *Political Affairs*, May 1977, p. 23.
12. Len De Caux, op. cit., p. 279.
13. Foster, *Railroad Workers Forward*, Workers Library, 1937.
14. Foster, *Stop Wage-Cuts and Layoffs on the Railroad*, Workers Library, 1938.
15. *Labor Fact Book, No. 3* and *No. 7*, International Publishers, 1935, 1945.
16. Foster, *From Bryan to Stalin*, pp. 342–5.
17. Foster, *The Negro People in American History*, p. 486ff.
18. Karl Marx and Frederick Engels, *The Communist Manifesto*, International Publishers, 1948.
19. Alfred Kazin, "Writers in the Radical Years," *New York Times Book Review*, March 23, 1980.
20. *Culture and the Crisis*, Workers Library, 1932, p. 30.
21. Matthew Josephson, *Infidel in the Temple*, Knopf, 1967, pp. 124–5, 149–54.
22. Joseph Freeman, *An American Testament*, Farrar & Rinehart, 1936, pp. 294–5.
23. Mike Gold in *Masses and Mainstream*, March 1951.
24. Conversation with Lloyd Brown, Dec. 20, 1979.
25. *The Path of Browder and Foster*, Workers Library, 1941.
26. Joseph North, *William Z. Foster*, International Publishers, 1955, p. 37.
27. Letter to author, Oct. 15, 1979.
28. H.L. Mencken, in *The Smart Set*, April 1923.

16. Fascism Leads to War

1. Foster, *History of the CPUS*, p. 323.
2. Ibid., p. 336.
3. Joseph Stalin, *From Socialism to Communism in the Soviet Union*, International Publishers, 1939, p. 15.
4. A brief but carefully documented account of the diplomatic steps in the months preceding the outbreak of World War II may be found in *History of Soviet Foreign Policy, 1917–1945*, Progress Publishers, Moscow, 1969.
5. Foster, "The Three Basic Tasks of the Communist Peace Policy," *The Communist*, July 1940, pp. 610–14.
6. *Labor Fact Book* No. 5, 1941, p. 57.
7. V.I. Lenin, *Collected Works*, Vol. 36, p. 297.
8. *Outline History of the Communist International*, Progress, Moscow, 1971, pp. 455 ff.
9. *The Communist*, July 1941.
10. Foster, *History of the CPUS*, p. 388.
11. Ibid., p. 392.
12. *Labor Fact Book* No. 5, p. 181.
13. Foster, op. cit., p. 394.
14. William Manchester, *The Glory and the Dream*, Little, Brown, 1974, p. 233.
15. *The Communist*, Dec. 1941.
16. Foster, *The Communist*, Sept. 1941, p. 793.
17. Ibid., p. 797.

18. Ivan Maisky, *Memoirs of a Soviet Ambassador*, Hutchinson, London, 1967, p. 292.
19. Gus Hall, *Peace Can Be Won,* New Century, 1951, p. 46.
20. Foster, *History of the CPUS*, p. 411.
21. Philip S. Foner, *Organized Labor and the Black Worker*, p. 261.
22. Foster, op. cit., p. 414.
23. Foster, op. cit., p. 415.
24. Foster, op. cit., p. 416.
25. Earl Browder, *Victory and After,* International Publishers, 1942.
26. Foster, op. cit., p. 366-7.
27. Foster, op. cit., p. 421.
28. Betty Gannett, "The Essence of Browder Revisionism," *Political Affairs*, Sept. 1969, p. 112.
29. Earl Browder, *The Communist*, January, 1944.
30. Earl Browder, *Teheran: Our Path in War and Peace*, International Publishers, 1944, pp. 11, 15.
31. Browder, in *The Communist*, July 1944, p. 597.
32. Foster, op. cit., pp. 425-7.
33. Browder, op. cit., pp. 70-1.
34. Foster, in *New Masses*, Dec. 14, 1943, pp. 11-13.
35. Browder, in *The Communist*, June 1944.

17. War Ends—Cold War Begins

1. Foster, *History of the CPUS*, p. 429.
2. Foster in *Political Affairs*, July 1945, p. 640.
3. *The Path to Peace, Progress and Prosperity,* Communist Political Association, 1944, p. 11.
4. Ibid., p. 137.
5. Ibid., p. 91.
6. See *Political Affairs*, July 1945, p. 655.
7. Foster, *History of the CPUS*, p. 428.
8. Geoffrey Perrett, *Days of Sadness, Years of Triumph,* Coward, McCann & Geohegan, 1973, pp. 423-4.
9. P.M.S. Blackett, *Military and Political Consequences of Atomic Energy*, Turnstile Press, London, 1948.
10. Tim Buck, *Thirty Years, 1922-1952,* Progress Books, Toronto, 1952.
11. Foster, op. cit., p. 433-4.
12. Jacques Duclos, "On the Dissolution of the Communist Party of the U.S.A.," *On the Struggle Against Revisionism,* Communist Party, U.S.A., 1946, pp. 19-33.
13. *New Masses,* June 12, 1945, p. 16.
14. Foster, op. cit., p. 435.
15. Ibid. p. 436.
16. Foster, "On the Expulsion of Browder," *Political Affairs,* April 1946, pp. 339-46.
17. Elizabeth Gurley Flynn, *Political Affairs,* July 1945, pp. 617-18.
18. *Highlights of a Fighting History,* International Publishers, 1979, pp. 225-28.
19. D.F. Fleming, *The Cold War and its Origins,* Doubleday & Company, 1961.
20. Foster, *The Menace of a New World War,* New Century, 1946.
21. George Morris, *American Labor—Which Way?* New Century, 1961, pp. 47-9.
22. Gil Green, *What's Happening to Labor?* International Publishers, 1976.
23. Foster, *The New Europe,* International Publishers, 1947.
24. Ibid., pp. 117-9.
25. Foster, *History of the CPUS,* pp. 490-1.
26. *Labor Fact Book, No. 9,* 1949.
27. Albert E. Kahn, *High Treason,* Lear Publishers, 1950, pp. 332-41.

28. Cited in, Karl Obermann, *Joseph Weydemeyer*, International Publishers, 1947.
29. Information now available under the Freedom of Information Act shows that the FBI had completed a massive amount of preparatory work for the Smith Act indictments before February 1948. We suggest that the moment chosen for announcing the indictments may not have been coincidental.
30. Foster, *In Defense of the Communist Party and the Indicted Leaders*, New Century, 1949.
31. Ibid.
32. Foster, "People's Front and People's Democracy," *Political Affairs*, June 1950, pp. 14–37.
33. Foster, *The Crime of El Fanguito*, New Century, 1948.
34. *The Case of Puerto Rico*, New Century, 1953.
35. See: William L. Patterson, *The Man Who Cried Genocide*, International Publishers, 1971. Patterson's book, his autobiography, deals with the cited cases and many others.
36. John Wexley, *The Judgment of Julius and Ethel Rosenberg*, Cameron and Kahn, 1955.
37. The cited reports were published in 1951 by New Century. The Main Resolution is in *Political Affairs*, January 1951. The February 1951 issue is a special enlarged number (254 pages) containing reports, speeches, and greetings, of the 15th National Convention.

18. Three Score and Ten Plus

1. *Political Affairs*, March 1951.
2. Foster, *Outline Political History of the Americas*, International Publishers, 1951.
3. Paul F. Douglass, *Six Upon the World*, p. 118.
4. Ibid., p. 119.
5. Foster, *Twilight of World Capitalism*, p. 162.
6. Foster, *Outline Political History of the Americas*, p. 11.
7. Ibid., p. 12.
8. *Labor Fact Book, No. 11*, 1953, pp. 63–5.
9. *New York Times*, May 26, 1953.
10. *Daily Worker*, April 2, 1954.
11. *Labor Fact Book, No. 13*, 1957, pp. 124–5.
12. Foster, *History of the CPUS*, p. 551.
13. *Political Affairs*, March 1951, p. 5.
14. Gilbert Green, *The Enemy Forgotten*, International Publishers, 1956, contains in Chapter XIII a full and thoughtful discussion of the Black liberation question as it appeared in this period.
15. *Village Voice*, Nov. 4, 1980, pp. 21–3.
16. Foster, "Left Sectarianism in the Fight for Negro Rights and Against White Chauvinism." *Political Affairs*, July 1953.
17. Gus Hall, *Racism: The Nation's Most Dangerous Pollutant*, New Outlook, 1971, pp. 14–5.
18. Foster, "Notes on the Struggle for Negro Rights," *Political Affairs*, May 1955, pp. 20–42.
19. Foster, *The Negro People in American History*, p. 13–14.
20. Foster, op. cit., p. 557.
21. The figure 286 is for the year 1900.
22. *The Communist Position on the Negro Question*, New Century, 1947.
23. "On the Negro Question in the United States," *Political Affairs*, Feb. 1960, pp. 43–57.
24. *The Struggle for Afro-American Liberation*, New Outlook [1979], pp. 8–9.

25. William Z. Foster and Benjamin J. Davis, "Notes on the Negro Question," *Political Affairs*, April 1959. See also: James E. Jackson, *Revolutionary Tracings*, International Publishers, 1974, pp. 149ff, 233ff.
26. Foster, "Reply to a Priest's Letter," *Political Affairs*, Oct. 1954, pp. 45–8.
27. Foster, *Twilight of World Capitalism*, pp. 158–9.
28. Foster, "Is the United States in the Early Stages of Fascism?" *Political Affairs*, pp. 4–21.

19. One Final Conflict

1. *Political Affairs*, March 1956.
2. Foster, *Outline History of the World Tade Union Movement*, International Publishers, 1956.
3. Sidney Lens, *The Labor Wars*, Doubleday, 1973.
4. Eugene Dennis and John Gates, *What America Needs*, New Century, 1956.
5. Eugene Dennis, *The Communists Take a New Look*, New Century, 1956.
6. *Proceedings (Abridged) of the 16th National Convention of the Communist Party, U.S.A.*, New Century, 1957.
7. Gus Hall, "William Z. Foster—A Tribute," *Political Affairs*, Feb., 1971, p. 37.
8. Foster, "The Party Crisis and the Way Out," *Political Affairs*, Dec. 1957 and Jan. 1958.
9. Elizabeth Gurley Flynn, "Salute to William Z. Foster," *Political Affairs*, Feb. 1961.
10. "Foster Memorial Meeting in Moscow," *Political Affairs*, Oct. 1961.
11. Gus Hall, "William Z. Foster: American Workingclass Leader," *Political Affairs*, Oct. 1961.
12. Gus Hall, *Political Affairs*, Feb. 1971.

Index